HOMES IN THE HEARTLAND

Rural America

Hal S. Barron
David L. Brown
Kathleen Neils Conzen
Cornelia Butler Flora
Donald Worster

Series Editors

HOMES IN THE HEARTLAND

Balloon Frame Farmhouses
of the Upper Midwest, 1850–1920

Fred W. Peterson

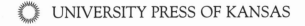 UNIVERSITY PRESS OF KANSAS

Photographs and floor plans are by the author unless otherwise noted.

Published by the University Press of Kansas (Lawrence, Kansas 66049), which was organized by the Kansas Board of Regents and is operated and funded by Emporia State University, Fort Hays State University, Kansas State University, Pittsburg State University, the University of Kansas, and Wichita State University

Library of Congress Cataloging-in-Publication Data

Peterson, Fred W.
    Homes in the heartland : balloon frame farmhouses of the upper
Midwest. 1850–1920 / Fred W. Peterson.
        p.   cm. — (Rural America)
    Includes bibliographical references and index.
    ISBN 0-7006-0536-3 (alk. paper)
    1. Farmhouses—Middle West—Design and construction—History.
2. Balloon framing—Middle West—History. 3. Farmhouses—Middle
West—History. I. Title. II. Series: Rural America (Lawrence,
Kan.)
TH4920.P48 1992
728'.6'0975—dc20   92-2833

British Library Cataloguing in Publication Data is available.

Printed in the United States of America
10 9 8 7 6 5 4 3 2

To my father, a carpenter and mechanic,
and to my mother, a practical person

CONTENTS

PREFACE

Discovery is the expansive quality that pervaded my experience while researching farmhouses of the Upper Midwest. Travel to areas that were new to me and returns to previously visited locations consistently resulted in collecting significant material. In every instance in which I learned more about the farmhouses of the region, I was informed by people who opened their homes to me for study, by people who believed their history was important and demonstrated interest in preserving it, and by people who trusted me with aspects of their past. In the early phases of my research, a trip to the prairies of North Dakota introduced me to the cultures of German-Russian and Ukrainian farmers. During my last ventures into the region, I returned to areas of early settlement to appreciate the building skills of Yankee farmers evident in the box frame farmhouses of southern Wisconsin and eastern Iowa. As a traveling scholar, I was a visitor, an observer who delighted in what I perceived and learned but who would never be an integral part of the history of the rural communities I studied.

The sense of being an outsider looking in was heightened by the realization that I was moving into an area of investigation in which few had pursued extensive fieldwork in this region. I was motivated by an urgency to collect as much information as I could about farmhouses before they vanished from the landscape, to record facts accurately, and to form concepts clearly, as well as to develop suitable ways to arrange the diverse materials I gathered. Work in libraries and archives, visits to state and county historical museums, and the primary research on farm sites generated a rich overlay of information.

Other challenges and excitements were encountered along the way. I could create a bestiary of the real and imaginary creatures encountered while working in farmyards and on the sites of abandoned farmhouses—the mild and the wild dogs, skunks, badgers, bulls, billy goats, and snakes. Bees by the hive, hornets in squadrons, flies by the hordes, and the persistent whining presence of mosquitoes. Storms, dense fog, oppressive heat, or strong winds delayed work or made it difficult to accomplish. When a warm sun illuminated white clouds above the prairie, it was good to work. The pace of research slowed during summer in Iowa corn country and in the Red River valley when a stifling humidity drenched the days and nights. Every one of these creatures and all of these weather conditions are good to recall because they created the texture of the times and places in which I worked. Each danger, discomfort, or pleasure contributed to a knowledge of the farmhouses and the quality of life experienced by those who made these dwellings their homes.

I was given support in numerous ways to initiate and to continue this study. I received grants from the Minnesota State Arts Board and the Minnesota Humanities Commission to research, create, and present two exhibitions that interpreted vernacular architecture in the area of the state where I teach art history at the University of Minnesota, Morris. The University of Minnesota has awarded me grants to fund aspects of the research as well as single-quarter leaves and sabbatical furloughs to devote full time to the work. A National Endowment for the Humanities Fellowship supported one sabbatical and a Bush Sabbatical Fellowship another.

A major influence and consistent inspiration in my work as an art historian comes from Professor Emeritus Dimitri Tselos, my mentor and major adviser in graduate school at the University of Minnesota. He not only taught me fundamentals of research in architectural history, he also instructed me through his example to be curious about everything that appeared meaningful and to investigate that curiosity with intellectual thoroughness and rigor. I would also like to acknowledge colleagues at the University of Minnesota, Morris, who encouraged and aided me in this work, especially the research librarian, Barbara McGinnis, who could find and deliver virtually every item I sought. Friends and colleagues outside this university to whom I am indebted include the late Larry Remele, editor of *North Dakota History*, who as a historian encouraged me to study farmhouses seriously and systematically. John McGuigan, now at the University of Virginia Press, convinced me that a study of the farmhouses of the entire region was indeed a reasonable and realizable venture. I am also grateful for the advice and direction from colleagues in the Vernacular Architecture Forum who helped me overcome the sense of isolation that seems an inevitable aspect of working alone collecting, analyzing, and interpreting data in remote rural areas of the nation.

More immediate and equally important as the support noted above have been the perspectives and insights gained from my wife, Vasilikie Demos, a professor of sociology. Our son, Caleb, has also been involved, because he grew as the study matured and I hope both he and the study are now ready to go it on their own. It has been almost fifteen years since I began this work. It's time to share the results and debate the issues. That, as my mother would say, is the only practical thing to do.

INTRODUCTION

The advent of balloon frame construction in the Upper Midwest fundamentally changed the way people conceived of and built structures with
wood. Invented in Chicago in the early 1830s, the popularity of balloon
frame construction increased with each new wave of settlement of a predominantly agricultural region. As farmer-builders and carpenters increasingly employed balloon frame construction, the logic of the system convinced them and others of its advantages. These were qualities we associate
with the positive results of industry and technology. Balloon frame farmhouses proved to be economical and efficient to build, convenient and flexible in use, and in time proved to be strong and durable against the wear
and tear of large families and the elements. These houses were secure shelters in which homes could be established in the heartland of the nation.

This revolution in building technology is best understood through analyses and interpretations of farmhouses in Wisconsin, Minnesota, Iowa,
South Dakota, and North Dakota from the 1840s to the 1920s—the period
when farmers and local builders gradually adapted traditional house forms
and architectural stylebook designs to the new means and materials of
building. The new way of building was seldom performed in an ostentatious display of design and ornament. The best qualities of balloon frame
construction were demonstrated in simple, nonassuming ways. It was a
manner of building that did not draw attention to itself as it became virtually the only reasonable way to plan and realize a house.

This study is a series of essays that interpret related balloon frame farmhouse types in the rural Upper Midwest in the context of the values that
gave them form and meaning. It discusses these forms both as a technical
approach for creating structures and as a manifestation of the culture that
developed during a rapid period of growth. First, there is a detailed descrip-

Building supplies storage building, Morris, Minnesota

tion of the basic construction techniques that define balloon frame buildings. Chapter Two sets out a typology for balloon frame farmhouses, based
on a broad survey of the region. The greatest part of the migration to the
Upper Midwest did not occur until the mid- to late nineteenth century. As
a result, settlers moved from their first subsistence shelters of log, sod, or
wood directly to balloon frame dwellings, products of the Industrial Revolution. Chapter Three discusses those subsistence shelters, their construction, the people who built and occupied them, and even how they were often incorporated into the larger, more comfortable houses that were built
after these farm families achieved some degree of material stability.

The remaining five chapters are devoted primarily to defining and illustrating farmhouse types. After discussing specific farmhouses, the origins of
each type will be traced from traditional sources, models adapted from architectural stylebooks, and designs taken from local lumberyard pattern
books. It will become evident that balloon frame farmhouses resulted from
an interplay of traditional forms and popular styles embodied in a new
building technology.

Economic, aesthetic, social, ethnic, religious, and technological factors
contributed to the planning of a new house and influenced the shape and
uses of the completed dwelling. For instance, gabled rectangular farmhouse
types will be presented on a continuum from small to large in order to illus-

trate the range of scale possible in balloon frame farmhouse construction and also to provide the basis for discussing the effect of changes in domestic science on the family farmhouse from the 1870s to 1920. Ell- or T-plan farmhouses will be interpreted as expressive of the rapid, widespread settlement of the region from the 1860s to the mid-1880s. Because of their great popularity, ell- or T-plan farmhouses will be the basis for discussion of a vernacular aesthetics of building. The formal, impressive qualities of double-wing houses will be interpreted within the context of rural community in which social and economic as well as religious values contributed to the meaning of the home. The popularity of foursquare house types from the mid-1890s to the 1920s indicates a move toward consolidation and standardization expressed in the fourfold symmetry and centrality of design. Finally, the myths and realities attending success on the homestead will be investigated through an interpretation of farmhouses that communicated achievement and position within the context of ethnic and local values. Although the order of the chapters suggests a chronology that traces developments from one decade to the next, I do not intend to present a developmental treatment of the farmhouse types. Rather, I mean to provide analyses and interpretations of the revolution in building that paralleled the transformation of the region's virgin land into the specialized, technological agriculture that exists today.

This book is an attempt to understand a particular time and place. One approach to that understanding is to study the landscape where the people lived and the structures they built to adapt it to their ways of living and working. Standing on the site of an abandoned farm, it is tempting to glorify what was created and accomplished there. Romanticizing the past is a common tendency; we must guard against it. The abandoned buildings are remnants of the history of that place and its inhabitants; they must be considered in the context of their own time. In order to "return" to a particular space and a particular time and to measure those dimensions of human life, it is necessary to have many means available to delineate the ways people lived.

Because the balloon frame farmhouse is treated as a type of building, concepts and methods related to the study of material culture in a vernacular tradition are fundamental.[1] A geographic survey of the region, the development of a typology for farmhouses, extensive photo-documentation of structures, the creation of floor plans, and structural analyses of selected dwellings were important means of gathering data. Concepts and methods of social history aided in understanding patterns of collective behavior, the dynamics of community, and the contributions of ethnic groups to the mainstream of industrial and technological change in America from 1840 to 1920.[2]

The perspective of art history contributed to understanding farmhouses as architectural monuments and the importance of studying these structures as they were initially planned and realized. I could then subject the "original" of the farmhouse to a stylistic analysis in order to identify a consistent and characteristic choice and handling of architectural elements and then infer an underlying predisposition, an inclination, a preference to build a house in a particular way.[3] A full analysis of farmhouses includes consideration of the farm family as its central theme or subject and how this subject relates to the functions of the house in the context of the farm. It is at this point that one approaches a fuller interpretive statement about farmhouses, in which data from material culture and social history can be related to insights gained from art historical inquiries. Knowledge of farmhouses based upon field studies is basic. A perspective on the historical and socioeconomic situation of the region is essential. And a thorough, sensitive synthesis of those approaches focused upon the meaning of a farmhouse is the goal in understanding the structure as a work of art.

1. THE BALLOON FRAME STRUCTURAL SYSTEM

Balloon frame farmhouses are characteristic and important features of the upper midwestern rural landscape. Their simple shapes sharply defined and differentiated from their natural surroundings and their starkly white planar surfaces illuminated by the sun express qualities inherent in the structures and the way they were put together. These dwellings constitute approximately 90 percent of existing farmhouses in the region. The adoption of balloon frame construction on such a major scale suggests that the structural system became the norm, the basis of a way of thinking of, planning for, and realizing a farmhouse in the practice of local carpenters and farmer-builders. Further, the origins and development of balloon frame construction from about 1840 to 1920 are an integral part of the history of the period in which technological and industrial aspects of American culture increasingly shaped the way of life for people in both rural and urban sectors. The gradual adoption of the structural system by farmers in the Upper Midwest parallels their gradual acceptance of mechanized and commercial agriculture.

An extended description of the balloon frame structural system and a discussion of its development provides the basis for interpretation of specific buildings and the people who built them as an essential part of the agricultural enterprise called the American farm. The description of balloon frame construction will begin with a listing and illustration of the somewhat specialized parts and a discussion of structural details. Although customarily presented as a relatively simple way to build, the system does incorporate some complexities and subtleties that are not immediately evident when it is given a cursory treatment (Figure I.I).

The materials used to build a balloon frame structure are the various sizes and lengths of milled lumber fastened together with nails. The frame is

Carpenters building Peder Weeg house, Glenwood, Minnesota, 1914. From left to right: Ed Tate, Albert Wollan, Oscar Kirkwald, Arnold Gunderson, and Hagen Moe.

composed of dimension lumber such as 2 × 4, 2 × 6, 2 × 8, and 2 × 10 inch boards. These sizes are used for the studs, joists, and rafters. Boards measuring 1 inch thick, such as 1 × 4, 1 × 6, and 1 × 8 inches, are used as bracing, flooring, or external sheathing. The smallest members of the frame are wall laths measuring ½ × 1¼ inches and supplied in lengths of 4 feet. Some lumber for a balloon frame structure must be shaped for special functions such as tongue-and-groove flooring or siding, shiplap siding, doors, and windows, as well as framing and trim for the same. The size of the nails used is measured by the weight of 1,000 nails of a given size. For instance, 1,000 tenpenny nails weigh 10 pounds, 1,000 sixpenny nails weigh 6 pounds, and so on. The word "penny" does not refer to a coin but is derived from the English word "pun," which was a vernacular abbreviation for pound.[1]

The following are the parts of a typical balloon frame assembly (see Figure 1.1):

1. A *sill*, made up of large dimension lumber or of two or more smaller pieces of lumber, is leveled and secured to the *foundation* of the structure and acts as the anchor for the rest of the frame.

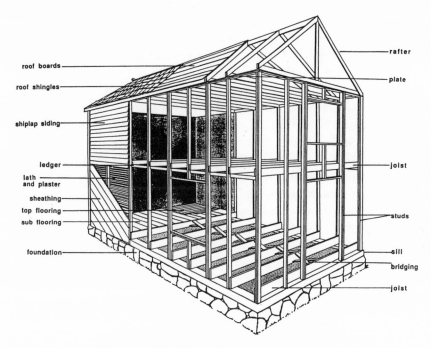

roof boards
roof shingles
shiplap siding
ledger
lath and plaster
sheathing
top flooring
sub flooring
foundation

rafter
plate
joist
studs
sill
bridging
joist

Figure I.I. The balloon frame structural system

2. The *joists* for the first floor are fastened to the sill and to the studs of the exterior walls. Both joists and studs are usually placed at intervals of 16 inches on center. First-floor joists are sometimes supported by a *girder* that is held in place by posts set on footings in the floor of the basement. In a balloon frame structure, the *studs* of the exterior walls rise from the foundation to the plate. Studs at the corners of the structure and at window and door openings are usually doubled or made of 4 × 4 inch posts or two 2 × 4 inch boards nailed together. The corners of the frame are sometimes reinforced with 1 × 4 or 2 × 4 diagonal bracing.

3. The joists for the second floor are supported by a 1 × 4 or 1 × 6 inch *ledger*, or *ribbon*, that is "let in" the vertical studs. Both ledger and joists are firmly nailed to the studs.

4. The top of the studs is capped with a *plate* composed of either one 2 × 4 inch board or two 2 × 4 inch boards nailed together. Ceiling joists for the second-floor chambers are nailed to the top of the plate.

5. After they have been properly cut for the form and pitch of the roof, the *rafters* are nailed to the plate. Rafters are usually placed at intervals of

24 inches on center from one another, although they are sometimes set at 16 inches on center to align with the second-story ceiling joists.

6. Joists and sometimes the studs of the structure are laterally reinforced by *bridging* made up of 1 × 4 or 2 × 4 inch boards that have been mitered to fit at an angle between these members of the frame.

7. Interior walls are composed of 2 × 4 inch boards placed 16 inches on center and nailed to a bottom plate of one 2 × 4 inch board and a top plate of two 2 × 4 inch boards. In some instances in which interior walls align on the first and second floors, the studs for the walls can be run continuously from the first-floor plate to the plate at the ceiling of the second floor.

8. Two layers of *flooring* are nailed over the floor joists. A subfloor of rough boards measuring 1 × 6 or 1 × 8 inches supports the finished floor, usually made of tongue-and-groove material.

9. Two or more layers of material are applied to the external surface of the studs. A rough *sheathing* of 1 × 8 inch boards is usually nailed on the studs in a diagonal pattern followed by the horizontal application of ship-lap siding. Sometimes *insulation paper* is tacked over the sheathing before the shiplap siding is put on the surface of the structure.

10. The rafters are covered with 1 × 6 and 1 × 8 inch boards, sometimes further protected by insulation paper before overlapping *roof shingles* are nailed to the surface.

11. The interior walls and ceilings of chambers are first lined with *lath* that acts as the support for the *plaster* finish of these surfaces. The 4-foot length of the lath is the basic module or unit of measurement upon which the entire structure can be based, that is, joists and studs are placed at 16-inch intervals so that the studs can receive the 48-inch length of the lath over a section of three studs spaced to span 48 inches on center.

12. Openings in both exterior and interior walls for *doors* and *windows* are also usually based upon multiples of the 16-inch spacing of the studs. Doors and windows 30 inches wide are common because they fit into a frame of 1-inch material between the 32-inch spacing of two studs. Placement of windows and doors on both exterior and interior walls is sometimes influenced by the regular spacing of the wall studs.

Balloon frame construction results in a tightly integrated system of parts that are proportioned to and that contribute to and increase the strength of one another. The structure has been likened to a basket in which all the parts are tightly woven together in a unified enclosure or container of space. Although composed of relatively lightweight members, the framework is extremely strong because each part, when joined with the others at the proper place in the proper sequence, creates the integrity of the entire network of members. Consequently, if a builder makes a mistake in part of the frame, it results in a pervasive weakness or fault in the whole building. For instance, floor and ceiling joists are not to be measured flush with the external edges of the studs to which they are nailed. A small mismeasurement, making some joists too long, would eventually cause bulging in the entire wall. Joists, therefore, should be cut somewhat shorter than the width of the house and nailed to sill and studs as well as notched into the ledger on the second floor to prevent such a fault. In some cases a builder has assembled sill, studs, joists, and flooring in such a way that the shrinkage of the wood parts together causes the wall and floor to draw away from one another, resulting in drafty openings at the first-floor level (Figure 1.2). In another faulty sill execution, space between the studs of the outer walls is left open under the flooring, creating conditions for the rapid spread of fire inside the walls of the structure (Figure 1.2).[2] Sills have been designed in various ways to solve structural and material problems in the system.

Contractors and carpenters benefited from years of apprenticeship and experience before they realized the positive qualities of balloon frame construction. One needed a thorough knowledge of all the parts of the structure and how they relate to each other. In addition to this comprehensive theoretical and practical understanding, one had to be able to read floor plans and specifications accurately or to follow intuitively "a plan in the head." The importance of the simple act of measurement is recognized in the adage, "Measure three times, cut once." Measurement is crucial at every step in construction and can become relatively complicated when calculating the cuts for roof rafters or staircase framing. Should the full scope of the building project be assigned to the carpenter, he had to also know how to estimate completely and accurately the amount and cost of materials needed for the building to be constructed. Given the large number of individual pieces that compose a balloon frame structure, this task can be rather difficult to accomplish.

Qualities inherent in the balloon frame structural system ensured its eventual and virtually universal adoption in the Upper Midwest. A skilled carpenter and just one helper could erect a small one-story house measuring 14 × 20 feet in about one week. Each member of the frame was light enough for one or two men to carry, set in place, and fasten to the frame with nails. The traditional mortise-and-tenon method of framing a structure, on the other hand, necessitated a skilled housewright to measure and cut the joints of the frame and a crew of at least five to six men to help raise it and set its heavy members together (Figure 1.3).

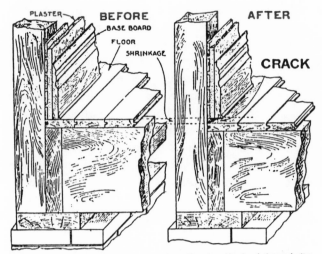

·Built-up T sill with flooring and base board in place *before* and *after* shrinkage. *See that crack?* Such cracks will invariably occur with such sill construction unless the lumber has been thoroughly well seasoned because there is no provision for shrinkage.

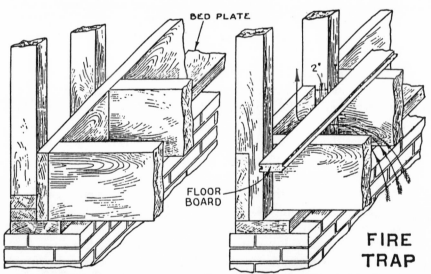

·Built-up T sill with combination three-piece bed plate, and beam spaced for external studs. The bed plate is reinforced by two layers of studding laid along the outside edge and forming a stiff footing for the wall studs.

·Built-up L sill with internal let-in studs. This construction is faulty in that the sapce between lath and siding is not shut off from the cellar, allowing access of rats and draughts, as indicated by arrow. *Such construction is a fire trap and should not be permitted.*

Figure I.2. Balloon frame sills

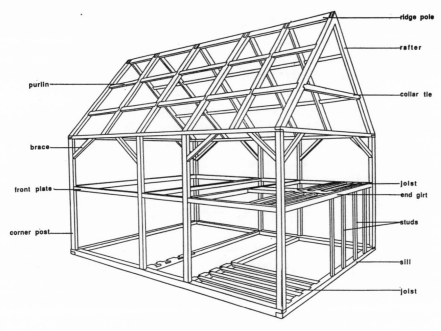

Figure I.3. The box frame

The availability of milled lumber also facilitated the speed with which a balloon frame house could be built. Preparations for building a heavy mortise-and-tenon box frame house began two years before actual assembly of the frame to provide time for cutting timber, forming the posts and beams, and seasoning or drying these large sections of wood. The relative simplicity and efficiency of balloon framing not only saved time and energy, it also saved money. One could save approximately 40 percent by building a balloon frame rather than a heavy box frame house.

The name given to the structural system suggests that a house built this way would blow or float away because it appears so lightweight and perhaps weak and vulnerable.[3] Balloon frame structures did, however, pass the test of standing against the strong winds of the prairie and bearing up beneath the heavy snows of the region. In addition to strength and durability, the system provided flexibility in planning, adapting, maintaining, and moving a structure. Wings or "add-ons" could be joined more easily to the existing house than with other framing systems. A wing could be moved from one side to the other of the central core of a structure; old, damaged, or worn parts of the structure could be replaced with relative ease. One could either move an intact structure to another site nearby or dismantle it and carry it for reassembly to a distant location on one or more wagons. The mobility of balloon frame structures constitutes a separate study. There are many records of individual houses being moved within the limits of a town or city and accounts of farmhouses being moved from one farm to another or relocated on a farm site. In some instances citizens actually moved their houses and businesses as small communities so they could live in a county seat that had been newly established nearby. Zealous town boosters stole neighboring town halls during the night by transporting them to their town in order to relocate a disputed county seat.

Some qualities of balloon frame construction resulted in positive side effects. People without architectural training could learn to plan and utilize the system after a relatively short apprenticeship or by studying balloon frame houses already built in their area. Architects and planners who published pattern books during the second half of the nineteenth century addressed their work to all levels of society. Through the model homes they illustrated and discussed, they inadvertently educated their readers in ways to plan and build balloon frame houses. Milled lumber and mass-produced nails allowed almost everyone to become his or her own architect and builder. In addition to pattern book sources, the nonprofessional could find plans published in agricultural journals, ladies' magazines, and etiquette books and supplied at local lumberyards.

Whatever the source of a basic plan and elevation, the farmer-builder and his family could build their own balloon frame house or alter their present dwelling. Local carpenters satisfied rural clients by working from a "plan in the head" that permitted them to build a basically similar house for many families but to alter elements within the whole to meet the preferences and needs of the occupants. This popular, democratic approach to building resulted in a quality evident in a cursory study of structures in the field—variety. Standardization of lumber dimensions and regular measurements used in balloon frame construction would seem to yield structures of generally similar appearance. Variations in buildings often resulted from economic reasons, but they also reflected the tastes of the builder-occupants. The system was inherently easy to adapt to individual needs and preferences, and because it was new, builder-occupants seemed less resistant to change and more inclined to experiment with variations in plan and elevation.

The emergence and widespread use of the balloon frame structural system was dependent on two by-products of the Industrial Revolution—the mass production of inexpensive nails and ready availability of lumber cut in standardized dimensions. Before the nineteenth century, nails were hand forged in iron and were relatively rare and expensive. The technology to mass-produce nails developed in America during the last decade of the eighteenth century. Ezekiel Reed is given credit for inventing a machine in 1786 that would cut nails from a strip of iron. Each slice of hot iron was caught in a vise while a hammer flattened the wide end of the strip to form the head of the nail.[4] By 1820 cut nails were being mass-produced and sold at reasonable prices. The process had so improved that cut nails could be made with strong points and shanks equal in quality to hand-forged heads. The machines developed to make a variety of cut nails in a wide range of sizes did not, however, put out a perfect product.[5] The long taper and flat ends of these "square" nails made them difficult to drive into thick dimension materials. They also tended to turn at an angle once they were driven into the wood, which caused problems, especially in fine work of small dimension material. Whether fine or rough work was involved, the cut nail tore at the fiber of the wood rather than passing through it.[6]

Round, sharply pointed wire nails, which could be driven through wood more easily, became available by the 1870s. By the mid-1880s, they were made of steel. As the high cost of these superior steel wire nails decreased, their use in balloon frame construction increased. Because nails were used by the thousands or by the pounds to tightly fasten members of the frame together, their effective design and low-cost availability were extremely important for the development of balloon construction.

Sawmills powered by waterwheels provided the first ready-to-use lumber to settlers in the Upper Midwest. Although slow in cutting logs, the mills antiquated the laborious method of cutting lumber with one- or two-man handsaws. Sawmills greatly increased the quantity of milled lumber for building as well as began the standardization of lumber sizes. By 1860 most of the lumber used in the nation came from the forests and mills of Wisconsin, Michigan, and Minnesota. By that time, steam-driven gang saws and circular saws had further increased the power, accuracy, and speed of cutting dimension lumber. The more efficient and economical band saw came into use in the 1880s, and by the 1890s only skilled operators milled lumber. Steam-driven saws and carriages cut the logs into large sections. A conveyor sent these slabs to another saw to be cut into dimension lumber, trimmed to standard length, and sorted according to size. After being stacked and dried, the wood was ready to be used. In settlements close to forested areas and local sawmills, farmers hauled the lumber on wagons to building sites. When railroad lines were laid through distant towns on the prairie, lumberyards were established to supply the building needs of the growing communities.

The system as well as the materials of balloon frame construction are closely linked to the basic sources of power and modes of production of the Industrial Revolution. Efficiency, cost effectiveness, adaptability, mobility, and standardization—qualities that formed the essence of industrialization—are embodied in this building technique.

George Washington Snow is called the inventor of the balloon frame structural system, but evidence also suggests that a carpenter, Augustine Taylor, is the originator. In 1833 Taylor built St. Mary's Church in Chicago, the first structure identified as balloon frame. During that building season and in subsequent years, many carpenters built this new kind of framed structure in the city, and others predicted that as soon as newly settled farmers had paid for their land, they too would erect balloon frame houses and outbuildings. More than a generation would pass, however, before farmers and local carpenters fully endorsed balloon frame construction. Rural Americans preferred to build in time-tested traditional ways. Professional architects and planners also had reservations about this new way of building and were reluctant to use it.

As carpenters became familiar with and trusted balloon frame construction, they began to use varying versions of the system. Eventually the building technique became common throughout the Upper Midwest. In addition to the instructive examples of actual buildings, articles in agricultural journals and newspapers and chapters in architectural pattern books provided a printed context in which the pros and cons of the new structural system were debated. These explanations, defenses, and critiques are important because they document different conceptions of the structural system after it was "invented" and indicate major reservations that many critics had about adopting it.

The balloon frame construction illustrated in Figure 1.1 and described above is an ideal type. A perfectly rational structural system did not spring forth, fully conceived, from the minds and practice of architects and carpenters in America from the 1840s to the 1880s and afterward. Considerable controversy surrounds the gradual dissemination of this way of building. Although some put forth positive explanations, many more presented arguments against balloon frame construction—some appearing as late as the third decade of the twentieth century. Many conservative Americans in the new and expanding nation were deeply skeptical about radically new theories and procedures.

This skepticism crossed social classes. Architects and planners during the nineteenth century were predominantly Anglo-American in ethnicity and British in allegiance. They had a vested interest in preserving the techniques they judged to be appropriate. In addition, they were reluctant to champion anything novel that originated from the lower ranks of mechanics. Yankee merchants and farmers, who were usually the first to arrive in newly opened areas of the Upper Midwest, tended to rely upon the time-tested methods of building permanent structures in box frame, stone, or brick.[7] Farmers of other ethnic origins used their own traditional methods. In fact, although it might seem that settlers were progressive in adapting new techniques, that was not the case. Instead, they approached change and innovation cautiously. One encounters the deep-seated traditions or ways of doing things "right" when one studies pioneers actually constructing buildings on the frontier.

The period from 1830 to 1900 is recognized as a time of many changes in the technology of farming. Farmers in the Upper Midwest accepted these changes in the same wary way they had adopted balloon frame construction. For example, the first cast-iron plow was made as early as 1797, and improvements in both manufacturing and quality occurred over the next generation. However, it was not until 1845 that the iron plow replaced the wooden plow. Farmers initially rejected iron plows because they seemed to provide no real economic advantage over the old way of turning the soil, but as soon as there were concrete economic reasons for adopting the new design and material, the iron plow was rapidly accepted.[8] American farmers tended to learn by experience and were forced by necessity to accept and exploit the new industrialized way of doing things because greater economies and efficiencies resulted not only in success but frequently in simple survival. Balloon frame construction was one of many new ways of doing things that the farmer observed, evaluated, and eventually adopted when its benefits became evident through use.[9]

Solon Robinson, a pioneer farmer and entrepreneur from Indiana, wrote the earliest published explanation of "ballooning" in the *American Agriculturalist* in February 1846. For nearly a decade Robinson had been writing articles on agriculture as well as various accounts of using light wooden frames in building. In the 1846 article, however, he offered a plan for "A Cheap Farm-House" (Figure 1.4) "intended for the *new settler*, and to be built on the *baloon plan*, which has not a single tenon or mortise in the frame, except the sills; all the upright timber being very light, and held together by nails, it being sheeted under the clapboards, is very stiff, and just as good and far cheaper than ordinary frames."[10] Robinson provided no construction details of the frame house and he described the framing

FRONT VIEW OF COTTAGE.—FIG. 11.

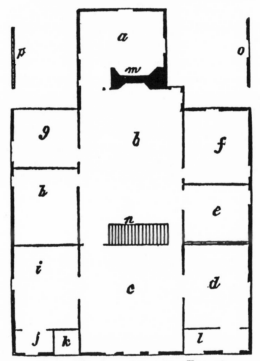

GROUND PLAN OF COTTAGE.—FIG. 12.

Description.—*a,* Wash-room, 13x13; *b,* kitchen, 16x24; *c,* parlor, 16x16; *d, f, h, i,* bed-rooms, 10x12; *e,* store-room, 8x10; *g,* pantry, 8x10 *j, l,* clothes press; *k,* entry; *m,* fire-place; *n,* stairway; *o,* wood-house; *p,* garden gate; the pump should be in the wash room.

Figure 1.4. "A Cheap Farm-House," 1846. From Solon Robinson, "A Cheap Farmhouse," *American Agriculturist* 5 (February 1846): 57–58.

method in a misleading manner. Even so, he presented an all-nail balloon frame and extolled its economy and adaptability.[11] He claimed that his "cheap farm-house" cost less money and could be built in fewer than four to five stages, as funds became available. The scale and arrangement of the first two chambers of the "cheap farm-house" were remarkably similar to a "Western Prairie Cottage" plan that Robinson had had published in the *Cultivator* in 1839.[12] This plan, as the author acknowledged, was of his log house in Indiana. Robinson must have been able to observe and study balloon frame structures being built in and around Chicago by the late 1830s. However, his description seems to be based more upon his experience in creating functional domestic space in log cabin construction. Josiah T. Marshall's *The Farmer's and Emigrant's Handbook* in 1851 included another of Robinson plans for "prairie" farmhouses.[13] This plan was similar to the earlier projects except it was somewhat smaller. The reason for its appearance in the handbook is unclear. Robinson's plan, with no explanation of the framing system, is sandwiched between two other projects for farmhouses that were to be built in box frames. It would be possible, therefore, to assume that his plan had nothing to do with "the baloon plan."

Solon Robinson's description of the balloon frame also appeared in Gervaise Wheeler's *Homes for the People in Suburb and Country*. This piece is based upon Robinson's talk before the American Institute of Farmers in New York in 1855 which the *New York Tribune* published that year. No plans or elevations appeared with the text, making it difficult to determine if Robinson was still thinking of "ballooning" in terms of traditional log building. He did begin his explanation by specifying only three dimensions of lumber or boards—2×8, 2×4, and 2×1. He claimed that these could be best obtained at a sawmill, but, if necessary, they could be hewn or split by hand from rails or round poles that were straight and the same thickness on at least two sides. Further, Robinson's description of constructing a balloon frame structure does not suggest the use of any plan or predetermined measurements. For example, he suggested that instead of precisely measuring the first-story floor boards, they could be laid to run over the ends of the sill and then simply cut to fit. Next, the builder would install the vertical corner posts and locate the door and window openings. The remaining space along the sill would be measured at 16-inch intervals for the studs. However, the exact height of the studs was to be of little concern because the builder could cut them off at the proper place after he had worked up that high in nailing sheathing boards to the exterior of the studs.

Robinson's account could not be expected to win many converts because his description makes it seem impractical and wasteful. It is difficult to understand how one could keep the studs in plumb while nailing on individual sheathing boards before the plate and ceiling joists were nailed to the top of the studs after they had been cut to level. Practical builders carefully measured and used material to conserve time, energy, and money. If floor boards were to overlap the sill and then be cut flush, the excess lengths of boards would best fit in another section of the floor and not be cast away as waste. Robinson's imaginative and often ambiguous presentations of the system cast doubts on the extent of his practical experience with balloon frame building.

Robinson's early presentation of balloon frame construction initiated a discussion that lasted for generations. By the 1860s George E. Woodward, an architect and engineer, and James H. Monckton, a practical carpenter, had come forth with the most complete and positive explanations of balloon framing. Others—like William Bell, who authored *Carpentry Made Easy* (1858), and H. Hudson Holly, a professional architect—suggested ways in which problems they perceived in balloon frame structures could be solved. Another professional architect and stylebook author, E. C. Gardner, undertook a hesitant look at the system and concluded by forcefully rejecting it. There were those who simply ignored it and continued to instruct in traditional ways of framing. Andrew Jackson Downing established the earliest and most pervasive opposition to any kind of frame building by generally dismissing construction in wood as unworthy of true and lasting values in architecture.

Woodward offered the strongest support for adopting the balloon frame, but even he did not present a completely consistent argument for or conception of the system. The *Cultivator* published his first discussion of balloon frame construction in a series of fourteen articles in 1860–61. In them, he explained and extolled an all-nail process of joining structural members. Woodward's training as an architect and engineer may have enabled him to present a clear and logical description of the balloon frame and an easy-to-follow explanation of how the frame was to be assembled in the sequence of building from sill to rafters. He also summarized the advantages of the system:

1. The whole labor of framing is dispensed with.
2. It is a far cheaper frame to raise.
3. It is stronger and more durable than any other frame.
4. Any stick can be removed and another put in its place without disturbing the strength of those remaining—in fact the whole building can be renewed stick by stick.

5. It is adapted to every style of building, and better adapted for all irregular forms.
6. It is forty per cent cheaper than any other known style of frame.
7. It embraces strength, security, comfort, and economy.[14]

Responding to common fears about weaknesses and durability, Woodward cited an exceptional incident in which a balloon frame house was blown from its foundation by a tornado and tossed about but not damaged. He compared this with similar situations in which box frame structures had collapsed. He suggested that the balloon frame system be called the "basket frame" in order to convey a better impression of its nature.[15] Woodward further characterized the adoption of the balloon frame as a positive and progressive way to build.

> It takes many years to overcome popular prejudice. . . . [W]e look with suspicion on any one who has the energy, the courage, the impudence to pronounce the old fashioned mortise and tenon timber frame . . . a relic of by-gone days handed down to us with all the prejudices and ignorance clustered around it. . . . We see no objection whatever in the way of freely adopting the balloon frame, and very much can be said in its favor; it is absolutely safe and secure, and its economy a strong recommendation.[16]

Woodward also understood how the balloon frame system would be used by the farmer-builder on the frontier. The new system, he claimed, placed the art of building in "the control of the pioneer." In fact, Woodward implied that it was on the frontier, beyond the influence of the mechanic, that the balloon frame system was developed and that it afforded all who wished to build "a cheap and substantial manner of any class of buildings."[17]

Woodward's views on domestic architecture had a great influence upon popular taste during the 1860s. He wrote books that offered a wide range of styles, sizes, and costs of dwellings. These works were done in collaboration with designers such as E. C. Hussey, G. E. Harney, and others. Possibly because of the number and variety of contributors to his stylebooks and a desire to appeal to a wide clientele, no consistent description of balloon frame construction can be found in his publications. House elevations and plans were offered in stone, brick, and box frame, as well as balloon frame.

In his *Architecture and Rural Art, No. 2*, Woodward provided specifications for a dwelling that included a brief description of a balloon frame.

The dimensions for the members of this frame are heavier than those of the framing system described in the *Cultivator* articles of 1860–61.[18] The later version seems to be a regression to the dimensions and weight of the box frame. Nails would be used, of course, at all joints, but the heavier version also included strong recommendations for bracing or bridging the "floor beams" and instructions to "gain in" the girts on the studs. One can only speculate why Woodward published a more conservative description of the heavier framing system after using such progressive rhetoric in presenting and explaining the earlier version. The conclusion remains that no standardized version of balloon frame construction was conceived or practiced during this time.

James Monckton wrote *The National Carpenter and Joiner*, which was published by Woodward in 1872. In addition to instructions about how to make moldings, stairs, and window sashes, the book contained a section on balloon framing. Introducing the system, Monckton stated that it had been in use for more than twenty-five years and was superior to the old method of framing "because it ties and combines the least amount of material with the greatest strength and with the least labor."[19] Monckton listed the members of the frame according to one-story and two-story structures. The taller, larger dwelling contained slightly heavier members with instructions for bridging the floor joists. Floor plans featured large fireplaces and chimneys that necessitated special framing to support the hearthstone as well as the floor around the hearth. Monckton recommended that joists carrying the weight of the hearth be twice as thick as the others. In the diagram showing their configuration, the joists appear to be mortised and tenoned together and perhaps joined by nails.

William Bell's *Carpentry Made Easy* is an example of a practical text that expresses a reserved acceptance of balloon construction as one way of framing in wood; it also offers ways to improve faults in the system. The book contains information on mortise and tenon framing and diagrams for one-, one-and-a-half-, and two-story balloon frame structures. Bell's conception of the system retained some traditional framing practices, particularly where studs were fitted into the sill by a mortise-and-tenon joint. Two 2×8 inch boards composed the sill of the one-story project. The tenon end of a stud was to fit between the separated members of one of these boards. A larger 8×8 inch sill had to be mortised to receive the tenon end of the studs for the two taller and larger projects. The remaining parts of the frame were to be joined together solely by nails.[20]

Bell's combination of old and new framing techniques illustrates a reluctance to adopt wholeheartedly a new system of building until all aspects of its strengths and weaknesses could be thoroughly tested. Some feared if the balloon frame did not float of its own accord, then it might be blown from its foundation. An Iowa farmer writing to the *Cultivator* in 1860 explained that he had created a version of the balloon frame to build a two-story farmhouse and advised his carpenters to use plenty of nails to firmly join together every member. He went on to describe a method of anchoring the sill to the foundation by fastening the sill to the floor joists and filling the spaces between the joists over the foundation wall with bricks so that the frame's superstructure would be immobile. The bricks were also intended to act as insulation.[21]

Another practical acceptance of and approach to the balloon frame structural system originated from H. Hudson Holly's *Modern Dwellings in Town and Country* (1878). Concerned about the shrinkage of lumber in frame houses, Holly recognized the balloon frame as a system that allowed the manipulation of members to avoid such problems. The sill, for instance, when composed of two or three 2 × 8 inch boards laid flat, supposedly took more compression and minimized shrinkage. Studs and posts, because they rise continuously from the foundation to the roof, allow for the omission of interties that cause shrinkage problems. Holly claimed that the balloon frame system was "invented by our pioneers" to reduce the problems he had cited. "Yet, notwithstanding all the ridicule to which it was subjected, it has steadily grown in favor, and is now, in modified form, accepted by our best builders. The system upon which it is based is simply to avoid, as far as possible, resting the frame on girders or interties."[22]

In *Homes and How to Make Them* (1874), E. C. Gardner presented a grudging description of balloon frame construction; by the early 1880s he had soundly rejected the system. In *Homes* he specified studs of 2 × 5 inches set at 12-inch intervals rather than 2 × 4 inch studs set at 16 inches. He further advised the use of tenpenny nails to the extent that the house be "peppered with them." Still doubtful of the strength of the frame, he suggested two layers of exterior sheathing.

Even after boarding, your walls will have less than two inches of solid wood. If you wish to make an example of yourself, lay this boarding diagonally; and, to cap the climax of scientific thoroughness, having given it a good nailing and a layer of sheathing-felt, cover the whole with another wooden garment in the same style as the first, and crossing it at right angles. All of this before the final coat of clapboards, or whatever it may be. A house built in this way would laugh at earthquakes and tornadoes. It couldn't fall down, but would blow over and roll down hill without doing any damage. . . . It would hardly need any studs except as furrings for lath and plastering, and would be very warm.[23]

Indeed, the studs seem to have been nailed in place only as a means to attach the sheathing. What Gardner described is not a reinforced balloon frame structure. Rather, he seems to have had in mind a double-walled box incidentally supported by 2 × 5 inch boards.

Gardner's suspicions about the soundness and style of frame structures, both old and new, became explicit in a lecture delivered in 1880 and published in 1882 as *Farm Architecture: Houses and Barns*. After providing advice on remodeling old frame farmhouses, he thoroughly disparaged the balloon frame house as "a rectangular cell with smooth, straight walls, and white, square flat ceilings."[24] He characterized the spaces between joists and studs as avenues for mice, rats, and roaches as well as conduits for all kinds of cooking odors and worst of all for smoke and flames that would quickly engulf the structure. In short, the architect declined to recommend balloon frame construction to his clients and concluded his lecture by predicting that the farmhouse of the future would be built primarily of brick or stone. It was a vision biased by the conventional wisdom that stone and brick were the best building materials to communicate permanence and substance.

Gardner was certainly not an accurate prophet. He was, however, a spokesman for the conservative opinion of his time—as late as the 1880s! He based his judgments on what seemed to him to be the apparent frailty of the balloon frame. He also expressed an aesthetic preference for architectural spaces more complex and varied than the right-angled interiors created by joists and studs and planar surfaces of plaster.

Amid these varying and changing conceptions of balloon frame construction, it is not surprising to discover a variety of terms used to identify the same parts of the structure. Both E. C. Hussey's *Home Building* (1876) and S. B. Reed's *Dwellings for Village and Country* (1885) confuse the reader with their terminologies. Neither Hussey nor Reed were consistent. Hussey offered plans and elevations for smaller houses to be built in what he called "semi-balloon construction, thoroughly braced and spiked together complete."[25] For larger dwellings, Hussey specified a "skeleton frame" that was composed of heavier corner posts, beams, and girders. This frame was to be truss-braced in all the partition walls, and long braces were to be installed on each side of the corner posts. In addition to adding thick girders to support the floors of a house, Hussey identifies joists as "beams" and studs as "wall strips."[26] Reed used the same terms to identify these two members of the frame and, like Hussey, increased the use of heavier members for larger structures.

In addition to these descriptive inconsistencies, the visual presentation of balloon frame construction in plans and elevations in nineteenth-century stylebooks and technical manuals is frequently misleading. Estimates for the kinds, quantities, and costs of materials needed to build a particular design are also sometimes impossible to relate to the plan and elevation of the house presented in a stylebook or lumberyard book of plans. Throughout the 1870s A. J. Bicknell included diagrams for framing various houses in the balloon frame that were not drawn to the scale specified with the illustrations. The diagrams inaccurately portrayed the number of studs or joists needed in the frame of a dwelling. With unwavering inconsistency Bicknell specified for one project studs of 2 × 6 inches set 16 inches on center, while for another he listed studs of 2 × 4 inches set 12 inches on center.[27] In his *House Plans for Everybody*, S. B. Reed suggested savings could be realized if "piece lumber" (studs and joists of the same length) were used in house construction. Further, he recommended using 2 × 3 inch studs not only to save more money but also to gain additional floor space because the walls would be thinner. When the specifications for such a house were given, the builder would have found it impossible to determine where "pieces" fit in the frame of the structure. The move toward these economies led to obscurity. Words and images bore no relation to one another.[28]

Considerable discussion about the proper way to insulate the walls of a balloon frame house added to the controversies about the system.[29] Some sources suggested that external 1-inch-board sheathing could be tongued and grooved to ensure tighter seams and keep out cold winter winds. Others recommended double plastering to create a tighter envelope in and around the frame. Lath was first applied to the external face of the studs. Wooden sheathing and siding were then nailed to the external wall and a rough coat of plaster was applied to the lath from the inside. Finally, lath was applied to the interior surface of the studs and then plastered. When finished, four layers of materials sealed the frame. Other insulation techniques involved stacking soft bricks in the spaces between the studs. If the proper clay was available, a builder could manufacture his own insulating brick by forming them and allowing them to cure in the sun. Some rural builders fashioned these bricks from a recipe of mud and straw, making the interior of the wall appear as if it were made of waddle. By the 1880s a variety of insulation papers were available to "wrap" the frame of the house. The paper was tacked over the exterior wall sheathing and on the roof boards before shiplap siding and shingles were applied. In rare instances, wood ashes were poured between the spaces of the stud to seal the frame tightly. Another uncommon technique of insulating the balloon frame involved stacking stovewood between the studs.[30]

By the late 1870s, balloon frame construction had become generally accepted in practice, and some standardization in terminology and technique had occurred in the architectural literature. Evidence of these changes is found in the many plans and specifications given for a variety of balloon frame houses in a trade journal, *Carpentry and Building*, published and widely read from 1879 through the early 1900s. During the same period, the balloon frame became more completely standardized through the development of precut, ready-to-assemble houses offered through mail-order catalogues. Balloon frame construction eventually became identified with progressive planning and home modernization through the popularity of mail-order designs that included the comforts of central heating, hot and cold running water, conveniences of kitchen planning, and a bathroom with sink, toilet stool, and tub. Despite the controversies and the criticisms, balloon frame construction in one form or another became the most popular and practical way of building with wood in the Upper Midwest. Each farmhouse built in the balloon frame method was a monument to the builder's ability to realize the fullest potential of the structural system in the time and at the place the farmhouse was conceived and finally realized. Indeed, it seems inaccurate to speak of only one system or one best way to build in balloon frame construction. Forty years after its appearance, the balloon frame was perceived as a means to an end that proved to be so economical, adaptable, and available that it became virtually the only way carpenters and farmer-builders conceived and constructed farmhouses in the Upper Midwest for almost seventy years.

2. A TYPOLOGY FOR BALLOON FRAME FARMHOUSES IN THE UPPER MIDWEST

Balloon frame farmhouses built in the Upper Midwest are of a bewildering variety. It appears as if each builder exploited the system's potential for creating a structure that was unique. Despite this great variety, it is possible to sort these farmhouses into discernible groups or types.

Two fundamental qualities of architecture are used to type farmhouses in this study—the basic shape of a structure and its floor plan.[1] Shapes of balloon frame farmhouses are rectangular or square or combinations of these as realized by the way in which the walls and roof of the structure form exterior volume as well as define enclosed sheltered space. The height of exterior walls to one, one-and-a-half, or two stories affects the exterior shape of the structure as well as determines the number and nature of its interior spaces. The length and width of a house and, in some instances, the wings of a house also are fundamental determinants of type.

The floor plan of a structure as the second criterion for type diagrammatically indicates the way the interior of a house is divided by walls and how walls and portals determine movement through these separated spaces. As the exterior walls and roof form the house as shelter, the interior floor plan forms the house in terms of domestic functions. Interior spaces are created for the basic purposes of food storage and preparation, eating, sleeping, and other social functions.[2]

Upper Midwest balloon frame farmhouse types are, therefore, grouped according to basic shapes and similar divisions of interior spaces. Subgroups of general types can be identified by architectural elements such as dormers, bay windows, and porches that are important portions of a house but do not determine the structure's basic shape. For instance, subtypes of the two-story foursquare farmhouse can be established on the basis of the number, position, and shape of the dormers that are frequently part of the

25

Balloon frame farmhouse types. Top row: Type 1—Morrison County, Minn. (Minnesota State Historical Society); Type 3—Morrison County, Minn. (Minnesota State Historical Society); Type 1—G. W. Bysom farmhouse, Hettinger County, N.Dak. (State Historical Society of North Dakota). Middle row: Type 9—Pope County, Minn.; Type 10—Grant County, Minn. (Grant County Historical Society); Type 10—Douglas County, Minn. Bottom row: Type 3—Traverse County, Minn.; Type 4—F. Mastvetten farmhouse, Bottineau County, N.Dak. (State Historical Society of North Dakota); Type 3—Syver Ellingson farmhouse, Grant County, Minn. (Grant County Historical Society).

roof design. The simplicity and ease of adding, subtracting, or moving these kinds of architectural elements in balloon frame construction indicate that they cannot be reliably used in classifying basic farmhouse types.

Ten major balloon frame farmhouse types result from analyzing and grouping structures according to fundamental architectural traits (Figure 2.1). Farmhouse types 1 through 10 are presented in a logical progression from the simple to the more complex and are characterized by the two primary criteria: external shape/enclosed shelter and division of interior spaces for certain functions. A brief characterization of these ten farmhouse types will reveal how closely related these two criteria are in the nature of each type. Analyses and interpretations of these types will be expanded in subsequent chapters.

Farmhouse type 1 is the simplest of structures. The one- to one-and-a-half-story rectangular volume enclosed by exterior walls and covered by a saddle roof usually lends itself to only two interior spaces on the first floor and the half story divided more or less equally at or near the middle of the longer side of the rectangle. Because it is small and simple, the type 1 farmhouse functions primarily as shelter for the basic needs of eating and sleeping. The two-story gabled rectangular farmhouse, type 2, is a relatively large structure. The rectangular two-story interior covered by a saddle roof goes beyond the most basic needs for shelter to provide special-purpose spaces such as dining room, parlor, reception hall, private chambers for some of the family, and storage spaces. Houses of this type communicate a moderate level of achievement and stability through their broad extension and tall elevation on the farm site.

Farmhouse type 3 is an ell- or T-plan structure consisting of two gabled rectangles of one to one-and-a-half stories joined at right angles to one another. Interior spaces in each section provide for a greater variety and specialization of function than in the type 1 farmhouse. The taller section of the ell or T customarily encloses parlor, dining room, and bedrooms, while the lower wing contains the kitchen and pantry. Frequently built in two or more stages, this composition of extended volumes and the resultant floor plan express expansion and change. Farmhouse type 4 relates to type 3 in the same way as types 1 and 2. The ell- or T-plan house that is two stories in one or both wings of the structure is usually the result of careful planning and one-stage construction that results in a relatively prestigious display of balloon frame monumentality.

Farmhouse types 5 and 6 are one-and-a-half or two-story double-wing structures composed of combinations of gabled rectangular units in a formal, balanced elevation and plan. Relatively large and laterally extending from the central gable unit, these farmhouse types are classical designs that meet the needs of large families as well as serve the social functions of the rural community.

The double house, type 7, is so rare in the region that it will not be discussed here. In the few instances that it appears, it is characterized by a pair of identical architectural volumes, such as two gabled rectangular units built side by side.

The type 8 farmhouse, the one- to one-and-a-half-story foursquare, is composed of a square or almost square volume capped by a pyramidal roof. The small, centralized floor plan of these structures offers limited space to farm families. Sometimes a small kitchen wing is added to the basic unit to provide additional special-purpose space, but chambers on the half story

Type	Description		Number	(%)

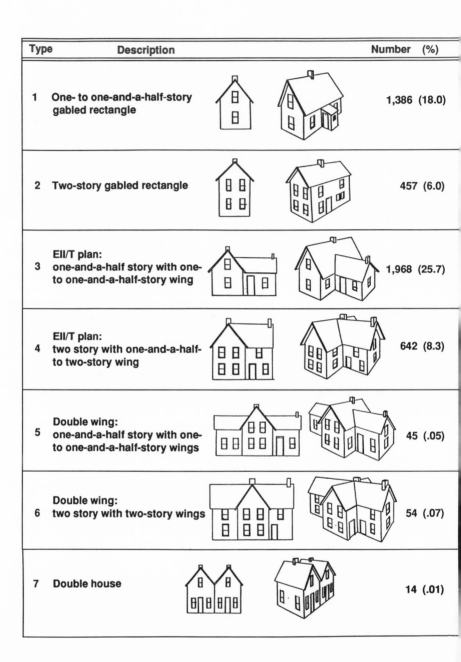

Type	Description	Number (%)
1	One- to one-and-a-half-story gabled rectangle	1,386 (18.0)
2	Two-story gabled rectangle	457 (6.0)
3	Ell/T plan: one-and-a-half story with one- to one-and-a-half-story wing	1,968 (25.7)
4	Ell/T plan: two story with one-and-a-half- to two-story wing	642 (8.3)
5	Double wing: one-and-a-half story with one- to one-and-a-half-story wings	45 (.05)
6	Double wing: two story with two-story wings	54 (.07)
7	Double house	14 (.01)

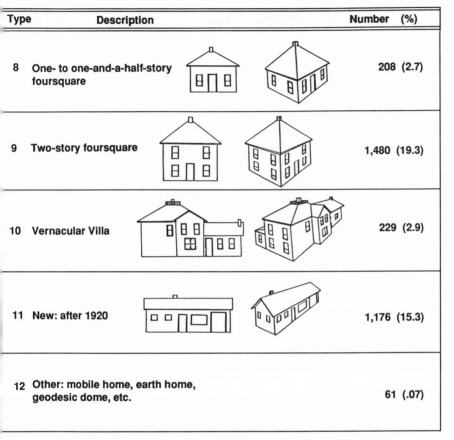

Type	Description		Number (%)
8	One- to one-and-a-half-story foursquare		208 (2.7)
9	Two-story foursquare		1,480 (19.3)
10	Vernacular Villa		229 (2.9)
11	New: after 1920		1,176 (15.3)
12	Other: mobile home, earth home, geodesic dome, etc.		61 (.07)

Figure 2.1. Typology of balloon frame farmhouses of the Upper Midwest based on a survey of the region

under the pyramid roof remain cramped. The type 9 farmhouse is a two-story foursquare structure that constitutes a simple cubical enclosure centrally crowned by a pyramidal roof. Interior spaces on both stories are divided and designated in general areas of related functions such as food preparation, serving, and eating; reception and entertainment of guests; workrooms; and private family chambers. The essential traits of this farmhouse type—symmetry of floor plan and cubical volume of enclosure—facilitate the grouping of related domestic and social functions in the centralized, consolidated space of the structure.

Vernacular Villa, the type 10 farmhouse, is identified by its similarity to professional stylebook designs of dwellings for country gentlemen. This impressive and sometimes elaborate structure is built on a scale intended to com-municate substance and economic status—the home of a successful farmer.

The New and Other categories, types 11 and 12, are not structural but temporal categories that define the historical framework of the study. Be-cause structures built after 1920 are not included in this study, everything after that date is excluded except as survey information that roughly indi-cates the proportion of "new" to "old" farmhouses. The Other designation includes mobile homes, prefabricated houses, geodesic domes, and earth houses. These types of structures are rare in the rural Upper Midwest but do occur and so were counted as a fraction of the survey.

All of the house types illustrated and discussed in this study appear in villages, towns, and urban residential areas in the Upper Midwest. The ge-ographic location of a farmhouse and its specific functions in the context of the farm distinguish it from other dwellings. A farmhouse is a free-stand-ing, single-family dwelling, usually with its major façade toward the road or lane and protected from the prevailing northwest winds of winter by a grove of trees. Although many aspects of farm work occur in the farmyard, outbuildings, and fields, an equally important portion happens in the farmhouse. The farmhouse in the Upper Midwest is a dwelling that is situ-ated in the farmyard as part of the complex of structures that comprise the physical, functional, and human dimensions of the farmstead.

Two traditional house types built in areas of the region settled before the Civil War are the I-house or I-house with wing and the upright and wing, or the temple-form, house. The existence of impressive examples of these designs led to their adaptation throughout the region as balloon frame farmhouses of types 3 and 4. Structural analysis of these older dwellings documents a gradual change from building with the traditional box frame to construction in the balloon frame. I-house with wing and upright and wing farmhouses were not tabulated in the survey of upper midwestern bal-loon frame farmhouses but were studied as structures that documented this change from traditional to popular types of houses.

The identification of only ten major farmhouse types may seem to be too few in which to classify the great variety of structures existing in the region. Should one introduce the element of architectural style to this typology, the house types would increase tenfold. The revival of historic architectural styles of nineteenth-century America is characterized by surface decoration and the use of particular architectural features such as towers, turrets, ve-randas, and balconies. These seldom appear on simple vernacular farm-houses; when they do, they do not affect the basic shape of the building. In this study I recognize the important role of revival styles of the period but establish a typology on fundamentals, not fashions.[3]

It could also be argued that the identification of farmhouses according to elevation creates too many types. For instance, types 1 and 2 could be considered essentially the same kind of structure and therefore an increase in scale would not be sufficient cause for the creation of another house type. Interior shelter and floor plan function are, however, other basic qualities considered for classification. Farmhouses of one story are fundamentally different from those of one-and-a-half stories and both of these are not the same as two-story dwellings.

This classification of balloon frame farmhouses in the Upper Midwest will not satisfy every scholar involved or interested in this area of inquiry. Those whose studies have concentrated upon the older building traditions of New England and the mid-Atlantic seaboard of the United States might object to the absence of familiar labels such as Georgian, I-house, or upright and wing. This criticism might arise from an ethnocentricity that assumes most traditional house forms in America derive from Anglo-American models. The majority of balloon frame farmhouses in the Upper Midwest were not built by or for Americans of English descent, and although sometimes influenced by an Anglo-American way of building, they are not dominated by this tradition.

Another objection to this classification of balloon frame farmhouses could originate from those devoted to the study of an architectural history that focuses upon structures of clearly identifiable stylistic traits. The subordination of the revival styles in architecture in America from 1850 to 1920 might seem a denial of historical reality. The analytical approach to the basic architectural qualities of structures recognizes the importance of such styles but does not use them as primary means of identification.

A third argument against this set of farmhouse types might come from those who conceive of type and typology as a manifestation of a reality higher than the individual examples from which they were derived. This ontological argument rests upon philosophical premises that are incompatible with the empirical approach followed in this study. Although this orientation toward types as universal realities has been useful in areas such as linguistics, it would attribute to building patterns of Upper Midwest farmers a logic and syntax not appropriate and never intended.

Other studies of domestic vernacular architecture are based on house types identified by the basic shapes of structures or various stylistic features or by both fundamental forms and stylistic features. Most of these sets of house types do not consider the floor plan and use of interior space in relation to the exterior shape as a criterion for classification as is done in this study. Consequently, other studies of houses in the Upper Midwest have been based upon either a larger or smaller number of house types. For instance, twenty-two kinds of houses were identified in *South Dakota House Types*.[4] The basis of classification in that guide is primarily historical stylistic traits. Data cards used by surveyors in an Illinois study of rural houses listed eighteen different house types that ranged from traditional ethnic types to professional architectural styles popular from 1850 to the 1920s. *The Iowa Farmhouse (1857–1950): A Literature Survey* is, as the title suggests, a review of the writings about farmhouses in Iowa that appeared in agricultural journals such as *Wallace's Farmer* and the *Western Farm Journal*.[5] Based upon such evidence, the document catalogued only five house types from the ell- and T-plans to the bungalow. In another in-house, unpublished guide, the State Historical Society of Wisconsin defined only nine vernacular forms of housing by focusing upon essential structural traits and classifying houses as Front Gable Form or One-Story Cube Form.[6]

In a major, more inclusive study, *American Vernacular Design, 1870–1940*, Herbert Gottfried and Jan Jennings posit thirty-six house types. A series of design concepts that determine the basic shape of a structure combined with architectural elements such as window style and placement, porch and entrance system, or gable shape and decorative treatment are criteria that interact in the vernacular design process that generates house types. The authors "note that vernacular buildings are composed of arithmetic and geometric progression of elements and concepts, that is, elements and ideas have been added to one another in single or multiple steps."[7] The resultant house types are identified as Gable Cottage: Colonial, Hipped Cottage: Italianate, or Bungalow Cottage. Rather precise identifications of house types are possible within this system of classification, but the method becomes too complex and cumbersome to use for balloon frame farmhouses in the Upper Midwest from 1850 to 1920. Examples of Hipped Cottage: Colonial or Hipped Cottage: Rectilinear are in rural areas of the region but are more generically identified in this study as the basic two-story foursquare, or type 9 farmhouse.

Two other architectural guides present relatively large numbers of house types because both studies are of national scope. In *A Field Guide to American Houses*, Virginia McAlester and Lee McAlester present a method for identifying houses that includes historical architectural styles of the nation from the 1600s to the 1970s. "Ground plans," elevations, and "families of shapes" are categories that classify an extended, and perhaps necessarily complex, series of house types.[8] Building materials and structural systems are also considered significant but not determinant of house style and form or type. *Common Houses in America's Small Towns*, by John A. Jakle, Robert W. Bastien, and Douglas K. Meyer, identifies as many as sixty-seven "structural forms" of vernacular dwellings from the Atlantic seaboard to the Mississippi valley.[9] The diagnostic characteristics used to classify types are floor plan, as it defines "perimeter outline and room arrangement, height (the number of occupied stories), and roof type." *Common Houses*, like the McAlester guide, covers a large geographic area and spans many historic periods, resulting in a complex set of house types.

One architectural guide has offered a typology similar to the one in this study. The similarity seems to be based upon the fact that the buildings typed are all mail-order houses produced by Sears, Roebuck, and Company. They represent an American commercial vernacular similar to the rural vernacular tradition of farmhouses. In *Houses by Mail*, Katherine Cole Stevenson and H. Ward Jandl collaborated to define fifteen house types that were available through Sears from 1895 to 1940. The criteria for the classification of these dwellings were the kind of roof, number of stories, location of the front door, and presence of dormers.[10]

In a less related analysis of folk housing in middle Virginia, Henry Glassie presented a classification of traditional type dwellings.[11] Beginning with the square of the floor plan as the basic geometric language of building, Glassie used a structuralist approach or grammar of building within the folk tradition of single-pen, hall-and-parlor, and double-pen houses to chart an inevitable logic of the transformation of dwellings over a limited time and space. Although the basic elements of the grammar are comprehensible, the application of that logic to the syntax of actual structures becomes excessively complex. My study of farmhouses in the Upper Midwest treats a wider variety of house types constructed by a greater diversity of people in a larger region during a longer period of time than Glassie's study. Any efforts to apply a similar structuralist approach to identify and analyze farmhouse types in the full range of balloon frame farmhouses would lead to extraordinary complexities.[12]

Currently there is no universally accepted method of classifying vernacular buildings. Each typology is based on a system of classification that depends upon objective data collected in a particular region of the United States and on each scholar's perceptions and interpretation of that data.[13] Thomas C. Hubka has suggested an approach involving interdisciplinary considerations of spatial organization, architectural style, structural system, social usage, and environmental context. I will be using many of these

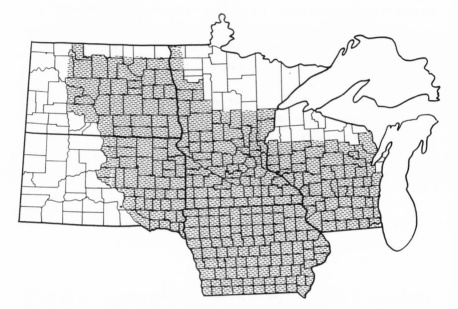

Figure 2.2. The upper midwestern states: Agricultural areas included in the survey of balloon frame farmhouses

approaches to understanding groups of farmhouses and individual dwellings.[14]

The typology for balloon frame farmhouses presented here is based upon several methods of collecting, analyzing, and interpreting the data. First, an extensive, long-term exploration of the region involved locating, counting, and studying existing farmhouses. Second, intensive study of individual farmhouses resulted in social and local historical information about the structure as a house and a home as well as specific technical data about how local builders used balloon frame construction. Third, a study of the history of the five-state region as part of national history provided a spatial-temporal framework to see the data in a broad perspective. Knowledge of the art historical traditions of Western civilization gave a broad and focused view of the aesthetic questions and concerns that directly affected the history of architecture and vernacular building in the nineteenth century.

In this survey, the Upper Midwest is defined as the primarily agricultural areas of Wisconsin, Minnesota, Iowa, South Dakota, and North Dakota (Figure 2.2). I did not survey as intensively areas in the western Dakotas, northern Wisconsin, and northern Minnesota, where ranching, mining, or

Table 2.1. The Upper Midwest Farmhouse Survey: The Three Phases

Type	1977–1981	1982–1985[a]	1985–1986
1	1,118(21.6)[b]	145(16.3)	123 (7.7)
2	359 (7.0)	30 (3.3)	68 (4.2)
3	1,249(24.1)	263(29.7)	456(28.5)
4	416 (8.0)	92(10.3)	134 (8.4)
5	32 (.06)	7 (.08)	6 (.04)
6	34 (.06)	6 (.08)	14 (.09)
7	13 (.02)	0 (0)	1 (0)
8	148 (2.8)	8 (.09)	52 (3.2)
9	1,007(19.4)	160(18.1)	313(19.6)
10	142 (2.7)	37 (4.1)	50 (3.1)
11	660(12.7)	137(15.4)	379(23.7)

[a]Lac Qui Parle County only.
[b]Numbers in parentheses are percentages.

lumbering were important. During the second half of the nineteenth century, parcels of land from 160 to 320 acres were either purchased, preempted, or homesteaded. These relatively small tracts were perceived as sufficient to operate a family-owned farm. During the same period, the focus of American agriculture shifted from subsistence farming to commercial agriculture. Therefore, I identify agricultural areas in the Upper Midwest as places that contained family farming operations involved in raising feed and/or cash crops and/or small-scale livestock operations. In the initial phases of settlement, the majority of farmers raised wheat as a primary cash crop, but by the late 1880s and early 1890s most family farms had diversified their efforts. By the 1900s farm management promoted more-specialized agricultural operations on farms somewhat larger than those of previous decades.[15]

I initially studied virtually every county in the region where agriculture prevailed with the windshield survey method. This method provided an efficient means to collect data from which to tabulate the number of existing farmhouses, classify those structures into one of the ten major farmhouse types, and compute the percentage of each type within the whole sample.[16] Early in the fieldwork, I postulated and tested a tentative set of farmhouse types against both the findings of the windshield survey and the nature of the farmhouses perceived and analyzed according to type. The result is the system represented in Table 2.1, which I modified from a more complex set of criteria. The chart gives the actual number of farmhouses classified according to the established types and then indicates the numerical proportion of the types to one another.

One must be careful and cautious in recording and analyzing the results of a windshield survey.[17] After farmhouse types are established, one consistently discovers exceptions that seem to prove the rule. For example, some farmhouses have undergone such extensive changes in basic structure and surface remodeling that it is difficult to determine the original shape and appearance of the dwelling. Classification of these kinds of structures must be postponed until there is accurate information about their histories.

One can devise checks and controls to test the reliability of a windshield survey. I accomplished the survey for this study in three phases (Table 2.1). My first research trips throughout the region began in 1977 and became more frequent and concentrated during 1980–81. In the next survey, from 1982 to 1985, I focused on one county in Minnesota (Lac Qui Parle) with a large number of farmhouses, both occupied and abandoned. I located, counted, classified, and tabulated every farmhouse in the county. The proportionate representation of each farmhouse type in the single-county survey was remarkably similar to that of the entire Upper Midwest region. The third phase of the survey, during 1985–86, included areas in Iowa and Wisconsin I had not previously covered. A substantial number of farmhouses were added to the survey and again the relative percentages of different farmhouse types remained consistent with the other phases of the survey. This kind of consistency does not prove that the survey is flawless, but it does demonstrate that this typing system is applicable to the entire region and that the numbers and percentages of farmhouse types are consistent throughout.

Further, when I related the results of the survey to the settlement history of certain areas in the region, it was possible to predict with some accuracy the types of farmhouses and their frequency in a given area. For instance, in some areas of the Dakotas where soil and climate make farming more difficult and less financially rewarding, one would anticipate farmhouses of the economical kind, most likely the one- to one-and-a-half-story gabled rectangular type or smaller versions of the ell- or T-plan type. My survey of such areas showed the supposition to be true. The converse is also possible. Larger farmhouses of type 9 (the two-story foursquare) or type 10 (the Vernacular Villa) were predicted and found in such rich agricultural areas as the Red River valley in Minnesota and North Dakota. In some areas such as southern Iowa, where many generations have worked the same farm, larger and more recent farmhouses shelter and serve the family. Again, one can predict that the two-story foursquare farmhouse type would appear as a large percentage of the dwellings in this area because it was popular from about 1895 to 1917, when farm families decided to replace these old, small, and inadequate structures with new houses.

During the survey, approximately one thousand five hundred farmhouses were photographically recorded. In many instances, I photographed a dwelling extensively to record at least four perspectives of the structure, distinctive ornamentation, structural details, and orientation of the house on its site and in relation to the outbuildings in the farmyard. This documentation built an extensive file of visual information about farmhouses in the region. As I gained experience and the farmhouse types became more clearly established, I became more selective in photographing them to document the "right" example of a farmhouse type. Photographs that were copied from nineteenth-century originals on file in state and county historical centers or in family memorabilia also became important resources. Issues of local newspapers that commemorated a seventy-fifth or one hundredth anniversary of a community frequently reprinted old photographs of farmhouses. The Andreas atlases for Iowa, the Dakotas, and Minnesota contain helpful engraved images of farmhouses that suggest farmhouse types. The farmhouses from these indirect historical sources were, for the most part, identified by name and specific place, but they were not included as data in the survey. Although historically valuable, they remain two-dimensional images of three-dimensional structures. Both the photographs of farmhouses I took during the survey and the photographs and engraved images from collections and atlases served as the visual means to postulate and test the set of farmhouse types I used as a basis for this study.[18]

The concept of artistic style is used in two relatively different ways in defining and identifying farmhouse types.[19] The first use is primarily as a means to discern the essential and recurring formal qualities in farmhouses that lead to the establishment of consistent and characteristic traits shared by a group of structures. As architectural monuments, farmhouses were stylistically analyzed according to essential qualities of visual form—basic geometric masses evident in the elevation of the structure, perimeter of the floor plan, surface articulation and division of exterior walls, and proportional qualities of the whole. Here the concept of artistic style is used as a diagnostic, nonaesthetic tool to identify individual dwellings as belonging to a particular farmhouse type.

The second use of the concept of artistic style is as a means of identifying and dating a structure according to its historical architectural style.[20] During the second half of the nineteenth century, revivals of style from throughout history were applied one after another, changing with fashion and as quickly as the decades. However, there were basic farmhouse types that remained independent of the latest trends. For example, type 9 farmhouses can be identified as Italianate in style, be noted as a Sears, Roebuck version of its kind, or be recorded as a plain and unadorned example of the type (Chapter Seven, Figures 7.12, 7.8, and 7.6, respectively). In using the concept of artistic style to aid in the typing of farmhouses, the focus is initially upon essential formal, nonhistorical properties. It would be misleading and insufficient, however, not to recognize that farmhouse types take on attributes of time and place according to prevailing fashions or stylistic preferences.

Finally, it should be noted that essential qualities of balloon frame construction have contributed to the nature of farmhouse types of the Upper Midwest. The origin and spread of balloon frame construction did not necessarily generate house types that were unique or distinctly different from many traditional house types built with the box frame method or of brick or stone. The balloon frame did provide an excellent means to adapting old house forms to the new industrially milled, standardized framing materials and method. The efficiency and economy of balloon frame construction was most fully realized by using the geometrically simple shapes and floor plans of most traditional house types. The farmhouse types in this study manifest the qualities inherent in this new system: They are based upon the volumes, planes, and spatial enclosures readily derived from balloon frame construction.

The balloon frame structural system possesses an internal logic founded on consistent measurements and proportions. The vertical studs are spaced 16 inches apart on center so that they can accept the 48-inch lath on the interior wall. The basic module of 48 inches, if put consistently into practice, would generate standard room sizes as well as regularized placement of doors and windows in both exterior and interior walls. The module of 16 inches is repeated in the spacing of the floor joists and the studs to provide more efficient joining of members and greater structural strength and integrity. If thoroughly understood and applied as a system of building, balloon frame construction would result in a few basic kinds of structures or, in the case of this study, farmhouse types. Local carpenters and farmer-builders did not customarily use plans or blueprints. They did not incorporate an ideal system of measurement and proportion based upon philosophical or practical values in their work. Many vernacular builders relied upon "a plan in the head," "knowing how to start, get along, and finish" and using techniques that were passed through tradition or learned through experience. Contractors, carpenters, and farmer-builders intuitively adapted popular designs from professional pattern books, proven plans and elevations from local lumberyards, and "model" houses already built in areas of previous residence or in newly settled areas.

The repertoire of house types a local carpenter could build was usually quite small and limited to meet a conservative preference for the successfully tested. The items in the repertoire would be repeated frequently because, after a carpenter learned plans and construction procedures for one or two house types, it was easy to achieve modifications in scale, proportion, and external finish to satisfy individual clients. Actual farmhouse dimensions were frequently determined on the basis of the lengths of the least expensive milled lumber available at the local lumberyard. It was sometimes most economical to buy lumber by the boxcar lot; this realized savings for the builder but also influenced the size and proportions of the dwelling, depending upon the amount, sizes, and lengths of the material. An abstract theory of measurement and proportion did not contribute significantly to the specific, practical factors that caused variety in real balloon frame farmhouses. The results that were achieved were of the most practical nature and the means to achieve them were usually the most economical and expedient.

The farmhouse types in this book are, therefore, derived from direct study of structures in the field through broad survey techniques and intensive examination of individual dwellings. The study of the history of the Upper Midwest region in the context of national history provided a perspective in which to understand qualities of form, technique, and style of farmhouse types in the region. The concept of artistic style furthered this comprehension, first as an analytical tool to perceive and identify essential formal traits of the structures and then as a historical tool to recognize and evaluate the changes of architectural fashions prevalent during the period. Finally, a knowledge of the qualities of the balloon frame structural system and also an awareness of the practical ways builders employed the method contributed to understanding how they were built according to discernible farmhouse types.

3. SETTLEMENT AND SHELTER

Before balloon frame construction became the primary way to plan and realize houses on farms in the Upper Midwest, settlers built small shelters intended to last for a limited number of years. These temporary dwellings met basic needs with minimum resources and taught most settlers how to "make do" with essentials for survival. Although balloon frame farmhouses differed from the shelters they replaced, the form and finish of the permanent dwellings were influenced by the practice of expedience and economy necessary to survive on the frontier.

Pioneering began in the region when southern Wisconsin and eastern Iowa opened for settlement in the mid-1830s, after the federal government had negotiated treaties with Indian tribes on those lands. Most of these pioneers were Yankee farmers from New England, New York, and Pennsylvania searching for good land. As late as 1900, eastern European immigrants began developing marginal cutover forest areas of northern Wisconsin and Minnesota. After 1900, grasslands west of the Missouri River were the last prairie areas to be cultivated (Figure 3.1). From about 1830 to the early 1900s tens of thousands of people from more than thirty-five ethnic groups arrived in the Upper Midwest and made their homes there. Those who settled in rural areas frequently had traveled with family and friends to establish ethnic communities in the new land. Most were farmers, who developed the most characteristic feature of the region—the family farm.

Before the Upper Midwest was transformed into a center for agriculture, other forces had shaped the environment. Before the second half of the eighteenth century, explorers, trappers, and hunters, the first white intruders, had come to the region, but their numbers were small and their tenure brief. Surveyors had platted the land into the rational gridwork of square-mile sections before most settlers arrived. Within this practical ge-

William Knowles farmhouse, Morton County, North Dakota (State Historical Society of North Dakota)

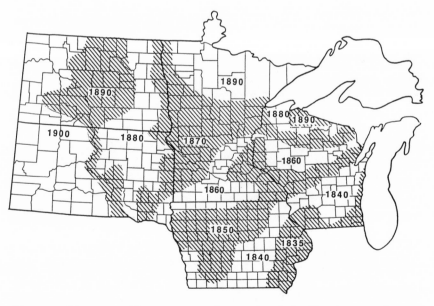

Figure 3.1. The upper midwestern states: Areas and periods of immigrant settlement

ometry, entrepreneurs developed towns—essential trade centers that served the region's emerging agricultural economy. The geographic structuring of the land also facilitated the formation of local governance and education. Each rural township level was divided into thirty-six sections, and land within it was reserved for or had to be sold to fund government facilities and schools. The country schoolhouse became the center of civic life that focused on education and participation in government.

Travel to and within the region was initially accomplished by difficult journeys on waterways, turnpikes, wagon trails, and ox-cart trails and across open land. Railroad transportation began to develop in the region by the 1850s. Continued rail expansion both stimulated and coincided with settlement and growth. In 1830, only 23 miles of railroad track served the nation; by 1860, the railroad had built 30,626 miles of track.[1] Railroad expansion increased after 1860 when railroad corporations received large grants of lands from the federal government on which to lay track; they financed this construction through land sales (Figure 3.2). Iowa, Minnesota, and North Dakota were most affected by this transfer of extremely large tracts of land from the public domain to corporate possession. Railroad companies actively encouraged settlement along their routes by developing towns, selling farmland to immigrants, and embellishing a glowing rhetoric about the agricultural and economic future of the region as the Promised Land or New Eden.[2]

Through a refinement and extension of 1830 federal preemption laws, settlers in 1841 could acquire land from the government for towns or farms if they were the head of a family, a widow, or a single male who was a citizen or in the process of becoming a citizen and who was twenty-one years old or older. Such a person could file claim on land and purchase no more than 160 acres at the price of $1.25 per acre. The settler had to demonstrate improvement of the land for habitation by digging a well and building a house or suitable shelter on the property. In 1862 Congress passed the Homestead Act, which superseded the preemption process of obtaining public lands. Any adult head of a household who was or was becoming a citizen could, through homesteading, pay a $10 fee, file on 160 acres of land, and live on and improve that land for at least five years. After that period, a final filing fee of $5 would secure full title to the land. By 1873, supplemented by the Timber Culture Act, the Homestead Act encouraged the planting and nurturing of trees on prairies. It provided a tree claim of 160 acres in addition to the quarter section of land entitled in the homestead claim. The settler was required to plant trees on at least 40 of the 160 acres of this additional claim. An individual could, therefore, acquire up to

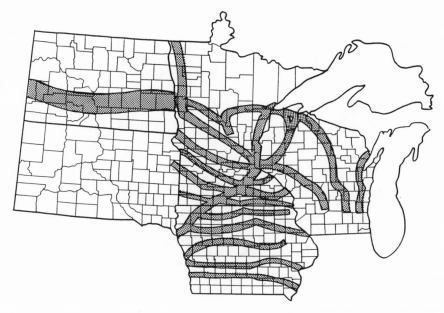

Figure 3.2. The upper midwestern states: Federal land grants to railroad corporations, 1850–1890

320 acres of public land in some areas of the region. Enterprising couples who were engaged to be married or "children" over age twenty-one who were within a larger household could file as individuals to take advantage of their separate homestead rights and tree claims. By claiming land on adjoining sections, a couple or family could obtain a small empire of a section or more of land.

Railroad corporations were involved in real estate trade as much as in transportation and commerce. Owning land for miles on either side of their rights of way, their representatives actively promoted emigration from Europe and sold land to newcomers at varying costs. Land close to the railroad could be sold for more than $70 per acre, even though it was poor farm property. Despite high prices and the availability of virtually free federal land, many had the means and inclination to buy a farm on railroad land to ensure easy access to transportation. Land transactions also took place through wealthy speculators who as groups or individuals purchased large tracts at low cost to sell at a profit, to develop estate farms, or to rent to tenant farmers. Iowa was so affected by the latter practice that in 1880 up to 23 percent of its farms were operated by tenant farmers.[3]

The vegetation and soil confronting the pioneer varied greatly according

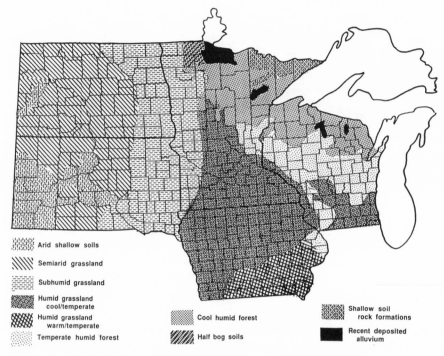

Arid shallow soils

Semiarid grassland

Subhumid grassland

Humid grassland
   cool/temperate

Humid grassland
   warm/temperate

Temperate humid forest

Cool humid forest

Half bog soils

Shallow soil
   rock formations

Recent deposited
   alluvium

Figure 3.3. The upper midwestern states: Soil types

to location. The soils of the Upper Midwest suitable for agriculture have been analyzed and grouped into six broad zones (Figure 3.3). Eastern and south-central Iowa is characterized by rolling grass-covered hills through which numerous streams and rivers flow in deep, forested valleys. The climate there is moderate and humid. Beginning with the narrow southern section of Wisconsin and fanning out to almost the full extent of the western borders of Iowa and Minnesota is a vast open prairie. Stands of trees grow along rivers and streams, on lake shores, and on escarpments. Here for the first time in their movement westward, settlers experienced the full horizon of the earth and the seemingly endless expanse of light across the sky. Stretching across Wisconsin and bordering both shores of the Mississippi River a hardwood forest grows upon undulating hills and valleys. North of this warm, humid deciduous forest region, the larger cool, humid forest of conifers constitutes the great pineries of Minnesota and Wisconsin. The subhumid and semiarid grasslands of South Dakota and North Dakota presented settlers with their last obstacle to establishing farms, dairies, and/or cattle ranches to gain a livelihood from the land.

In addition to various soils and vegetation, settlers also experienced a change of seasons and a variety in daily weather conditions. In the southern sections of the prairie and in the temperate humid forests, the growing season for long-maturing crops was sufficient, rainfall usually dependable and adequate, and winters cold but tolerable. On the northern stretches of the prairie and in the subhumid and semiarid grasslands, the time between planting and harvest was less than ninety days, rainfall scattered and unpredictable, and winters severely cold with low temperatures intensified by strong winds. Blizzards and thunderstorms, hail and tornadoes, could create havoc on the open lands; torrential rains and floods could destroy crops and property in the hill country. Sometimes drought affected only certain areas; at other times it became a catastrophe endured by all.

Where, when, how, from whom, and at what price farmers acquired, rented, or worked lands in the agricultural areas of the Upper Midwest had great bearing on farm development and house construction. Obviously, pioneers met the various circumstances in each area and during each phase of settlement. Greatly differing terrains fostered widely differing kinds of agriculture, from the relatively small dairy farms in Wisconsin and Minnesota to huge wheat farms in the Dakotas.

It cannot be assumed that all, or even a majority, of the immigrants who came to the new territory acquired land, built a habitation, began to cultivate the earth, reaped bountiful harvests, and improved and expanded their estates from profits made through the sale of cash crops. One had to have a relatively large amount of money to purchase land and to plant and harvest crops. Getting started necessitated an initial capital outlay of $500 to $1,000 or more. Solon Robinson, an experienced pioneer in northern Indiana in the 1830s, itemized the costs as follows:

160 acres at $1 25, is	$200
Timber, say 40 acres, which is more than enough, at $3,	120
Breaking up the prairie, at 1 50,	240
Fencing it into four lots, eight rails high and stakes, 960 rods, or 3 miles, 15,366 rails at 1 ct. 153 66; 3,840 stakes, at ½ ct. 19 20,	173
A good comfortable double log cabin, such as first settlers generally occupy,	50
Other small buildings and temporary sheds,	50
Average cost of a well with pump, $30, with buckets, $15,	15
I will add to cover contingencies, such as a half an	

acre of land well paled in for garden, a cow yard,
hog pen, and other "fixings,"   72
This makes the cost of the farm, independent of the
woodland, just $5 an acre—the total, $920[4]

When Horace Greeley went west in 1859, he provided a higher estimate "for the farmer who comes with liberal means." Greeley laid out a program that involved buying 160 acres of land at $10 per acre, hiring two good farm laborers, buying a yoke of oxen, two wagon horses, a milk cow, and two heifers, putting up "a cabin that will just do," and planting as much winter wheat as one can before the ground is frosted in late fall. During the winter, wood was to be processed for a better house to which one would welcome the family members when they arrived in spring. By then one would plant spring wheat and other crops, build fences, put in a garden and tabulate the accounts that established the farm at a cost of $5,000. Greeley admits, "He who comes in with but $2,000, $1,000, or $500, must of course be much longer in working his way to a position of comfort and independence."[5] Many who came to the new region did not even have $100 to purchase essentials and finance beginnings. Some pioneers were virtually penniless and had to hire themselves out as farm laborers or servants to survive and eventually, if fortunate, save enough to purchase land or pay filing fees on public lands acquired through homesteading.

Whatever one's circumstances, the first stages of agriculture were minimal. The farmer was a "farming hunter" involved in the most important business of surviving. He subsisted by using the land's resources as much as possible and relying on his skills and those of his family.[6] It is in this context of survival and subsistence that basic pioneer shelters should be understood. Much has been recalled and written, even by those who endured the hardships of life in a cabin, or "soddie," that romanticizes the nature of these dwellings and perpetuates a myth that "the good life" was something forged in simple circumstances and rudimentary existence. The temporary quality of almost all subsistence shelters on the frontier indicates that "the good life" in these mean surroundings was soon abandoned for an even better life in a larger, more convenient, and comfortable house.

The most primitive kind of shelter on the upper midwestern frontier was the dugout. The settler chose a hillside or gully in which he dug a room and covered the extended entrance with a minimum of natural materials—usually branches and thatch, logs, or prairie sod—collected near the construction site. One settler described this first, primitive shelter.

Dwellings for the colonists themselves were next constructed. For this purpose hillsides were selected in which small cellars could be excavated, with an opening facing south. Over the opening, walls were built of logs fashioned from trees that grew along the lake shore. A door and a window was placed in each log wall. These cellars furnished the first homes to which the settlers could move after having spent an entire summer with "prairie schooners" as their only living quarters. There was nothing elaborate about these humble dwellings, but they furnished protection from the cold and snow. They were the forerunners of hundreds of modern farm homes that since have been reared above the prairies that these colonists were the first to venture upon.[7]

The other type of dugout was made by using sod slabs to make walls projecting from the hillside cellar. A wooden frame supported a roof covered with sod.

The log cabin was the kind of subsistence shelter that pioneers most frequently built in the Upper Midwest. That choice is not unusual for those settling in the region's forested areas, but it is somewhat surprising that in supposedly treeless areas such as North Dakota, the log cabin was the most prevalent type of house on the prairie until milled lumber became available to build shanties.[8] Wherever trees of suitable size grew along streams, rivers, lakes, and hillsides, settlers used them to construct cabins, sometimes hauling the logs for miles across the prairie to the home site.

Logs were favored as construction material because they had customarily been used on the frontier. Without rehearsing the entire history of and controversy about the origin and geographic dispersion of the log cabin in America, it should suffice to say that the building type was imported to the New World in the seventeenth century by Swedish immigrants who settled in Delaware and German immigrants who settled in Pennsylvania. From there, the log cabin became commonplace in the westward settlement of the nation.[9] Another reason for the popularity of the log cabin was that except for some nails, metal hinges, and glass for windows, it cost virtually nothing. It was not unusual for cabins to be built without these items. The log cabin also had the advantage of being a relatively permanent structure that could eventually be joined to a larger balloon frame house or used as an outbuilding on the farm.

An account by Olaf Erickson, a Norwegian immigrant to Wisconsin, relates a typical series of events that led up to the attainment of his family's first home in the New World.

They reached their destination about the middle of September and found work almost immediately near Springville, Wisconsin. . . . They stayed there about a year, Father working most of the time grubbing out trees and stumps at a fixed sum per acre. He cleared two acres of timber land for one man and received a two-year-old brindle heifer in the exchange, the first livestock my parents owned in the New World. . . . In the fall of 1868 the little family, now with their second son . . . moved to what was destined to be their home for the rest of their lives—a valley called Brush Creek. . . . [t]he first winter they lived with Bugbee's son Moab. . . . Father worked at 50 cents a day whenever he could get work; days when he could not, he spent clearing ground and cutting logs for their first house. By spring he had the log house completed, 16 × 24 feet and about a story and one half in height. None of the material was bought except the windows, the hinges, and the nails; even the shingles were hand split. In the spring of 1869 they moved into their own home. What a day it was! How wonderful to be in their own house![10]

Olaf's father did not build their cabin by himself. Raising a cabin was a community effort that was a special social event. After family members had cut and dragged the logs to the building site, they prepared other equipment, such as smooth, slender trees and some strong forked branches used for rolling logs in place on the upper part of the walls of the cabin. Men with experience rived shingles from sections of hardwood and cedar logs for the roof covering. Others sawed puncheons for the broad, rough floor boards of the cabin. Joists were cut to be mortised into the sill for the ground floor and sometimes into the logs above for the floor of a half-story loft. Planed wood planks were prepared for window and door frames. Those who were especially skilled with the ax and experienced in raising a cabin stationed themselves at the corners of the structure to cut the notches before the construction crew raised and set them in place. After the exterior walls were erected, door and window openings were cut into the perimeter of the shelter, and construction of the roof began with placement of the rafters and ridge pole over the substructure. In some instances, part of the day's informal ceremony was the telling of tales and jokes, passing around a jug of whisky, and sharing a meal prepared by the women. The small scale of the log cabin made it possible for several men to accomplish most of the construction in one day.

The day the Ericksons occupied their cabin must have seemed a special occasion because it was the result of years of journey and labor. The finished structure probably looked much like the William Krueger cabin (Fig-

Figure 3.4. The William Krueger log house, Jefferson County, Wisconsin, no date
(State Historical Society of Wisconsin)

ure 3.4). The shape and location of the chimneys on these log cabins were
different from those of cabins built earlier in the westward movement of the
frontier. The iron stove that pioneers brought with them or purchased after
arrival was usually centrally placed in the cabin's interior so it could better
heat both stories. Frequently only a half chimney rising from the second
floor near the center of the house marked the location of this appliance.
The Fingal Enger log cabin and floor plan illustrate a typical way that interior space was divided (Figure 3.5). The half-story loft was customarily an
open, undivided space where children and visitors slept. Like many log
houses in the region, the Enger house was home for the growing family for
almost twenty years. These first structures, now sheathed in clapboard, still
serve farm families as the core or wing of a balloon frame farmhouse.

Unlike log cabins, sod houses were seen as ephemeral by most settlers.
They built these earthen shelters when the only material available was the
tightly woven root system of prairie grasses. Sod house builders cut broad
fibrous ribbons from the prairie by turning the sod with a plow and using

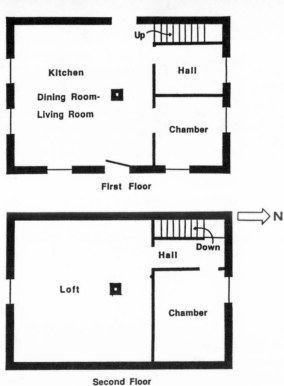

Figure 3.5. The Fingal Enger log house, Steele County, North Dakota, 1875

a straight edge spade to slice it into slabs 12 to 18 inches wide. The first two layers began as parallel rows defining a square or rectangle measuring about 14 × 14 or 14 × 20 feet. Atop this, more slabs were pounded into place at right angles to the first, alternating until they reached 7½ to 8 feet. Window and door frames, constructed in advance, fit into the walls as sod slabs that rose to the full height of the walls. Tree branches and slender tree trunks or milled lumber supplied the framework for a low, sloping roof. Tar paper covered the frame, and a layer of sod completed the roof of the shelter.[11]

Two examples of sod houses will illustrate the range of possibilities in using earth materials. The Art Ogdall sod house in western Minnesota (Figure 3.6) has thick walls that taper toward the center of the small interior like the sides of a tent. The John T. Wallace sod house in North Dakota (Figure 3.7), built after 1900, is a one-and-a-half-story house with a wood frame superstructure. Considerable care and precision was used in creating the substructure for the framed half story so that the downward diagonal thrust and the weight of the roof would be supported adequately.

One had to step down into some sod houses because the floor was below ground level. This feature gave the house a low profile that made it look like a grassy knoll on the open land. A twofold division customarily defined the interior as kitchen/living room and bedroom. In some locations settlers used lime from natural deposits or purchased it in town to make a mortar covering that protected both the exterior and the interior surfaces. The white coating did much to brighten the interior of the thick-walled structure.

Almost every recollection of life in a sod house asserts that it was warm in the winter and cool in the summer because of its thick insulating walls and its low profile in the prairie winds. The sod roof also aided in keeping the interior of the house comfortable. Other recollections note the effects of natural elements and age. Birds collected nesting materials from the sod walls. Mice, rats, and snakes burrowed into and through the walls. The roof weakened, leaked, and sometimes collapsed. As this frail structure returned to its natural state, the house became a haven for small wildlife and increasingly cold and drafty as the tight seal of sod slabs was perforated or gradually eroded. Once abandoned, a sod house soon returned to the earth from which it came.[12]

A description of a sod house by a pioneer woman who first lived in one on the South Dakota prairie provides a glimpse into this type of shelter.

When we came near the Home Farm I asked Christian to show me the house from a distance so I could see if it looked nice—Oh, well! if one

Figure 3.6. The Art Ogdall sod house, Stevens County, Minnesota, ca. 1875 (Stevens County Historical Society, Morris, Minnesota)

Figure 3.7. The John T. Wallace sod house, Burleigh County, North Dakota, ca. 1910 (State Historical Society of North Dakota)

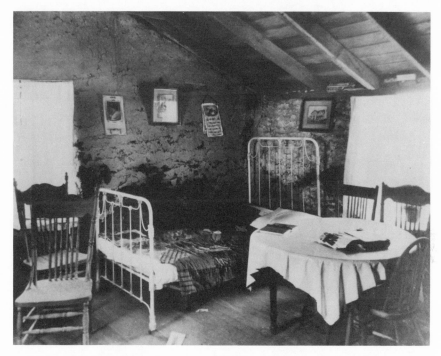

Figure 3.8. The Elling Onstad sod house, Walsh County, North Dakota, 1923 (North Dakota Institute for Regional Studies, Fargo)

isn't too spoiled it perhaps can pass, although without a doubt the interior is much more inviting than the exterior. . . . The interior is like a fairy palace. We have first a kitchen, which is also Christian's bedroom, our dining room, and usually our sitting room, as we have there a pretty hanging lamp and our largest table. . . . In my salon, besides my bed and a pretty little table (all carpenter work is done by Christian, likewise the buildings) a metal rocking chair, a cupboard, and two chairs with cane seats, so it is very fine.[13]

A rare photograph of the interior of a North Dakota sod house shows a relatively finished space with a stuccoed wall and wooden floor (Figure 3.8). The picture of a large frame farmhouse hanging on the wall over the bed seems to express a hope for better things to come. This shelter is like a sod house described by another South Dakota pioneer woman. She explained that the dwelling in which she lived was divided into two spaces—one contained three to four beds and the other held a kitchen range, a table for nine people, a sewing machine, and a rocking chair. The floors were wooden, and a small cellar under the kitchen was used for storing produce and canned goods.[14] This description was in a letter written to relatives in Norway. Its positive tone was probably to assure folks at home that all was well in the New World. Many in America also needed reassurance that the presence of sod houses on the frontier was not a sign that the settlers had lapsed into a state of "barbaric laziness."[15]

In 1874 an illustrated article about sod houses appeared in the *American Agriculturist* (Figure 3.9). It described this type of subsistence shelter as suitable for pioneers carrying culture to the wilderness. The journal's editors described sod houses as

> the home of a hardy, industrious, worthy representative of the spirit of adventure and enterprise, who carves a home for himself out of the wilderness. Each frequently shelters beneath its roof a settler who is poor of everything but hope and determination to succeed, but yet in each we have seen a home where an intelligent family has lived in comfort and has enjoyed many of the advantages of what is called civilized life. Books, pictures, and music are sometimes seen in such habitations, occupied by well-educated and intelligent settlers.[16]

The illustrations portray an idealized, architecturally geometric image of the sod house and its occupants involved in domestic labors and cultural pursuits. Compared with the organic irregularities of actual sod houses and the accounts of struggle for survival in them, the views of the East Coast editors of the *American Agriculturist* appear inaccurate and overly positive.

The construction of dugouts, log cabins, and sod houses taught settlers to build with scale and proportion commensurate with natural materials and to "make do" until larger and more convenient accommodations could be constructed. The claim shanty was akin to a balloon frame house because it was a wooden building made with milled lumber joined with nails. A shanty was a small structure, usually one room, that was built on the prairies of the Upper Midwest at places where lumber could be purchased and hauled to the homestead (Figure 3.10). In some places, settlers could pay $50 to $60 for lumber, its delivery to the building site, and construction of the shanty.[17] Settlers built shanties in western and northwestern Minnesota and in South Dakota and North Dakota from the 1860s to the early 1900s as one of the requisites to prove up the homestead claim. A typical shanty had a lightweight sill with 2×4 inch studs nailed to it and capped by a 2×4 inch plate. A thin, low-pitched roof covered the shelter. Since the sill was usually set directly on the ground, the floor of the shanty

SOD HOUSE—EXTERIOR.

SOD HOUSE—INTERIOR.

Figure 3.9. "The Sod House." From "The Sod House," *American Agriculturist* 33 (1874): 179–80.

Figure 3.10. The W. T. Batty shanty, North Dakota, no date or place (State Historical Society of North Dakota)

was earth. When rough boards were used as siding, tar paper was laid over them and fastened by nailing lath over the surface. Clapboards or vertical boards and battens were also sometimes used as siding. Lath and plaster were not used for interior walls, but sometimes newspapers were pasted on them for insulation. Some settlers shoveled dirt around the sill over the first tier of siding to insulate the shanty and to deter small wildlife from entering. Others used a tier of sod strips to encase the exterior for insulation. This method of enclosure and insulation became important whenever green lumber was used, because these boards cracked as they dried, leaving gaps through which the prairie winds could blow.

The W. T. Batty family built a shanty of about 10 × 20 feet on their homestead in North Dakota (Figure 3.10). The tent where they lived before they occupied the framed "tent" is visible in the photograph. Randomly placed rocks support the sill of the shanty. The 2 × 4 inch rafters for the roof are unevenly spaced; the vertical studs are also set haphazardly. They did not have to be placed 16 inches on center because no lath and plaster were to be applied to the interior walls. The principle of building a shanty seemed to be to use any method that utilized the lumber available. A metal stovepipe could pierce the roof wherever a small heating stove or cooking range was placed. However primitive their environment might appear, the Batty family had all the essentials to begin farming on the prairie. They even had the rudiments cultural life—components for a strange musical ensemble were displayed on the exterior wall of their dwelling.

Figure 3.II. The James Ward shanty, Walsh County, North Dakota, 1913. (North Dakota Institute for Regional Studies, Fargo)

A somewhat older shanty in a second stage of development illustrates the makeshift measures that settlers were forced to employ (Figure 3.II). Because these subsistence shelters have not survived as human habitations, one must closely examine these vintage photographs for every scrap of evidence that explains how the structures were built and the patterns of work and leisure carried on around them. The four people in Figure 3.II are wearing their "Sunday best." The only decorated part of the shanty is the border over the back door, which also holds a horse shoe for luck in the risky venture of farming on the prairie. The shelter does have a screen door and it appears that screening has been tacked to the shanty window. The stove and stovepipe are centrally located, which may indicate that the interior of the shanty was divided into two rooms. The two barrels on the roof caught rainwater. Although a well certainly was dug on this claim, the water in many parts of North Dakota was either hard or alkaline, making soft rainwater quite desirable. Garden tools, a wooden crate to haul produce from the garden, and a basin to clean the produce are "stored" on the roof of the lean-to.

The size of the cottonwood trees planted behind the shanty indicate that the first part of the structure was built about five years before the photograph was taken. By that time, the settlers had added the lean-to and insulated the floor and walls by stacking sod around the footing and tacking lath along the eave of the slightly arched roof. The roof on this shanty was apparently unique to North Dakota and may have originated from the design of cook cars used on bonanza farms. Many homesteaders in eastern North Dakota who worked on bonanza farms learned about these portable structures and adapted them as shelters.[18] Since the cook car was on wheels, it was an apt model for claim shanties on the prairies. Because they were so small, the shanties could be moved intact. One could also carry the materials for a shanty on one wagon from a local mill or the last railroad stop where lumber supplies were available. There are records of people building a shanty before they start their journey west, tearing it down, and reassembling it on the new claim.[19]

Even though the shanty was a practical and inexpensive first shelter for settlers, few if any recall them with fondness. They were not perceived as the homes of future presidents. Nor were they remembered as "warm in the winter and cool in the summer." The interior of a shanty was a cramped multipurpose space. An author who had thoroughly researched his family's pioneering history on the prairie related an account by his grandfather of occupying a shanty on his North Dakota claim.

This evening I write from the shelter of a claim shack—my new home on my new land. Although I have slept several times without shelter, I now have at least the rough beginnings of a home. I got the dimension lumber from Capt. Herman's saw mill. He set up a mill in the woods of oaks along Devils Lake. . . . Now he cuts lumber for claim shacks. He owed me some pay, but I took 2 × 4s instead. I used some of my railroad pay to buy the rest of the lumber—mostly shiplap—from the Northwestern Lumber Company in Minnewaukan. It's a familiar pine from the northern loggings of Minnesota. The railroad brings it to the railhead at Creel Bay. From there, one of the ferries . . . drays the lumber to Minnewaukan. My shack is 10' long, 6' wide, and has a sloping roof 7' high at the front and 6' high at the rear. The double sash window and door face the south—toward the sun and away from the northwest wind. I covered the outside with tar paper and vertical battens. . . . I used some leftover shiplap and dimension lumber to build a low platform which serves as my bed. A bundle of dry Buffalo grass suffices as a soft, sweet-smelling mattress. My immigrant trunk serves as my table, work bench, and seat. Soon I will get a small stove for heat and cooking. My coat and hat hang on a long-handled shovel plunged into the ground. I have learned to make do. In this, my new world is centered.[20]

Figure 3.12. A small claim farmhouse, Ward County, North Dakota, ca. 1900.

One other example of a larger, more finished claim shanty (Figure 3.12) provides an appropriate point of transition to farmhouses of balloon frame construction. There is a qualitative difference between this structure and log cabins, sod houses, and many claim shanties. The scale and proportions of this small structure are not determined by the dimensions of logs or sod or the casual use of milled lumber. This house is built in balloon frame construction with studs placed 16 inches on center to receive the 48-inch lath for interior plaster walls. Further, the exterior walls at 12 and 16 foot lengths and widths allowed for regular, even placement of studs and joists on the sill.

This dwelling documents a revolution in thought and practice about building balloon frame structures—a revolution characterized by a *turn toward* a relatively new orientation but not a complete *turn away* from traditional perspectives. Traditional types of houses were not abandoned when the new method and new materials began to be used. Balloon frame construction offered a logic of geometry and measurement inherent in the size and spacing of the members that formed each dwelling. Relatively new types of houses developed as builders adapted traditional house types to balloon frame construction. The result was a building practice that retained some formal patterns of the past and incorporated a new and more flexible way to conceive of and realize architectural space.

Migrants from the eastern United States and immigrants from western and eastern Europe could not foretell how they would alter the landscape during the initial phases of settlement and before they built permanent houses on their land. They already lived and worked in the grid pattern of township, section, and quarter section of land that government surveyors had platted before their arrival. Plowing for seasonal planting further marked the land with furrows parallel to the straight boundaries of fields. Eventually, the established farmer would plan and build a house that reflected the planar geometry and regular dimensions of the landscape. He would utilize balloon frame construction as the most economical and efficient means to shelter his family. The following chapters develop several interpretive perspectives toward how balloon frame farmhouses resulted from the creative interaction of vernacular builders with their time and place in the history of the nation.

4. FARMHOUSE TYPES 1 AND 2: WHAT MAKES A HOUSE A HOME?

People who pioneered in the Upper Midwest from 1830 to 1920 experienced rapid and enormous changes in almost every aspect of their lives. They changed the physical environment from what they considered wilderness to a garden of productive farms. Entrepreneurs developed towns and cities as important trade centers, while others built railroad lines that commercially linked the rural and urban sectors of the nation. Agriculture that began as subsistence farming quickly became large cash-crop operations, which grew into diversified livestock and crop farming, and finally became specialized commercial ventures. A scientific approach to agriculture improved the quality of seeds and livestock, suggested better methods for nurturing crops and animals, and outlined ways to manage the business aspects of farming. The growth of technology and industry developed implements and machinery, making farm labor easier, faster, and more efficient. These broad changes in lifestyle and labor are reflected in the kinds of farmhouses built in the region during this period.

A discussion of dwellings representative of farmhouse types 1 and 2 (Figures 4.2–4.6 and 4.10–4.13) will illustrate a development of ideas and values pertaining to the farm family home. These two farmhouse types include examples of the smallest and simplest of structures as well as some of the largest and most fully appointed houses in the region. This range provides the context in which to perceive and understand the limits in which architectural ambitions in rural America operated. A conception of the farmhouse as a shelter performing basic functions changed to an ideal of a home that could provide comforts, amenities, and planned efficiencies.

A simple rectangular shape covered by a saddle roof that created gables at two ends of the structure describes the fundamental architectural qualities of farmhouse types 1 and 2. These gabled rectangular dwellings consis-

Farmhouse kitchen

tently vary in elevation from one to one-and-a-half to two stories. This continuum of vertical scale results from qualities of the balloon frame. The length of the studs in the side exterior walls of the structure determines the elevation (Figure 4.1). For instance, a dwelling built with 9-foot studs creates one story with interior space about 8 to 9 feet high and a loft space on the half story. A farmhouse of 12-foot studs in the exterior side walls allows for a 9-foot ceiling on the first floor the full width and length of the structure; but on the half story, the interior side walls of the structure must be set in at least 3 feet from the exterior walls in order to provide a moderate height of about 6 feet before the ceiling slopes to a full 8-foot height in the middle of the chamber. Studs of 18-foot length in the exterior side walls provide a 9-foot ceiling on the first floor and an 8-foot 6-inch ceiling on the second story without a narrowing of the floor space on the second story. Farmhouses of types 1 and 2 have in fact been built with studding in the exterior side walls of 8 to 20 or more feet. It is sometimes difficult to tell whether a farmhouse is a one story with loft or attic, a one-and-a-half story, or a full two story.[1]

The one- to one-and-a-half-story gabled rectangular farmhouse was frequently the kind of affordable structure built when circumstances permit-

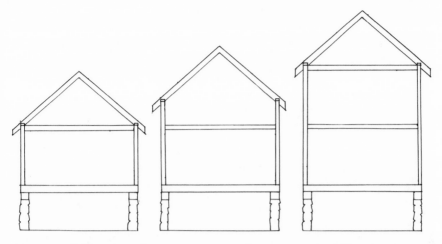

Figure 4.1. Balloon frame house cross sections of one-, one-and-a-half, and two-story structures

ted the family to move from the temporary subsistence shelter to a more permanent dwelling.[2] These structures were but one step beyond the original claim shanty or sod house, which sometimes still functioned as an attached unit (Figures 4.2 and 4.3). Expansion from the subsistence structure to these balloon frame dwellings was a change from a minimum of space to adequate space and involved a move from a one-room interior where al-

Figure 4.2. The Joseph Filbeck farmhouse, Almont County, North Dakota, ca. 1915 (State Historical Society of North Dakota)

Figure 4.3. The Thore Olstad farmhouse, no place or date (State Historical Society of North Dakota)

most all household functions took place to the beginning of specific functions for spaces in the frame house. The new house, however small, enclosed a kitchen and living room–dining room on the first floor and an open sleeping loft under the low sloping roof on the half story.

In these dwellings, interior space was organized in a traditional way by focusing upon the central hearth. As noted above, when farmers began to build balloon frame shelters in the Upper Midwest, iron cooking ranges and heating stoves replaced the central cooking and heating fireplaces of earlier American dwellings. In most instances, farmers connected these industrially produced appliances to a central chimney set in the interior wall that divided the house into two equal or almost equal spaces. A small balloon frame farmhouse in western Minnesota embodies this traditional floor plan (Figure 4.4). The plan includes an entry, kitchen, bedroom, and front hall on the first story with a steep staircase that ascends to an unfinished, undivided loft on the half story. The structure reminds one of log cabins such as the Enger log house in which the ladderlike, angled staircase quickly ascends to the sleeping-storage area close beneath the roof (see Figure 3.5). A hole in the kitchen ceiling of the Minnesota house provides a passage for the stove pipe of the cooking range, connecting it with the chimney in the center of the loft. The practice of focusing interior space on

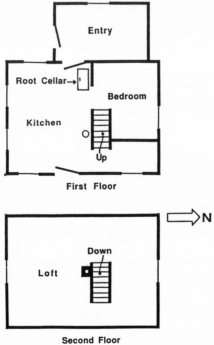

Figure 4.4. Farmhouse type I, Pope County, Minnesota, ca. 1870

the food and warmth of a central hearth dates from antiquity and is preserved in this 1870 farmhouse.[3]

A larger type I farmhouse preserves this simple, traditional division and function of space (Figure 4.5). This structure contains four spaces of almost equal size. The food-preparation and heating functions are focused on the central chimney, where the range and stove are located. A staircase ascends along the north wall to two ample rooms on the second story. The second floor is not an open loft. There is some differentiation of these spaces as bedrooms, but no passage was planned that would fully separate the two chambers. One chamber acts as a passage to the next. The Iowa farmhouse is 28 feet long and 14 feet wide, with exterior walls 14 feet from foundation to eave. This 2-to-1 proportion is evident in the 14-foot width of the lean-to set on the center of the long wall and balanced by windows on the 7-foot section of the remaining wall. A central window and door also equally divide the gabled walls. Moreover, the house displays a structural harmony insofar as twenty studs and joists can be evenly spaced at 16 inches on center on the 28-foot-long sill. An even number of roof rafters (fourteen) are nailed to the plate at 24-inch intervals. The simplicity of a balloon frame gabled rectangular farmhouse lends itself to this kind of proportion and integrity of construction that conserves time, energy, and money and also generates an internal logic of design that is both expedient and classical.

The design of a Swift County, Minnesota, farmhouse built about 1900 (Figure 4.6) reveals an effort to create specialized spaces within the limitations of the small one-and-a-half-story gabled rectangular farmhouse. The first floor provides an adequate kitchen functioning in relation to a somewhat large entry-storage-pantry wing. The parents probably used the small downstairs bedroom because it permitted easy access to the kitchen and the entry at all hours of the day and night. The largest space on the first floor is the dining room–living room with its separate and special doorway to receive guests. The upstairs hall also indicates some specialized functions of space. The hall acts as an antechamber to the three bedrooms, making each room quite private. Some rather complicated angling of walls and doors around the chimney was necessary to allow equal access from an adequately wide hallway. The broad gabled end of the house allows for this greater flexibility in dividing the spaces of the first floor and the half story because this plan accommodates two rooms across the width of the house. The added breadth also necessitates a median support in the foundation or basement of the house. In this instance, 4×6 inch posts support a 4×6 inch beam running centrally through the basement.

Some features of this farmhouse are found in plans for simple homes de-

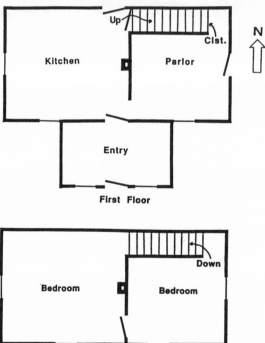

Figure 4.5. Farmhouse type I, Pocahontas County, Iowa, ca. 1880

Figure 4.6. Farmhouse type I, Swift County, Minnesota, ca. 1900 (above and opposite)

signed by professional architects as early as 1850. Architectural stylebooks of the second half of the nineteenth century in America prescribed qualities for a proper domestic environment in small to large houses. Carpenters and farmer-builders never precisely followed the plans and specifications in these stylebooks to construct actual farmhouses in the Upper Midwest. These publications did disseminate concepts and values of professional architects in rural America during the nation's biggest and longest building boom. Many stylebooks featured models for one- to one-and-a-half-story gabled rectangular houses as the most economical laborer's or farmer's cottages.

In *The Architecture of Country Houses*, Andrew Jackson Downing presented a Laborer's Cottage as Design I (Figure 4.7). Using costs that were effective on the eastern seaboard at midcentury, this wooden house, presumably with box frame, cost approximately $400. Because this simple plan is centered on the large cooking-heating fireplace, it is easily adapted to a balloon frame structure with a central chimney. Downing's plan specifies a generic "living room" in which functions of kitchen, dining room, and parlor are intended. The dimensions of the Laborer's Cottage approximate those of small balloon frame farmhouses, but Downing designated

First Floor

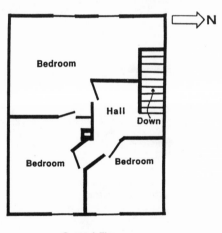

Second Floor

special functions for spaces that are usually absent in Upper Midwest farm-houses—pantry, porch, and closets.[4]

The Laborer's Cottage features fashionable decorative elements such as extended roof eaves with brackets and eaves with brackets over the doors and windows. These create variegated contours in the structure and generate dramatic patterns of light and shadow over its surface. Rough textures, warm colors, and some asymmetry of the façade are features intended to blend the geometric shape of the structure with its natural surroundings. In contrast to plain or nondescript houses, Downing identified this design as

DESIGN I

A LABORER'S COTTAGE

Fig. 5

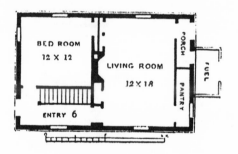

PRINCIPAL FLOOR
Fig. 6

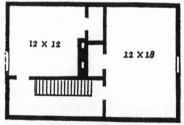

[Fig. 7. Chamber Floor.]

Figure 4.7. "Design I: A Laborer's Cottage," 1850. From Andrew Jackson Downing, *The Architecture of Country Houses* (New York: D. Appleton, 1850), 72.

picturesque, aligning it with the aesthetic taste that prevailed among the upper classes in America during the second half of the nineteenth century.

Working-class people had varying degrees of knowledge about and aesthetic preference for this kind of beauty. The picturesque was not the primary factor determining the designs and decoration of farmhouses in the Upper Midwest. If a farmer-builder or local carpenter used professional plans and specifications for a house, they were more likely to be adapted from plan books such as *Rural Architecture*, made available in 1888 through the auspices of the Northwestern Lumberman's Association of Chicago and locally at the Adams-Horr (Lumber) Company in Minneapolis. Design No. 7 from this pattern book is identified as "a very Cheap House for small Farm or Village Tenement" (Figure 4.8). Actual farmhouses are simpler than this lumberyard design. The latter designated pantry and closets and separate access to bedrooms as essential features of house design. These features were consistently absent in small farmhouse interiors. The Adams-Horr Design No. 19, "a very Cheap and convenient House," offers a plan including a hall, kitchen, living room, and parlor on the first floor (Figure 4.9). The Swift County Farmhouse shows similar intentions within a different configuration of rooms but did not contain a parlor separate from a living room (Figure 4.6). Despite the range of suggestions offered in stylebooks and plan books, the balloon frame houses built on the frontier in the Upper Midwest were consistently simpler and decidedly "cheap." Frugality was a virtue that farmers realized in the prudent operation of establishing and developing a farm. The added costs of beauty or extra conveniences were postponed until one could easily afford them—providing people wanted them in the first place.

In addition to stylebooks and lumberyard plans, agricultural journals were an important means of communicating new building ideas. Farmers who wrote to the editors of these periodicals usually offered advice of a fundamentally practical nature. E. F. Brewer passed along such information and advice to readers of the *American Agriculturist* in 1884 about "a Progressing Dakota Farm Home." Brewer outlined a process by which one could begin by building a small one-story gabled rectangular farmhouse and, through two subsequent additions, conclude with a large ell- or T-plan farmhouse. The first unit was a 14 × 18 foot shanty lined inside and out with "tarred or roofing paper" at an estimated cost of only $80 to $120. One year later, after the first crop had been harvested, an addition to the house measuring 8 × 18 feet was projected and the entire dwelling covered with clapboard. Brewer said that the roof could remain without shingles as long as the tar-paper covering remained securely installed.

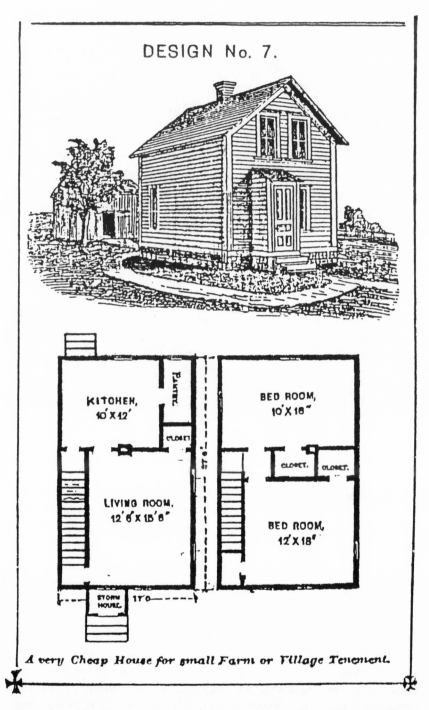

Figure 4.8. "Design No. 7: A very Cheap House for small Farm or Village Tenement," 1884. From Adams-Horr Company, *Rural Architecture* (Chicago: Northwestern Lumberman Print, 1884), 3.

DESIGN No. 19.

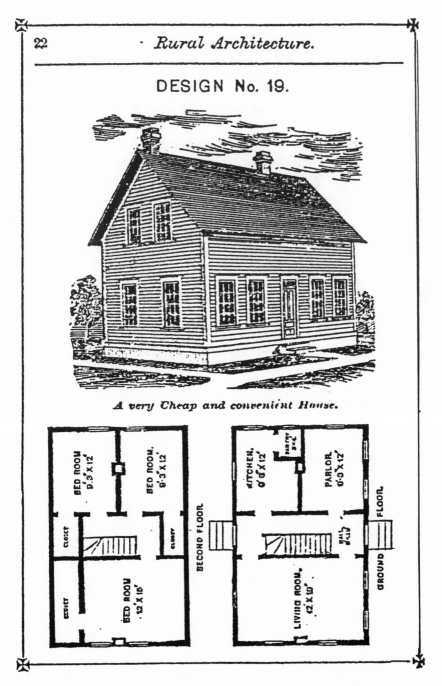

A very Cheap and convenient House.

Figure 4.9. "Design No. 19: A very Cheap and convenient House," 1884. From Adams-Horr Company, *Rural Architecture* (Chicago: Northwestern Lumberman Print, 1884), 22.

A temporary partition or drape sufficed to separate the kitchen and bed-room in the larger space of the house. "As soon as circumstances would permit," the third unit could be added. It would include a 16 × 28 foot space on the first floor and add a complete second story of four bedrooms and two closets.[5] Brewer's way of thinking about building according to one's means underscores the importance of simple beginnings embodied in the small one- to one-and-a-half-story gabled rectangular farmhouse.

A little book entitled *Tom's Experience in Dakota*, published in Minneapolis in 1883, also discusses values related to building a farmhouse. The story in-structs the reader about conditions on the western frontier and advises on matters of practical morality.[6] A portion of the narrative explains how in 1881 Tom had 180 acres of good Dakota land in cash crops and was speculating on the harvest to come. Calculating future returns and being "a trifle ashamed" of the little one-story 12 × 20 foot frame house in which he was living, Tom was persuaded by a local carpenter to build "the handsomest and handiest farmhouse in the county." Pride overcame prudence, and Tom not only had a new house, he also had a mortgage at the bank for $1,200. The large new house was named "Tom's Folly" because the year's crops turned out badly and foreclosure was imminent. Tom's house was eventually offered up at a sheriff's sale and purchased against the bidding of the town villain by an old, estab-lished farmer friend of Tom from Illinois! Tom was deeded the farm to buy back in two years (with interest), and his "Folly" was saved. Tom said, "My building that house was regarded as a piece of extravagance, and evidence of a lack of business prudence and sagacity. I was comfortable in that little house and should have lived in it another year, and so escaped this embarrassment." The moral of the story seems to work both ways. Yes, the first small house was something of which to be ashamed. Yes, building a house to make oneself proud can bring embarrassment if the decision to become architecturally re-nowned is based upon speculation and not money in the bank. Whatever side of the moral one is on, the small house was perceived to be only a point of de-parture to new and grander things.

Since the house that Tom built was not described, the reader could not visualize the type of structure it was. As "the handsomest" and "the handi-est," the dwelling probably satisfied the needs and comforts of domestic life as well as reflected the socioeconomic status that Tom had hoped to achieve. The two-story gabled rectangular farmhouse would have fulfilled these roles; the house type is sufficiently larger than the one- to one-and-a-half-story gabled rectangular farmhouse type, so it would have provided for more differentiation in the use of interior spaces, especially for social func-tions. Variations on the basic rectangular volume of the structure could be achieved by adding a bay window or a decorative porch to the exterior elevation and one or more dormers to the roof. Planning such a dwelling almost always occurred after the family had successfully worked the farm and securely established themselves on the land.

The origins of the two-story gabled rectangular farmhouse can be traced to the Elizabethan farmhouse of seventeenth-century New England. This line of descent is based upon external appearance and has an ancestry that includes the traditional box-frame I-house.[7] However, the two-story gabled rectangular farmhouse of the Upper Midwest was conceived and constructed with greater flexibility and variety of floor plan and elevation than the traditional house types. Balloon frame construction provided for this new freedom of design.

The two-story gabled rectangular farmhouse near Lilly in Day County, South Dakota (Figure 4.10), is on that continuum of scale and complexity that relates farmhouse type 1 to type 2. It is a full two-story structure with a lean-to porch across its southern façade. Its unadorned exterior is consistent with the simple divisions of space on both floors of the structure. Like smaller and simpler houses of type 1, this dwelling encloses only a kitchen and dining room–living room on the first floor. There is an added feature of a large closet behind the staircase on this level. The area above the closet is a second-story hall leading to two of the three bedrooms. A minimum number of ample spaces is provided under the full two-story height of the roof.

Whereas the South Dakota farmhouse exterior is severely restrained and plain, the Martinus Larson farmhouse in Grant County, Minnesota (Figure 4.11), is an elaboration of a larger two-story gabled rectangular structure. The simple rectangular mass of the house and the saddle roof are evident despite the added elements of a bay window on the dining room wall, a broad front porch, a cross gable on the roof, and ornamental scrollwork in the raking eaves. These decorative features indicate that the house was meant to communicate some measure of importance. The two-story elevation and half-story attic result in an impressive height. When the height is perceived in relation to the broad proportions of the house, the relatively simple planar surface and extension of the structure generate a balloon frame monumentality viewed best in the expansive space of the farmyard.[8]

When Oscar Borass and his family planned their farmhouse in western Minnesota, they were able to create a structure that economically and efficiently included the comforts and conveniences of a modern home (Figure 4.12). Oscar's father, Ole, homesteaded the farm in 1871, lived thirteen years in a dugout, finally built a frame house, and enlarged the farm to

Figure 4.10. Farmhouse type 2 near Lilly, Day County, South Dakota, ca. 1880 (above and opposite)

about 400 acres. When Oscar inherited the farm, he located his house on a different section of land. The farmhouse was constructed about 1915 in a county where Oscar could secure carpenters who had previously built a number of large and well-appointed farmhouses. Oscar and his wife were able to build a farmhouse that contained ample space for the family as well as for all the latest features of domestic convenience and comfort. The Doric columns that support the porch roof, the Palladian attic window, and the return at the eave of the roof all contribute to a classical effect. The plan of this farmhouse is similar to mail-order designs sold through Sears, Roebuck, and Company and other mass-production outlets from about 1890 through the 1920s. The house includes a complete bathroom and central heating. Other qualities of the design that contribute to ease and efficiency of housekeeping will be discussed later.

No one can debate that the John Olness farmhouse in Clay County, Minnesota (Figure 4.13), is also a top-of-the-line example of a stylish home. One may, however, argue against its inclusion as a two-story gabled rectangular farmhouse type. This structure could qualify as a Vernacular Villa type. The house is cited because it illustrates the range in size, scale, and elaboration of balloon frame farmhouses in the Upper Midwest. The essen-

First Floor

Second Floor

tials of the smallest and simplest one- to one-and-a-half-story gabled rectangular farmhouse are contained within the complexities of this large and elaborate dwelling. Behind the extended porch and bay windows lies a basic, broad rectilinear plan centered on an entry hall and staircase. The double doors of the major entry are reminiscent of the small entries of farmhouses discussed above. The axial orientation of the rooms is from the front to the rear of the house, despite the many specialized spaces such as halls, closets, and pantry. The spatial layout of other Victorian houses of this scale spin off in various asymmetries to create a fully picturesque effect, but the Olness house retains a vernacular equilibrium despite its various moves toward high style.

John Olness was a dealer in lumber, first in Norway and then in America. In Minnesota he was both an entrepreneur and a farmer who wanted

Figure 4.11. The Martinus Larson farmhouse, Grant County, Minnesota, ca. 1890 (Grant County Historical Society, Elbow Lake)

Figure 4.12. The Oscar Borass farmhouse, Lac Qui Parle County, Minnesota, ca. 1915 (above and opposite)

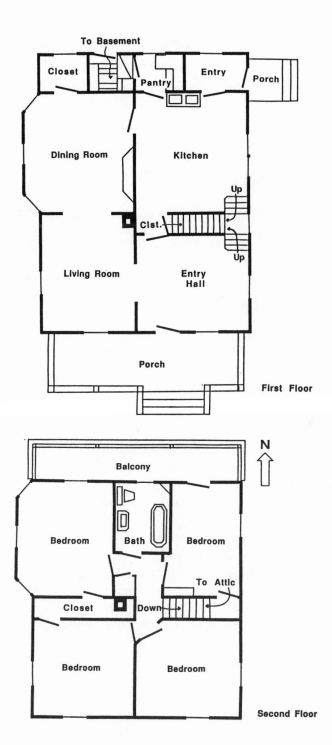

To Basement

Closet

Pantry

Entry

Porch

Dining Room

Kitchen

Up

Clst.

Up

Living Room

Entry
Hall

Porch

First Floor

Balcony

N

Bedroom

Bath

Bedroom

To Attic

Closet

Down

Bedroom

Bedroom

Second Floor

Figure 4.13. The John Olness farmhouse, Clay County, Minnesota, 1893 (above and opposite)

his personal and professional reputation to be expressed in the appearance and appointment of his home on the prairie. The house was constructed in 1898 when farming in the fertile Red River valley was profitable and before the lumber supplied by stands of trees that grew along nearby rivers was depleted. Although the lumber business eventually failed, farming remained a successful venture.

A large and substantial home was an ideal promulgated by most professional architects and social reformers in Victorian America. This ideal was not desired by or possible for all farm families in the Upper Midwest. Practicing frugality as a moral virtue, many large farm families chose to continue to live in small dwellings. The simple adage, "The house doesn't pay for the barn," communicates a belief that frames architectural ambition in the proper context of the farm as a working enterprise where one ought to accomplish "first things first."

More could be learned about the beliefs, values, and behavior patterns the occupants of these farmhouses if one were able to visit these houses as they were originally furnished and to follow the family through their daily

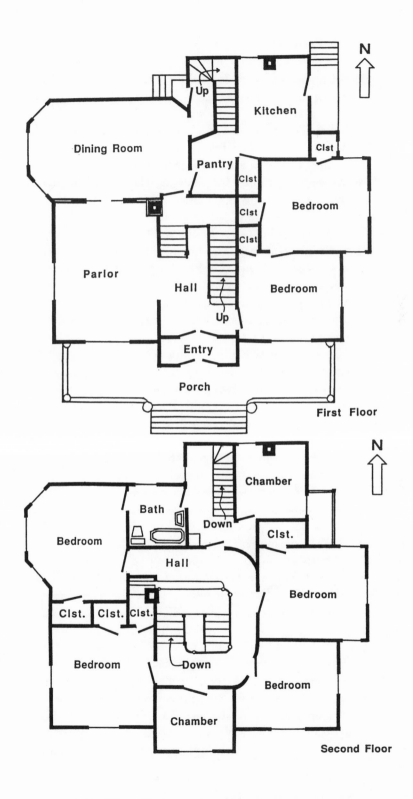

N

Up

Kitchen

Dining Room

Clst

Pantry

Clst

Clst

Clst

Bedroom

Parlor

Hall

Bedroom

Up

Entry

Porch

First Floor

N

Chamber

Bath

Down

Clst.

Bedroom

Hall

Bedroom

Clst. **Clst.** **Clst.**

Bedroom

Down

Bedroom

Chamber

Second Floor

and seasonal routines of work and leisure. The furniture, appliances, utensils, and tools were mediators between each member of the farm family and his or her environment. To know what these items were, how they were used, and what they did to facilitate life for family members is an important aspect of the study of farmhouses as homes.[9]

Insights gained from this kind of specific observation should be understood in the broader context of changing theories of domestic science about the proper way to run the house. A shift in house design and function is evident in architectural stylebooks and professional literature about housekeeping from the 1840s to the 1920s. During this time home economists studied ways to manage the home systematically and scientifically. *Convenience* is consistently noted as an important element of house design, and *efficiency* as a rewarding way to do housework and improve home life was presented as an increasingly important goal to homemakers.

When agricultural journals appeared in the 1840s, editors and readers began exchanging strategies on how to improve ways of doing housework. Ideas for floor plans and labor-saving techniques were regular features.[10] Catherine Beecher became an effective voice for these "progressive" planners. She crusaded for domestic economy through lectures and publications such as her *Treatise on Domestic Economy* first published in 1841. This work went through fourteen printings before it was enlarged under the title *The American Woman's Home* in 1869.[11] In her writings Beecher intended to identify practical ways that permit a house design to "provide in the best manner for health, industry, and economy, those cardinal requisites for domestic enjoyment and success."[12] To achieve this goal, she offered plans for a house that included many innovative features for its day. A centrally located, well-planned kitchen was the nucleus of a design based on her study of the best way to accomplish household tasks by organizing the house to that end.

Beecher's efforts appear sporadic and intuitive when compared with the principles of household management that Christine Frederick offered in *The New Housekeeping* (1912). Frederick, a disciple of Frederick Winslow Taylor, applied the master's principles of efficiency to domestic life by rigorously and thoroughly organizing work in the home ranging from "attitudes of the mind" to "scheduling" and "standardized operations." Beecher's way was "to choose the best means for accomplishing the best end."[13] For Frederick, "there is just one best way, one short way to perform any task involving work done with the hands, or the hands and the head working in cooperation."[14] The best and shortest way to do a task became the standardized way, the only way, of accomplishing housework.[15] This new domestic science became available to the rural population through publications such as *Farm Knowledge*. Volume 3 of that study contained practical advice for the construction of farmhouses, with emphasis upon utilitarian features. It describes the farmhouse as "an all-day workshop" in which "the least expenditure of time and energy" should be used to meet the demands of running the household. In addition to convenient and efficient arrangement of rooms, new technologies such as good indoor plumbing and central heating are noted as necessary to make the well-designed house work well.[16]

Exhortations toward convenience, comfort, and efficiency were not heard by some farm families who settled in the Upper Midwest. They were initially too busy establishing the farm and accommodating themselves to the confines of a small balloon frame farmhouse. A farmhouse the size of the Pope County, Minnesota, structure (Figure 4.4) did not provide enough space to realize any of the new methods for rural living. A remarkably complete account of a similar one-and-a-half-story gabled rectangular farmhouse in North Dakota describes how a family actually did furnish a small house in which only three people lived. Barbara Levorsen, a foster child, provided the description:

> Their house possibly 12 to 18 feet, was built. I think Germund Tweeten built it. I heard much talk on how well it was done. It was a plain house. Two windows faced east and two faced west. The door was on the south side, and beside it there was another window. The north wall was, as in so many dwellings thereabouts, blank. The upstairs remained unfinished all the time we lived there. . . . A three to four foot wainscotting lined the walls of the main room. This room served as kitchen, dining room, sitting room, and sometimes bedroom as well. Here mama washed clothes and ironed them, cooked, baked, sewed and mended. . . . A tiny bedroom and "buttery" took up one end of the house. A narrow stairway led upstairs through the buttery. A tight trap door at the head of the stairway shut out winter cold. Sacks of flour and sugar and boxes of other staples were stored upstairs as well as extra clothing. Outside the door was a tiny entry, the walls of which were papered with old "Decorah Posten" newsprint. This Norse language paper printed in Decorah, Iowa, was widely read in our settlement, and later used for lining dresser drawers or wooden grocery boxes. Some women, fancier than mama, cut scalloped edges in the paper before using it for shelf paper, and many papered walls with it. From my first remembrance of the house until the day I went away, the furniture always remained in the same place. In the very beginning mama must have used grocery boxes

for her cupboard too. Then one day Uncle Andrew had come pulling a two-piece cupboard on a sled. This became the only cupboard that mama ever had. Uncle Andrew, who was handy with tools, had made it out of shipping boxes and grocery crates. . . . This cupboard stood in the northwest corner of the room. Next came mama's choicest possession— her sewing machine. . . . In the northeast corner stood a large dresser, called "Kommoden." Below the east windows there was a clock shelf on the wall and below it the table. Between the buttery and bedroom doors stood the cookstove. . . . A few chairs and a neat little washstand made by Uncle Ole finished the inventory.[17]

Levorsen mentions that she could recall the interior of these small houses so well because the furniture was never rearranged and the rooms were never redecorated.

It will be necessary to discuss larger structures of type 1 and 2 to illustrate how families originally furnished their farmhouses and understand how they functioned as homes. The 1880 farmhouse in Pocahontas County, Iowa (Figure 4.5), and the Oscar Borass dwelling of 1915 in Lac Qui Parle County, Minnesota (Figure 4.12), can be compared as examples from two different decades in the history of farming in the Upper Midwest. All the necessities and most of the amenities of life in rural America could be experienced in either farmhouse. The Iowa farmhouse reveals less deliberate planning to be efficient than the Minnesota dwelling. It was built to satisfy basic needs of shelter with some conveniences in the most practical, direct, and money-saving manner. The Minnesota farmhouse incorporated comfort and the principles of saving time and energy in performing household chores by careful attention to the layout of rooms and the inclusion of specific household technologies, such as central heating and indoor plumbing.

Pocahontas County was an isolated part of the rural Upper Midwest when the Iowa farmhouse was built in the 1880s. Free mail delivery in rural areas was still a service of the future. Travel to and from the farm for limited household goods and furnishings in local markets was difficult on the dirt and gravel roads. Mail-order catalogues did not yet extend the dreams and actual purchases of this Iowa farm family. In short, they were insulated from "new-fangled" ways of doing things, even if they would have been interested in modifying their lifestyle to keep up with the times. By the time the Borass family occupied their farmhouse, there was an improved road nearby at which they received mail delivery, linking them more closely to commercial urban centers of the region and nation. It is possible that this family enjoyed telephone service because a cooperative telephone company had been built in their section of the county. Rural life was less insulated and became more complex for them as they experienced opportunities to alter the conditions in which they lived. Labor on the farm also became less strenuous as modern technologies eased the burdens of continuous strenuous work.

The simple act of going in and out of a house indicates something about the work patterns and social life of farm families. Both the Iowa and Minnesota houses have three separate entrances serving similar purposes and communicating particular family and community meanings. Where, how, and when one entered these dwellings was determined by family membership, family relationship, social class, position in the community, the day of the week, the time in the church year or secular calendar, and the nature of the task, event, or ceremony being accomplished inside or near the house. "Back" doors were the portals to the outbuildings or the vegetable garden and intended primarily for members of the family—those engaged in working the farm. One welcomed guests at a front door and then invited them directly into a parlor or living room. The Iowa farmhouse had two family doorways. There was one at the rear that allowed easy access to the vegetable garden, chicken coop, water pump, and farmyard; it also opened to the path that led to the outdoor privy nearby in the grove of trees to the north. Two doors at which one could enter at the rear of the Borass house led directly to either the kitchen or the basement. Women working in the kitchen could easily pass from the pantry to the food-storage and laundry areas in the basement and back again. A doorway in the Iowa farmhouse that faces the farmyard lane serves as the designated entrance directly into the small parlor. The more formal front entry of the Borass home is sheltered by a classical porch and introduces visitors to a front hall that probably accommodated a hall tree, a small table for a lamp, a chair, and an umbrella stand. The closet for visitors' wraps is below the stairs and immediately adjacent to the hall. If you arrived at the "front" door of either house, you were a guest to be received in the parlor or the living room.

It might be necessary to clean boots or shoes on a mud scraper implanted in the ground or pavement near the back door before using the family entrances of either farmhouse. Mud and manure created what some called too much "atmosphere" in the small spaces of entry halls. Coat hooks line the walls of the lean-to on the Iowa farmhouse, providing an open area for work clothes to hang and air. The space was also used to store the buckets, wringer, and bench for laundry and was large enough to store ample fuel for the kitchen range and heating stoves. The kitchen entry in the Minnesota house held warm clothing for someone doing errands in the farmyard during the winter. The rear entry to the basement allowed the storage of work clothes conveniently near the laundry area, where a water supply could help keep the area clean. Two or more kerosene lanterns hung near the back entries in both houses where it was easy to light a taper from the kitchen range or reach for a match before going out do evening chores after dark.

The kitchen was the heart of the farmhouse. It is here that family members performed fundamental activities of food preparation and eating. Many other work and social spaces inside and outside the farmhouse functioned in relation to the kitchen. Errands to get foods involved fetching fresh vegetables or eggs from the garden or chicken coop in the farmyard. Processed foods were procured from the root cellar or basement. Large storage spaces for foods to last weeks or months were necessary to preserve the bounty of the farm and supply the table between infrequent trips to town.

The Iowa farm wife did laundry in the lean-to by the kitchen whenever weather made it impossible to work outside. Women pressed the laundered clothes near the kitchen range on which they heated their irons. Family members bathed in a portable tub near the cooking range that heated the water for the occasion. The iron cooking/heating range was the most important item in the kitchen. An ample wooden box to hold fuel for the firebox was near the range. In addition to an iron poker to stir the fire, a bucket and shovel to empty ashes and a broom and dustpan to clean the area were kept there. A hand bellows or flat wicker fan might be used to ignite lingering embers to a full fire each morning.

In the Iowa farmhouse, a kitchen cupboard contained the table dishes and flatware as well as pots, pans, and crocks. Hooks and shelves on the wall near the stove and the sink held various utensils and possibly a small mantle clock. A dry sink and small counter were used for washing and drying dishes; water was hauled from the farmyard pump and heated on the range. Water buckets, dippers, homemade soap, washcloths, and towels were always nearby. A bucket for food scraps to feed the pigs might be next to the sink. Six simple chairs surrounded a rectangular or round dining table. A baby's high chair near the table or a small rocking chair by the stove would have been "extras." Kerosene lamps resting on tables and shelves or bracketed on the wall radiated a warm light that was visually soft, dim, and smelly. Combined with the aroma of cooking foods was the sharp tang of smoke from the firebox and the heavy sensation of kerosene and human perspiration. An unorchestrated ensemble of odors, scents, and "smells" usually filled the kitchen throughout the day and well into the night.

In the decades between the building of the Iowa farmhouse and the building of the Minnesota one, many kitchen amenities became available to the farm wife and her helpers. Indoor plumbing provided the luxuries of a laundry area in the basement and a full bath on the second story. The kitchen became a single-function space for food preparation. A hand pump above a basement cistern, which was filled from gutters and downspouts channeling rain from the roof, supplied soft water to the kitchen sink. A drain from the sink into a septic tank permitted safe disposal of dirty water. The sink's location next to the pantry facilitated carrying pots, pans, and dishes back and forth for washing, drying, and "putting away." The pantry was also conveniently near food-storage areas in the basement. Some food items could now be stored in an icebox, which was supplied with blocks of ice from a nearby lake or pond that were stored in an insulated space in an outbuilding. Sufficient floor space in the kitchen permitted two to three people to move about easily, mixing ingredients, cooking, setting the table, or washing dishes. Essentially the same chores were performed daily and seasonally in both farmhouse kitchens, but the Minnesota farmhouse was consciously planned to serve household functions efficiently and pleasantly.

The pots, crocks, pans, utensils, and special items used to prepare the family's meals are too numerous and varied to go into detail here.[18] Almost everything except sugar, salt, and coffee was prepared and processed on the nineteenth-century farm. Foods were prepared by pickling, salting, smoking, canning, drying, and freezing (the last process was possible in northern areas of the region where winter was predictably intense and long). These processes can be multiplied by the kinds of food kept in these ways. Food was processed whether it was preserved for a long period or consumed when ready. Making butter with a churn was a universal method for processing milk or cream. Other staples were cleaned, cut, mixed, boiled, baked, fried, roasted, or broiled in pots, pans, crocks, or bowls and served on platters and plates. The process of cleaning foods involved scraping, soaking, scrubbing, scaling, skinning, plucking, singeing, or scalding, depending on whether one was working with carrots pulled from the garden or a pig butchered during the cool autumn season. The variety and complexity of preserving and processing food in the farm kitchen demanded a large inventory of utensils and containers to get the job done in a proper and safe way.[19]

Two entries in the diary of Sarah Jane Kimball of Jones County, Iowa, vividly illustrate the tasks she accomplished in the farmhouse kitchen and the way her work related this room to other spaces inside and outside the farmhouse. "Saturday lots of work to do for Mother and I. We churned [butter], made bread, dressed a chicken, made sweet pickles, made up a pail of apples into applesauce, cleaned my bird cage and then the rooms and did the work upstairs and it was nearly milking time. Tired at night." On another day she listed her chores without punctuation to separate phrases. Everything runs together in a continuous line of labors.

After I had done my out of doors work—feeding the cats and tending the chickens and emptying the ashes I commenced work on the house. Filled the lamps and washed the dishes. Close [family member?] came for the cream tended the birds got some apples ready to bake chopped up some cabbage made a cake and got the dinner. After dinner washed dishes rested awhile swept out the sitting room looked over the papers went and cut the sage buried a hen I found dead in the granary changed the pork cracklins from the box to some pails rested a little and then did the chores for the evening.[20]

The family ordinarily ate at the kitchen table. Special meals to which guests were invited were served in the dining room. This chamber, like the living room, oriented the farm family toward the community. A well-appointed dining room, such as the one in the Minnesota farmhouse, provided a significant place to share the results of one's labors with members of the extended family, neighbors, and special guests. More than any other room in the house, the dining room was the place where feasts for holidays and family celebrations were shared, marking some days and weeks of the year with these recurring gatherings, giving some regularity to the seasons, and supplying a sense of identity to the family that celebrated their own special occasions there and presented themselves to others as a family when they entertained guests at the table.

The table, chairs, dishes, flatware, and other pieces of furniture for the dining room were finer and more costly than the kitchen furnishings. Table settings numbered more than twenty at the extended dining room table. These items were stored in the built-in buffet. A machine-woven carpet covered the floor at the center of the room beneath the dining room table and chairs. A kerosene lamp with glass bowl and shade hung from the center of the ceiling over the table.[21] The bay window provided a pleasant place in which two sitting chairs might be on either side of a stand holding potted plants. There was enough space on the wall near the kitchen door for a secretary or combination cabinet and writing desk.

The style of furnishings in the dining room of the Minnesota farmhouse could have been consistent with the simple lines of the built-in buffet. This piece of furniture was advertised as a convenient and artistic item in mail-order catalogues such as Sears, Roebuck, and Company of Chicago or Aladdin Homes of Bay City, Michigan. The illustration from the latter for a fully appointed dining room indicates a rather simple, spacious treatment of the chamber in a Craftsman style that was popular during the 1890s and early 1900s. The parlor of the Borass farmhouse could have been furnished like the Boulevard model home illustrated in the Aladdin Homes catalogue (Figure 4.14). In reality, the chamber would have been furnished with both old and new pieces of furniture. The conservative tendencies of farm families meant they did not discard a useful item just because it was not the proper style.

Photographs of an earlier farmhouse parlor illustrate a fashion of greater visual complexity (Figure 4.15). An aesthetic preference to fill every available space and surface with patterned decor is evident from the papered walls to the pressed-wood designs on the chairs. The room was also a formal place to display photos of family members, leisure and devotional reading materials, and personal knickknacks and handmade items. It was not uncommon to have a pump organ in the corner around which the family rallied on formal and informal occasions.

Although it is difficult to determine where it was used, a treadle sewing machine certainly was present in both farmhouses. This item, "mama's choicest possession," was one of the first mechanical home appliances that heralded further changes that American invention and industry would introduce to housekeeping. For the farm wife and her daughters, the sewing machine provided the most practical way to mend clothes and a satisfying means to create garments for the family and themselves. After disputes about patent rights were settled in the early 1850s, production of these machines developed rapidly. By 1860 more than seventy-four companies supplied well over one hundred thousand machines to households throughout urban and rural America. Machine-sewn had replaced homespun.[22]

The windows in the special-purpose spaces—the dining room, living room, and parlor—deserved lace curtains and possibly some drapery. Most other windows in both the Iowa and Minnesota farmhouses received simple homemade broadcloth or pinafore curtains. In the 1880s window and door screens became available and were generally accounted as one of the

Figure 4.14. Aladdin Homes interiors from "The Venus" and "The Boulevard." From *Aladdin Homes: Catalogue #29* (Bay City, Mich.: By the company, 1917), 75.

Figure 4.15. Two views of a farmhouse parlor, ca. 1880 (Minnesota State Historical Society)

most practical developments in home comfort and health of the times. The Upper Midwest is abundant with insect life. Flies and mosquitoes of numerous genuses, species, and varieties were plagues upon any household that could not keep them outside. Even after screening provided safe ventilation of the house, farm wives used fly swatters and glued strips (flypaper) hanging from ceilings to destroy or "collect" the winged invaders. Almost everyone can recall the squeak and slam of a screen door. The desperate whir of a fly trapped on glue paper may be more difficult to remember, but it too was a sound that added to the heat of summer on the farm. Many might also recall the pungent odor of slow-burning punk used to fend off mosquitoes at night on the farm.

Private family chambers were on the second floor of each farmhouse. In the Iowa farmhouse, one bedroom served as a dormitory type chamber for the children. The other bedroom housed the parents and acted as a nursery for the infant of the family. Members of the family usually had only one or two sets of work clothes and one ensemble for formal occasions. Hooks along bedroom walls served as storage spaces for these small wardrobes. A full window on the gable wall and a half window on the south wall allowed illumination and some cross ventilation in these relatively small rooms. According to nineteenth-century theories of practical health, proper ventilation of the house and especially sleeping chambers was considered very important. Fear of bad humors or miasmas that could bring death overnight was the basis for advice against the bad odors that must have filled small sleeping chambers in nineteenth-century houses, whether they were in cities and towns or on farms. Some ventilation was possible in the Iowa farmhouse, but no passage separated the upstairs rooms for movement of air in and out of them.[23]

The bedrooms in the Iowa farmhouse were equipped with washstands and toilet sets ranging from six to twelve pieces that included basin and pitcher, soap dish, shaving mug, slop jar, and chamber pot. A mirror on the wall over the washstand was necessary for a sponge bath and especially for shaving. Although some of these practices were not necessarily done every day, they were done at least once a week. During the winter, these ablutions were more comfortably done in the warmth of the kitchen. Two small bedrooms usually proved inadequate for growing families. When the children of the Iowa farm family reached their teens, the boys may have taken one bedroom and the girls the other. The parents would then have used for sleeping quarters a section of the parlor furnished with only a bed.

In the Minnesota farmhouse, the central hall at the top of the stairs allowed access to each of the four bedrooms. A hierarchy of private chambers began with the master bedroom, which had a bay window and closet; the bedroom next in importance shared the closet with the master bedroom. The back bedroom included only a built-in clothes rack in the corner behind the door. A small linen cabinet was a special convenience built into the hall next to the chimney.

The beds that furnished the chambers in these farmhouses would have had frames of iron, wood, or brass. Mattresses filled with straw and pillows filled with down provided various grades of sleeping comfort. By the time the Borass farmhouse was furnished, spring mattresses were available as modern sleeping comforts. Blankets and handmade quilts covered the beds. A crib stationed in the parents' bedroom allowed care of the infant during the night. In addition to closets, dressers and wardrobes were used for clothes storage. Sometimes steamer trunks brought from the East or from Europe were used to store fine clothes and linens for the beds. Small tables near bedsides held candlesticks or kerosene lamps. One small heating stove was installed on the second floor of the Iowa farmhouse to warm both chambers, but during many winter nights the temperature in these rooms could drop close to freezing. The fuel box needed filling every day during winter.

The Minnesota farmhouse bedrooms were "modern" insofar as two had closets, all had heat from the central furnace in the basement, and all had access to the great luxury of an indoor bathroom on the second floor. This miracle of plumbing technology was possible when sink and tub units became affordable and energy could be harnessed to pump water under pressure to the bathroom faucets and toilet stool. In some instances gas motors were used to drive the pumps; in other cases windmills supplied the power to raise water to an attic reservoir.

In retrospect, the Borass farmhouse may appear to be an adequately convenient and comfortable dwelling. Perceived in relation to living conditions that prevailed on the frontier, the house documents an amazing transformation in lifestyle that took place in just one to two generations. This new kind of habitat became possible through the industrialized methods and materials of balloon frame construction. The added comforts and efficiencies of this kind of house were also the results of new technologies. After the wilderness had been changed into a garden, farmers and their families had the opportunity to experience some of the pleasures made possible through the machine-made comforts of a new domestic environment.

A Swedish immigrant to North Dakota could look back and claim:

The prairie has changed. When I think back, I realize how different it is now than when I came some 30 years ago [in 1883]. Where once miles of prairie waited undisturbed, houses and barns now stand, furrows are turned, and trees are planted. The two-tracked wagon trails that wove through the tall grass, dodging rocks and badger holes, are now straight roads with ditches and gravel crowns. And we are a community. We are people with different origins, different languages and different cultures, but we are united by our dreams, our work, and our quest for a better way of life.[24]

For some the demands of farming became an all-consuming task that ended in frustration, failure, and death. According to one who was born and raised on the land and also worked it:

On such a farm, life became a Greek tragedy—a man and his wife locked in mortal combat with the land, headed for inevitable destruction. "Victims of the land. Victims of the hard life of farming," people said. I don't think they were victims of the land at all. They were victims of their own folly. They could not accept and surrender to the superiority of the land. They had to keep trying to beat it, keep ahead of it, become its master. They tried. They sacrificed themselves, their sweat staining the land like blood. They died. Their bent bodies were forced straight in coffins and the immortal land went on.[25]

These two statements based upon direct, long-term experience farming in the Upper Midwest present the broad context in which human efforts to establish some meaning in a new and challenging environment should be understood.[26]

Some farmhouses offered amenities that seemed like luxuries to those who had experienced the hardships of homesteading. Most farmhouses met only basic needs. The shelter served as a station in the lives of members of extended families. Many of them were born there in their mothers' beds; they were nursed from injury or through illness in their own chambers; and they died in the fields or in the barn or in the house. The last departure was from the parlor where the survivors staged a wake for the deceased. This tangible experience of life and death within the walls of the house paralleled the cyclic pattern of planting, cultivating, and harvesting. All this while the house was transparently there, always present and functioning but never directly perceived. If a house "took on airs," it was usually a Vernacular Villa type—large scale and high style. Only then was it a conscious projection of the individual or the family to the rural commu-

Figure 4.16. The Martin Dahl farm, Burleigh County, North Dakota, ca. 1920 (State Historical Society of North Dakota)

nity. Otherwise one "wore" the house as naturally as the clothes one donned each day to accomplish the work of the farm.

A look at the Martin Dahl farm near Bismarck, North Dakota (Figure 4.16), will refocus our attention upon the economic reason for the farmhouse in American agriculture during the second half of the nineteenth century—it was the house that was subordinate to the barn. Since farming was perceived and practiced as a family enterprise, the most important structures on the farm were those that contributed directly to the material security and success of that business venture. Although the farmhouse was essential, it was not the structure to which the most money and care were given. Despite its secondary place in the values of commercial agriculture, it was home for those engaged in that way of life.

5. FARMHOUSE TYPES 3 AND 4: A VERNACULAR AESTHETICS

The most numerous and familiar farmhouse type in the Upper Midwest is the ell or T plan. Although farmers and carpenters built what seems an endless variety of these houses, many nostalgically recall them simply as "the house where Grandmother lived." Its asymmetry and the expansive capability of its wings make the house pleasing in appearance and economically practical for a growing farm family. Farmhouse types 3 and 4 are essentially two units of one structure right angled to each other, resulting in a cross-wing effect. That characteristic configuration is evident in the pattern of the saddle roofs sheltering the rectangular interior spaces enclosed by the outer balloon frame walls.[1] Farmhouse types 3 and 4 are distinguished from one another by the elevation of the two units that make up the ell or T. Farmhouse type 3 is made up of units that are less than two stories high—usually a taller unit joined with a lower wing. Farmhouse type 4 is a two-story unit joined to a one-and-a-half-story unit or two two-story units joined together in an ell or T configuration.

Small type 3 farmhouses suggest relationships with frontier subsistence shelters. The Wisconsin and Minnesota structures (Figures 5.1 and 5.2) are almost small enough to qualify as claim shanties. The Wisconsin farmhouse seems to be the result of an additive process that began with a one-room shanty. Stovepipes rather than permanent chimneys indicate the place where the cooking and heating stoves are centrally located between the kitchen and the bedroom. The frame house is minimal and temporary in nature and provides only the essentials of shelter. The appearance of the Minnesota farmhouse indicates that it was built in one stage as a clearly conceived T-plan structure. The vintage photograph provides sufficient information to create a hypothetical floor plan of the house (Figure 5.2).[2] The one-story wing contains the kitchen with the cooking stove on the outer

Moving house to Peter Mourer homestead, eastern North Dakota, 1903 (North Dakota Institute for Regional Studies, Fargo, North Dakota)

Figure 5.1. "Family and house," Jackson County, Wisconsin (State Historical Society of Wisconsin)

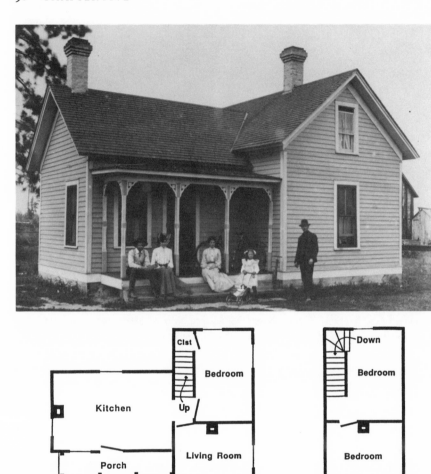

Figure 5.2. Farmhouse type 3, Morrison County, Minnesota, ca. 1880 (Minnesota State Historical Society)

wall, as indicated by the location of the brick chimney. The one-and-a-half-story unit is divided into a dining room and a bedroom downstairs and two small bedrooms upstairs. There is a compactness and clarity in the design of this structure. These qualities result from the regular dimensions of balloon frame construction and the proportioned geometric planes of the exterior walls and roof. The lower portion of the gable wall forms a square; the shape of the gables creates a triangle that is half as tall as the wall below. The kitchen wing joins the taller unit at its midpoint, forming a balanced T plan in a cohesive solid geometry of simple volumes. The sculptured posts and jigsaw brackets on the porch add just enough ornament to adequately decorate the house. It appears cozy enough for the family of three and ample enough to entertain a visiting couple.

An ell-plan farmhouse in Lac Qui Parle County, Minnesota (Figure 5.3), combines a similar architectural form with an interior plan that is elegant in its creation of simple related spaces. All evidence from the site indicates that the house was planned and built in one stage of construction. Despite its relatively small scale, the dwelling contains six ample rooms conveniently related to each other. A back entry room containing a pump and sink functioned as a passage to and from the summer kitchen, as a kitchen workshop, as a laundry room, and as an area to store fuel for the kitchen range and heating stoves in the house. The cellar is reached through a trap door in the kitchen floor, making errands to fetch food efficient and comfortable despite the weather outside. A hall and short, steep staircase off the kitchen introduce one to the other rooms in the house. This area conserves enough space for a moderate-size bedroom and living room on the first floor and two large bedrooms and a closet on the half story. A small covered porch off the living room introduces guests to this area, while a long porch on the kitchen wing provides a less formal entry to this work space. The porch itself becomes a protected outdoor work area spatially unifying kitchen and entry hall. The design of the house achieves this kind of convenience by using space economically and efficiently.

Many ell- or T-plan farmhouses are the result of "add-ons." The purpose of "add-ons" was to increase the size of the house according to need, expediencies of lumber available for the task, and aesthetic preferences. The add-on process was not thought of simply as remodeling because additions created fundamental changes in the design and function of the house. The add-on process does not appear to follow a predictable sequence. Sometimes a new kitchen wing was added to what became a parlor unit. In other instances a living room–dining room was added-on to a kitchen wing. A need for a lean-to entry hall, storage space, or bedrooms were other reasons add-ons were built. In rare instances, an entire house was jacked up so that a "first" floor could be built beneath the new "second" floor.

Sanford Olson built his farmhouse in three stages over approximately fifteen years (Figure 5.4). He accomplished the first phase of construction in 1881, when he was a bachelor requiring minimal space—a kitchen and bedroom in a 14 × 22 foot balloon frame structure. After he married, about 1890, Olson added a wing to the house that provided a kitchen and another bedroom. He made a trap door in the kitchen floor to reach the root

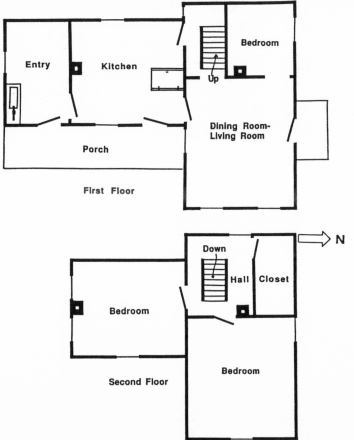

Figure 5.3. The S. M. Sjolie farmhouse, Lac Qui Parle County, Minnesota, ca. 1890

cellar under the "old" part of the house. A short time later he built the lean-to on the north entry to protect it from winter winds. The completed farmhouse had a T-plan configuration of wings one-and-a-half stories high.

Two factors determined whether one built a house using the add-on method. First, one began a project only if one had the economic means to build an addition and if each time an addition was finished it was completely functional. Second, the ultimate image or idea one had of the structure guided one in completing the entire dwelling. These practices manifest a conservative mindset based upon values that many farmer-builders shared. Each desired to save time, energy, materials, and money by preserving whatever they already had that might prove to be useful in the business of operating the farm. In terms of building a farmhouse, dimensions could be dictated by the measurements of lumber available at the lowest cost. The layout of rooms and interior and exterior finishing details might be determined by a careful measuring and cutting of materials resulting in a minimum of waste. Sanford Olson used standardized lengths of 2 × 8 inch joists and 2 × 4 inch studs to make cutting unnecessary. Floor and ceiling joists in both the first and second units of the structure were 14 feet long, and the vertical studs that permitted the tall one-and-a-half-story elevation measured 16 feet in length. When the wing was added to the first section of the house, the original chimney served both the heating stove in the new living room–dining room and the range in the kitchen. The door to the first unit, on the east side of the house, now acted as the passage between the kitchen and the living room–dining room. When Olson added the enclosed entry to the north side of the kitchen wing, he moved the original staircase, intact, to the second floor to provide a back hall passage to the upstairs chambers. This change cleared space in the downstairs and upstairs back bedrooms.

Sanford Olson had an image of how the completed structure would appear and perhaps how various spaces in the house would function at different stages of construction. He formed the general plan and elevation of the structure after he immigrated to America. His balloon frame T-plan farmhouse is a nineteenth-century American house type that he adapted from houses on neighboring farms. He may have studied T-plan house designs in architectural stylebooks or agricultural journals.[3] The interplay between stylebook designs and local lumberyard plans and the practical knowledge and aesthetic preferences of farmers and carpenters resulted in the kind of house that dominates the landscape of the region. The ell- or T-plan model became "a plan in the head" for some carpenters who built many versions

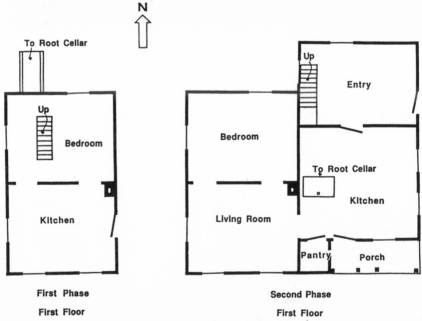

N

To Root Cellar

Up

Bedroom

Kitchen

First Phase

First Floor

Up

Entry

Bedroom

To Root Cellar

Kitchen

Living Room

Pantry

Porch

Second Phase

First Floor

Figure 5.4. The Sanford Olson farmhouse, Pope County, Minnesota, 1881–1895 (above and opposite)

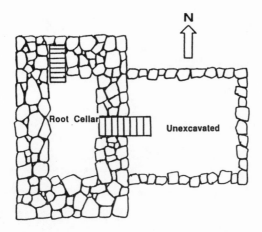

Foundation

Second Phase

Second Floor

of the same house type in their rural neighborhoods. Farmhouse type 3 also became the right kind of house for the farmer; it was the model for the finished farmhouse. Completion of the house was the result of a patient process associated with the long-term labors of developing the farm as a profitable agricultural enterprise.[4]

Farmhouses of type 4 are distinguished by one or two units of a full two-story elevation and by their ample proportions. Many farmhouses of this type were built in one stage of construction and reflect the kind of careful planning and attention to details that such full-scale projects require. The Mastvetten farmhouse, Bottineau County, North Dakota (Figure 5.5), pro-

Figure 5.5. The F. Mastvetten farmhouse, Bottineau County, North Dakota, ca. 1900
(State Historical Society of North Dakota)

vides an impressive example of such a dwelling. Its massive stone foundation increases the elevation of the house as well as gives the structure a
quality of permanence. A moderate use of surface ornament enables one to
perceive clearly the full height and breadth of the house. Decoration re-
stricted to porches and eaves gives a sufficient show of style and finish. The
major, symmetrical façade with a central double-story porch faces the
county road, offering a formal welcome to visitors. A side porch on the
kitchen wing introduces one to the less formal portion of the house. The
low, infinite reach of the prairie is the backdrop against which one per-
ceives the house. The view paradoxically increases the visual scale of the
structure because it is the only strong interruption to the open space. Its
vertical and lateral dimensions appear monumental in the clear light beneath the broad sky. It is the kind of architectural performance that is intended to communicate the secure and substantial position the farm family
had reached when the house was built in the 1890s.

A simpler, smaller example of farmhouse type 4 represents the other end
of the scale of this type (Figure 5.6). This ell-plan farmhouse is composed of
a one-and-a-half-story kitchen wing joined to a two-story unit. A small
porch indicates the entrance to the front parlor, which faces the county

road. A long porch welcomes visitors to the kitchen from the farm lane. This spatial ambiguity of dual orientations of farmhouse types 3 and 4 is a natural result of the directions of the two wings of the structure on the site. A rear entry and a pantry–work space elongate the kitchen wing of the house. A dining room and a parlor downstairs and staircase with hall and two bedrooms upstairs are in the front unit of the house. Another bedroom, illuminated by a window in a small gable, is over the kitchen. Two unfinished rooms that function as storage closets complete the second-floor wing.

The factory-made spindles that decorate the kitchen porch indicate the builder-occupants were concerned with ornament. The interior of the house provides further evidence of finish. An impressive sliding oak door divides the dining room from the parlor. The parlor door received a geometric relief pattern below and a beveled glass pane above. A wide window crowned by a stained-glass panel illuminates the parlor. These features provide the farmhouse with a reserved and economical elegance. That restraint is evident in the treatment of the woodwork on the second story. Here pine instead of oak is used for doors and trim around doors and windows, but wherever the woodwork faces the hall or bedrooms, it is finished with painted patterns to give the appearance of hardwood. Materials and finish were carefully planned throughout the house to give the impression of style and taste with a minimum of expense.

The clarity of design of the Tilly farmhouse near Howard, South Dakota (Figure 5.7), is evident in its external appearance, its arrangement and use of interior space, and finishing details. The solid, sober aspect of the full-width front porch sets the tone of introduction through a central door to a set of formal parlors. Guests could also be welcomed to dinner from a side porch flanking the dining room. A kitchen with a pass-through cabinet facilitated the serving of regular meals and special feasts in the central dining room. The pantry adjacent to the kitchen also led directly to food-storage areas in the root cellar. The problem of situating the staircase to the second floor is marvelously solved by installing it in a room of its own and combining that space with a closet off the dining room and an inside entrance to the cellar under the staircase. Upstairs, four bedrooms and two closets are conveniently arranged. The people who planned and built this house displayed a genius for creating a design of simple proportions and harmonious spaces.

The Vesledal farmhouse in Rice County, Minnesota (Figure 5.8), is similar to the Tilly farmhouse in elevation and plan. This dwelling is two stories tall with a half-story attic space above two units of the house. A large

Figure 5.6. Farmhouse type 4, Pope County, Minnesota, ca. 1895 (above and opposite)

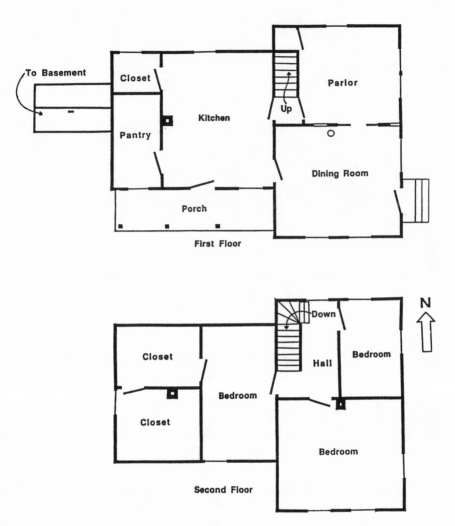

kitchen wing extends from the back of the house creating an ell extension from the basic T-plan of the structure. Syver and Margith Vesledal planned the house while they were living with their seven children in a log cabin measuring only 14 feet square. Built without a blueprint or plan, the proportions of the structure follow the 18-foot length of the floor joists that determined the width of each unit of the house.

In a house this size, some special features could be added to supplement essentials. A small hall off the front porch provides a protected entrance to the parlor for special guests. A small bedroom behind the parlor was reserved exclusively for visiting clergymen. A major staircase gives access to

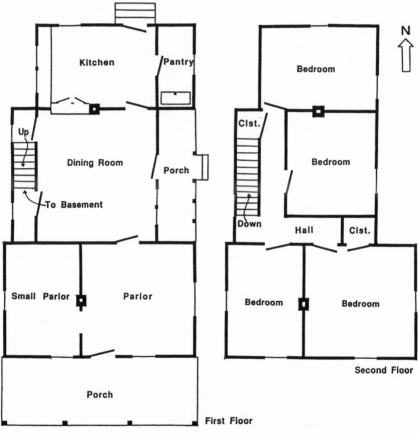

First Floor

Kitchen
Pantry
Up
Dining Room
Porch
To Basement
Small Parlor
Parlor
Porch

Second Floor

N

Bedroom
Clst.
Bedroom
Down
Hall
Clst.
Bedroom
Bedroom

Figure 5.7. The G. Tilly farmhouse, Day County, South Dakota, ca. 1895

the second story from the parlor–dining room area and another ascent to the second-story bedrooms could be used at the back of the house. A balcony over the front porch is reached through the central bedroom on the second floor. Every room of the house, even the pantry, closet, and attic, is illuminated by one or more windows. This natural light combined with the height of the ceilings gives every chamber of the house a feeling of comfort and spaciousness.

Each of these examples of farmhouse type 4 was a major building project that was planned and realized after the farm was established and the family had grown to a size requiring a large house. Each dwelling incorporates features that go beyond the minimal. Instead of growing in stages to meet family needs as did many examples of farmhouse type 3, the structures of type 4 were deliberate and complete architectural statements that were intended to communicate position and prestige.

One path in tracing the origins of farmhouse types 3 and 4 is evident in the elevation and floor plan of some balloon frame ell- or T-plan houses. Some are similar to the I-house with a kitchen wing or to the upright and wing house. These traditional kinds of houses were transplanted in the Upper Midwest by Yankee settlers from the eastern United States who were frequently the first to enter new areas on the frontier. They were at a time and place to perpetuate what they knew and practiced by constructing traditional house types.[5]

Some I-houses were built of stone, brick, and box frame in earlier settled areas of the Upper Midwest. A comparison of the Tilly farmhouse (Figure 5.7) and a Waupaca County, Wisconsin, farmhouse (Figure 5.9) illustrates how builders translated the traditional box frame house type into balloon construction. Both structures incorporate a tall, narrow front unit projecting a formal façade with a full-length porch. The side entrance and porch on the wing is another common feature. From the front, both designs appear to be traditional I-houses; but from the side where the porch is on the kitchen wing, they reveal a trend toward picturesque asymmetry and informality. The Wisconsin farmhouse was built with a modified box frame composed of 4×4 inch studs nailed together at some joints. Standardized milled lumber and nails compose the balloon frame construction of the Tilly house, which afforded greater flexibility in planning interior spaces than was possible in traditional I-house type and box frame construction.

The Willard Greenfield and Henry Bastien farmhouses (Figures 5.10 and 5.11) are examples of the old and the new in the upright and wing house. The structures may not initially seem similar because the Greenfield house is of heavy box frame proportions and its neoclassical elements add visual

Figure 5.8. The Syver and Margith Vesledal farmhouse, Rice County, Minnesota, 1894 (above and opposite)

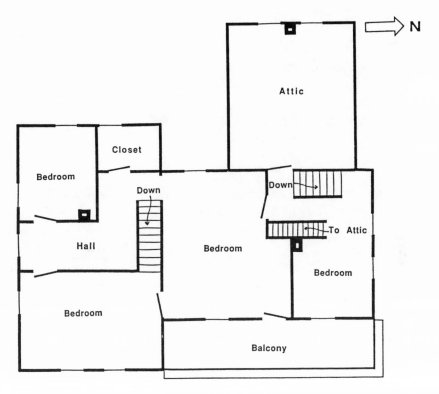

Second Floor

weight to its appearance. The lightness of balloon framing is evident in the simple planar surfaces of the Bastien house. In addition to the cross gable effect of its two units, the Bastien house does retain a characteristic layout of interior spaces of an upright and wing plan. Before the entry was added and the kitchen extended, the wing of the Bastien house contained a central dining room and balance of three smaller spaces at the end of the wing, similar to the Greenfield dwelling. Some qualities of the design of the Sjolie farmhouse (Figure 5.3) also bear a resemblance to the upright and wing type, although the time and place that it was built rule out any direct inheritance.

Another source for the origins of farmhouse types 3 and 4 is found in architectural stylebooks of the second half of the nineteenth century. These publications recommended ell- and T-plan cottages as popular designs that would satisfy a prevalent taste for the picturesque and for fashionable country life.

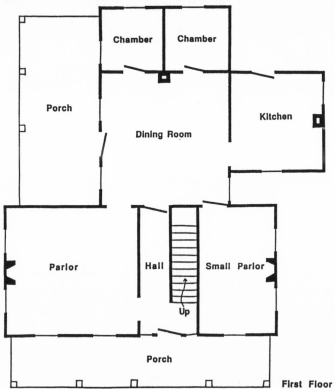

Figure 5.9. An I-house farmhouse, Waupaca County, Wisconsin, ca. 1860 (above and opposite)

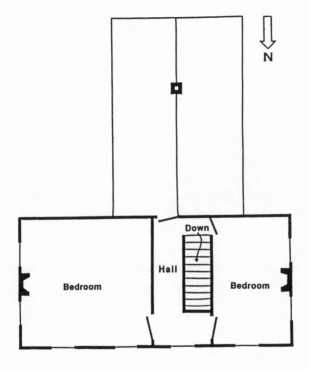

Second Floor

Of the cottages, farmhouses, and villas that Andrew Jackson Downing presented in *The Architecture of Country Houses*, he selected the cottage as "more picturesque, for its irregular form."[6] His "Design II: A Small Bracketed Cottage" (Figure 5.12a) became the stylebook prototype that indirectly inspired ell- or T-plan balloon frame farmhouses throughout the nation. In contrast to this picturesque elevation, he offered a plain version of the cottage that resembled vernacular farmhouses (Figure 5.12b). Downing described the simpler design for the cottage as based only upon a science or knowledge of architecture and claimed that it "lacked feeling." Downing believed that the picturesque was in part defined as a matter of sentiment relating to domesticity and the family. Through an instructive contrast of plain and picturesque, he illustrated how the addition of bay windows, rustic trellises, window canopies, and vines to a cottage design provide the necessary stimulants for such feelings.[7]

Downing's designs for ell- or T-plan farmhouses were also picturesque. He perceived that this form of natural beauty was consistent with his idealized concept of the American farmer. Farmhouses, according to Downing,

Figure 5.10. The Willard Greenfield farmhouse, Dodge County, Wisconsin, ca. 1850 (above and opposite)

were to express "forms of strength, simplicity, honesty, frankness, and sterling goodness of the farmer's character."[8] His "Design XVIII: A Bracketed Farmhouse in the American Style" (Figure 5.13) is a large, two-story ell-plan dwelling. He describes the house as broad and simple, but it is nevertheless ornamented with a bay window, a porch with vines on its posts and roof, a small gable at roof level, bracketed eaves, a rusticated roof line, and tall, complex chimneys. Downing believed that these picturesque features expressed "force or a certain rudeness of character" that suited the "strength, simplicity, and downrightness of character of the farmer."[9]

Farm journals contributed to the popularity of ell- and T-plan farmhouses. Building projects illustrating floor plans and elevations appeared during the 1860s and 1870s in the *American Agriculturist* recommending ell- or T-plan houses as the most convenient and economical to build in towns or on farms.[10] In 1881 the journal announced a contest for house plans. Of the nine awards given in three classes during 1882, two designs were ell- or T-plan houses.[11] The "Prairie Cottage" (Figure 5.14) project is a two-story T-plan reminiscent of an I-house design. The "Country House" (Figure 5.15)

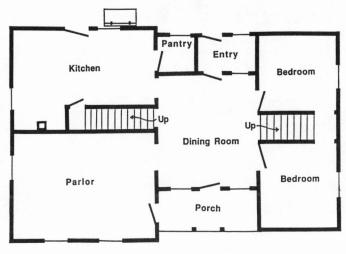

First Floor

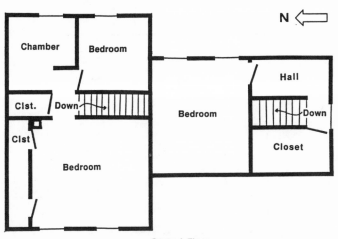

N ⇐

Second Floor

plan and elevation bears the greatest resemblance to type 3 farmhouses. Its design is attributed to "a practical farmer." Two criticisms from the judges claimed that the elevation of the house lacked ornament on the exterior. Some decoration costing $20 to $25 was added before the award was published. This may seem to be a small amount, but it was a substantial added cost to any house design for a farmer who might have preferred to invest in tools and equipment for his livelihood. The other shortcoming of the design was the absence of an entry hall to the parlor that could insulate that

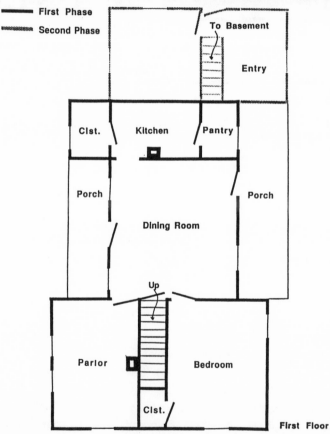

First Phase

Second Phase

To Basement

Entry

Clst.

Kitchen

Pantry

Porch

Porch

Dining Room

Up

Parlor

Bedroom

Clst.

First Floor

Figure 5.II. The Henry Bastien farmhouse, Washington County, Wisconsin, ca. 1860 (above and opposite)

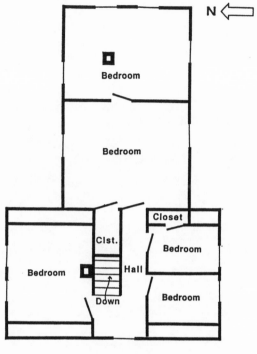

Second Floor

portion of the house from wind and cold. The essential quality of the design was identified as "the general convenience of the internal arrangements."[12]

The percentage of plans for farmhouse types 3 and 4 that appeared in practical pattern books such as Adams-Horr's *Rural Architecture* also indicates their popularity at the grass-roots level.[13] Of the twenty-seven house designs in the little book, eight were for ell- or T-plan dwellings, divided equally between farmhouse types 3 and 4. A comparison of the Adams-Horr "Design No. 1: A Five Room Cottage" (Figure 5.16) and Downing's "A Small Bracketed Cottage" (Figure 5.12) is instructive. Although the configuration of the units of the houses is similar, most of the other design elements are different. Much had changed in the conception of domestic architecture in America during the generation that separated these works. The Adams-Horr house is a balloon frame structure covered with horizontal clapboard siding. Downing's cottage is a box-frame building sheathed with broad vertical boards sealed with battens. Chimneys that served iron stoves replaced the large open fireplaces of the earlier design. In Adams-

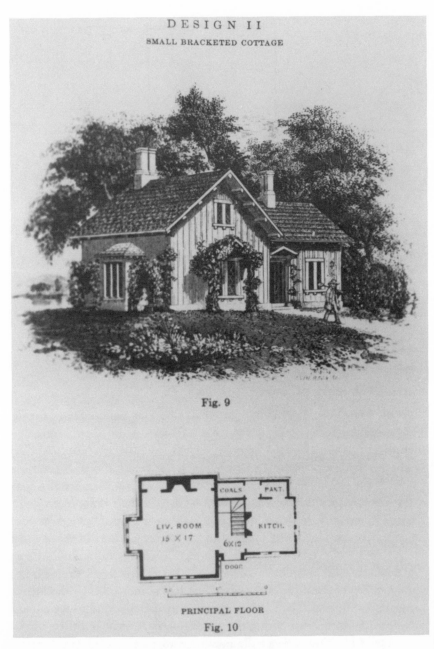

DESIGN II

SMALL BRACKETED COTTAGE

Fig. 9

LIV. ROOM
15 X 17

COALS   PAN.

KITCH.

6X12

DOOR

PRINCIPAL FLOOR

Fig. 10

Figure 5.12a. "Design II: A Small Bracketed Cottage," 1850. From Andrew Jackson Downing, *The Architecture of Country Houses* (New York: D. Appleton, 1850), 79.

Figure 5.12b. "House without Feeling," 1850. From Andrew Jackson Downing, *The Architecture of Country Houses* (New York: D. Appleton, 1850), 80.

Horr's design, full-pane sash windows illuminate the interior rather than the many smaller segments of glass, or "lights," that compose a window in Downing's structure. The increasing industrialization of house design and construction is a primary cause for the differences between the two dwellings. The Adams-Horr design is illustrated with a minimum of natural environment. It is shown as a stark and simple image—a product that could be efficiently and economically realized anywhere. Downing's cottage is portrayed in picturesque surroundings, and the house itself is appointed with finishing touches that blend it with its specific rural environment. Downing attempts to persuade his readers to accept a house design within an aesthetic-moral context for the home.

The Adams-Horr design is simpler than the plain cottage that Downing illustrated in his "Cottage without Feeling" (Figure 5.12). The lumberyard design is a plain, practical version of the fashionable country cottage. It is offered to a clientele who preferred the simple and economical version of the inherently irregular and picturesque profiles of ell- or T-plan houses.[14] The reason the Adams-Horr pattern book for *Rural Architecture* contained so many designs for ell- and T-plan houses is that they were the ones clients chose most frequently. The simplicity and economy of these structures

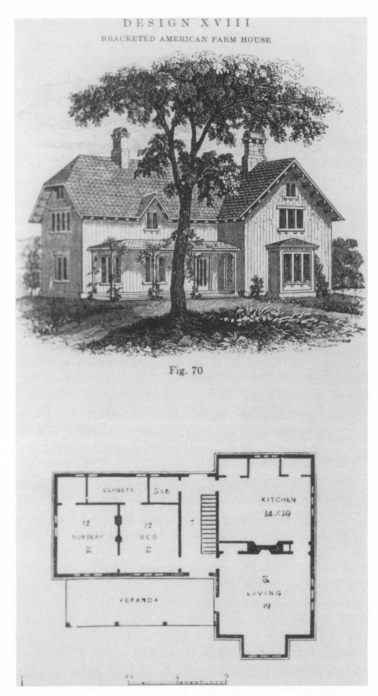

DESIGN XVIII

BRACKETED AMERICAN FARM HOUSE

Fig. 70

Figure 5.13. "Design XVIII: A Bracketed Farmhouse in the American Style," 1850. From Andrew Jackson Downing, *The Architecture of Country Houses* (New York: D. Appleton, 1850), 164.

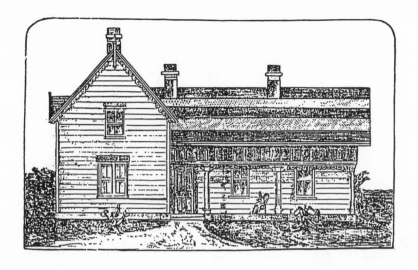

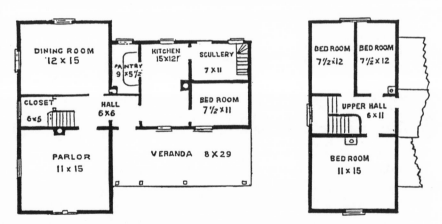

Figure 5.14. "Prairie Cottage," 1882. From "Prairie Cottage, Costing $800–1,000," *American Agriculturist* (1882): 360–61.

appealed to their sense of beauty. This does not mean those people "lacked feeling." It indicates that their sense of aesthetic pleasure was stimulated by sentiments different from those of people who were aroused by the picturesque.

Thus an aesthetics of vernacular building prevailed that differed from the aesthetic taste of Downing's clientele. A formulation of this vernacular aesthetics is a difficult and dangerous endeavor. It is difficult because the task

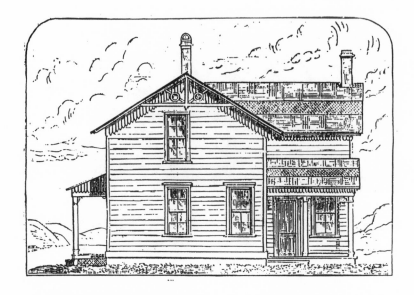

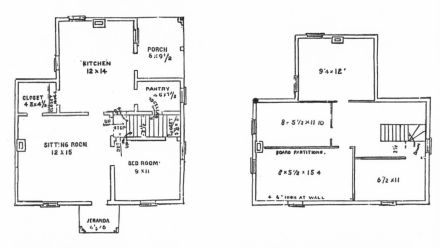

Figure 5.15. "Country House," 1882. From "Country House, Costing $600–800," *American Agriculturist* 41 (1882): 238–39.

necessitates interpreting the values and practices of a class of builders who were ethnically diverse, who worked over a relatively long period, and who operated in a large geographic region. The task is dangerous because the written sources that directly illuminate this creative activity of planning and building are extremely rare. The farmhouses do exist and it is from an

DESIGN No. 1.

Five Room Cottage.

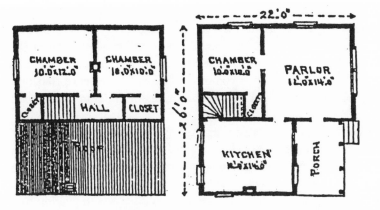

Very. Cheap and Comfortable.

Figure 5.16. "Design No. 1: Five Room Cottage," 1884. From Adams-Horr Company, *Rural Architecture* (Chicago: Northwestern Lumberman Print, 1884), 3.

analysis of these structures that one can infer principles that guided a vernacular aesthetics of building.[15]

The principles that created preferences to build in particular vernacular
ways were formed through the interaction of traditional building practices
and professional stylebook influences.[16] Farmer-builders, carpenters, and
contractors based their work upon values that emphasized practicality and
economy. Professional architects were primarily interested in offering designs that would house the client in the proper style at a cost commensurate with a sound and substantial structure. On the one hand, vernacular
builders were not blind to these professional ideals because they were pervasive in various publications and were considered "model homes" in
towns and cities. On the other hand, some house types of the vernacular
tradition were admired by professional architects and adapted as designs in
their stylebooks.[17] Both the professional architect and the vernacular
builder sought an ideal of beauty, but the latter tried to achieve that goal
through means and methods that saved time, labor, and money by accomplishing a project in the most direct and simplest way.[18]

Four qualities of farmhouse types 3 and 4 provide a basis for an aesthetics
of vernacular building: (1) economy and efficiency in construction; (2) flexibility and adaptability of use of interior spaces; (3) individuality of expression through design; and (4) perpetuation of traditional house types
through vernacular building practices and through adaptations of traditional house types published in professional stylebooks. Ell- or T-plan farmhouses were the kinds most often built because they allowed one to achieve
the qualities most prized by local builders and families in farming communities. Should the farmer choose to hire a carpenter and crew to build his
house, they would share a common place and experience that brought an
easy accord to their working together to realize the primarily practical qualities of vernacular building.

It has been demonstrated that the balloon frame method of construction
is more economical, more efficient, and easier than building the traditional
box frame or with brick or stone. Those values are especially evident in ell-
or T-plan farmhouses when built in two or more stages. This practical two-
to three-phase process of construction was discussed in relation to the Sanford Olson farmhouse (Figure 5.4) and applies to many examples of the
type 3 farmhouse. It is important to understand that the root meaning of
"economy" is the law of an estate or management of a household. It is a
term that originally referred to an orderly way in which the affairs of a family were run in the context of the place where they lived and the work that
they did there. Thrift and frugality became associated with this kind of

household management. When a farm family in the Upper Midwest practiced economy in domestic architecture, they considered all elements of the house to be nonessential that did not contribute to the maintenance of life and work on the farm. This practice resulted in a structure that incorporated only necessary spaces for eating, sleeping, and food preparation and storage. In some instances, a dining room was omitted and so the family would eat in the kitchen. The exterior of such a small house (usually a one-and-a-half story gabled rectangular farmhouse) was without ornament, perhaps even unpainted.

When the farm family increased in size, and/or the sons and daughters grew old enough to require separate sleeping quarters, and after the farm was established, the family could consider an addition to the house. Farm families expected to increase not only the size of the family and the structure that sheltered them but also the number and kinds of livestock and poultry kept, the variety of implements used and outbuildings constructed, and the amount of acreage added to the farm. Successful family farms in the Upper Midwest inevitably went through these stages of growth. The prospect of such increases was an article of faith expressed in the rhetoric of the American dream. Farming involved every member of the family in a process that necessitated perpetual annual rounds of tasks and chores.[19] Building a house in stages was a natural part of this rhythm. When the time arrived, a wing was added to the first unit of the house to form the characteristic ell or T configuration. The predominance of ell- and T-plan farmhouses indicates that this type was considered the right kind of house by these frugal people.[20] They would not consider tearing down the original house to build a new dwelling unless the first shelter was just a shanty. However, if the shanty had any structural strength, it would be attached to the new frame house as a kitchen or bedroom or it would be used as a free-standing summer kitchen or an outbuilding.[21]

The value of efficiency that relates to economy is used here to characterize the process of building the farmhouse. The reference for this value is not in the context of machine energies in which efficiencies are measured according to energy input and work achieved. Farmer-builders and local carpenters were not machines. When they worked efficiently, they worked in a competent manner that was learned from experience and guided by principles of economy. They possessed the requisite knowledge and practiced acquired skills to construct a dwelling. If a farmer did not have the skills to build a house, he hired a carpenter or enlisted the help of a neighbor who was capable of accomplishing the task. Every member of the family contributed to the project according to his or her abilities.

An extended description of the way a farmhouse was built will illustrate how the values of economy and efficiency were incorporated in construction. The statement is by Ann Davidson, a daughter of the farm family for which an ell-plan house was built.

When the house was being built the carpenters staid with us. Lyons and Pearson were the carpenters. Mrs. Lyons brought her baby—a little older than Matt, a month or so, and lived on us too. Those carpenters could put to shame any carpenters I have known since. They picked the lumber for the home and it was just boards. They made casings, matched floor boards and everything and they certainly built well. The casings and the c[asing] boards were all bevelled and *they* bevelled them too. They made tongue and groove boards too. They had planes and so forth for all that work. They built it for $75.00. It took them two months. They planed all the boards and sunk the nail heads in the casings and everywhere they would show. First a man by the name of Barrit dug the cellar, 18 × 34. Father put in a rock wall from the cellar floor to the surface and a rock foundation for the house. Then the carpenters came. People said on account of heavy winds they could not build tall or two stories high. Everybody in the country built shed fashion. The beams in that house of ours were very large—18 × 18 inches and mortised at the corners and then bolted, iron bolts with nuts to hold them. When they were laid on the rock foundation, Lu and I would walk around and around on it, side by side, arms around each other. The floors were wide matched lumber, covered with . . . paper. . . . The walls were wide matched boards first and tarred paper then regular siding. The roof was those wide boards—then tarred paper and shingles. The cornices were made the same way. Inside the house was lathe and plaster. The family did the lathing and father plastered and built the chimney while the carpenters took a vacation. The plaster came plumb against the window and the door frames and then the casings were put on. There were twin windows in the gables upstairs. House faced east. There was the living room which was also kitchen and dining room (until they moved the claim shanty against the south side and that was the kitchen, that was the kitchen where the knot hole was in the floor). There was bedrooms and pantry with buildt in flour and meal bins. That was at the very first. Upstairs was three rooms and closet. The stairs were made of 2 inch planks and with 8 inch treads and 4 inch risers. The stair way was three feet wide. There was an entrance on landing and at foot of stairs into which the front door opened, and also a door into the living room.

The cellar stairs were under the house stairs. That was the house at first. Several years later another room was built, the pantry and the bedroom were changed. . . . Perhaps all about the house does not interest you, but I sort of thought you might possibly like to know about it. I was always proud of the strong way it was built.[22]

Ann Davidson's last remark indicates how important strength was in a farmhouse. The sturdiness of the structure also seems consistent with the direct and practical way the project was carried out so that everyone in the family who was able contributed time and labor to the construction. Nothing is said of decoration or ornament on the interior or exterior of the house. In another section of her diary, Davidson describes how pleasant the front porch was because it was covered with morning glory vines and was a place where she played when she was a child. The description of the heavy sill was her only note on the frame of the structure. Although she does not comment on how carpenters cut the studs, joists, and rafters, it would be safe to conjecture they left very little waste lumber. Practical carpenters and farmers prided themselves on the careful calculations they used to determine the dimensions of a structure that permitted them to use materials in the most economical way.

The second set of qualities or values of an aesthetics of vernacular building is the flexibility and adaptability in the use of interior spaces in farmhouse types 3 and 4. Ann Davidson's statement and the varying functions of rooms in other ell- or T-plan farmhouses document that these farmhouse types could be readily modified to fit the changing requirements of farm families. A unit added at a right angle to the first gabled rectangular house conveniently linked and related interior spaces of both units by situating the new wing in line with existing portals on the first unit. The resultant ell or T configurations also provide an ample number of doors for easy passage in and out of the house as well as advantageous spacing of windows for good interior illumination and ventilation. It is easy to add an open porch to the front or side of the house and an enclosed back entry next to the kitchen at the back of the structure.[23]

A granddaughter of a homesteader in central North Dakota explains the practical approach farm families took toward building a house. She states, "It must have seemed like a miracle to them [the immigrant settlers] to be able to claim 160 acres of rich land. Having little or no money for making necessary improvements on their claims or for living expenses for themselves and their families, if they had any, led to a stringent economy. . . .

They were utterly practical people, wholly devoted to turning seed and toil into money with which to better their living conditions."[24]

This family's first shelter in 1888 was a claim shanty of 10 × 12 feet; the second house was a balloon frame structure of only 14 × 20 feet built in 1891–92. In 1904 a wing was added and the farmhouse was completed as an ell-plan structure. The add-on made it possible to alter the functions of interior spaces, rearrange furniture in appropriate rooms, and enjoy a doubling of space in the new house. One room in the first unit of the house formerly acted as a sitting room, sewing room, and bedroom. After the enlargement of the house, this became a dining room with space remaining for a sewing corner. Bedrooms became separate and private chambers. The uses of spaces in an expanding farmhouse remained fairly flexible. They were adapted for various functions at different times in the history of the house.

A third quality of farmhouse types 3 and 4 that furthered their popularity in the Upper Midwest is their potential for individuality of design. Ell- and T-plan farmhouses exhibit the widest variety of structures grouped as identifiable house types. Each farmhouse on its site seems to be a unique creation intended to reflect the design preferences of the builder-occupants. Other house types are relatively simpler and more symmetrical in design and lend themselves to more regular and standard solutions of planning and construction. However simple in appearance, the essential shape of the ell- or T-plan farmhouse was inherently picturesque. The two gabled units set at right angles to one another created an irregular profile that changed interestingly from varying points of view. If one were to choose a farmhouse type that could most readily be constructed over a period to express one's individual sense of domestic lifestyle and appreciation of fashion, the asymmetrical, picturesque qualities of farmhouse types 3 and 4 would serve best.

A basic level at which a structure communicates the thoughts and feelings of its creator is measurement. Measurement in turn generates the scale and proportions of the dwelling. Composed of two or more structural units, farmhouse types 3 and 4 permit many possible combinations in the number of stories of each unit—one plus one; one plus one-and-a-half; one-and-a-half plus one-and-a-half; two plus one; two plus one-and-a-half; and two plus two. When the relationships of units are combined with the scale and proportion of each and in relation to one another, there is opportunity for enormous variety. All of these factors directly determine essential qualities of the floor plan and shape the exterior of the farmhouse.

The way in which the two major units of farmhouse type 3 and 4 are joined provides some variations in structure design. The orientation of the farmhouse toward the road or farmyard lane also allows different visual presentations and impressions of the structure within the farmyard. An ell- or T-plan farmhouse might appear symmetrical and formal when viewed from the front or asymmetrical and picturesque when seen from the side.

The add-on process by which ell- or T-plan farmhouses were usually finished offers opportunities at different times to add architectural features that expressed the aesthetic preferences of family members. Choices for decorative features included ornamented porches, special material or finish for exterior doors to the dining room or parlor, bay windows, a stained-glass window in the parlor, a truncated or rustic roof line, gable ornament and/or vergeboard, patterned clapboard, or variously shaped and colored shingles. These kinds of decoration were common to the other farmhouse types, but they seemed especially appropriate on the more picturesque ell- or T-plan farmhouses. Farmhouse types 3 and 4 were most popular during the 1870s and 1880s, when such surface embellishment was the fashion. Milling plants in the Upper Midwest furnished local lumberyards with catalogues temptingly illustrated with a variety of ornamental devices to "beautify" locally built homes.[25]

A fourth and final reason for the popularity of ell- or T-plan farmhouses is their perpetuation of traditional house types such as the upright and wing and the I-house with wing. This relationship should be understood in the context of the values of a vernacular aesthetics. The values of economy and efficiency in construction and adaptability and flexibility in use were practiced by farm families whose attitudes and lifestyles were conservative. Both farming and building practices tried to preserve tested ways of doing things. Regional examples of the traditional upright and wing and I-house with wing document a gradual adaptation of the box frame to the new balloon frame construction. These adaptations were made during the generation that passed before the balloon frame was widely accepted and used in the region. A significant result of this slow adoption of balloon frame construction was the ell- or T-plan farmhouse. Davidson's statement in her diary that the foundation of the farmhouse was sufficiently massive to hold the superstructure confirms this cautious use of new methods. Also, the carpenters who built the farmhouse selected the materials from a local lumberyard as "boards" that the carpenters beveled and grooved by using special hand tools. In the late 1870s, when the house was built, these traditional techniques of the housewright were already generally replaced by machines that milled lumber for special functions and that made it available in lumberyard inventories. The Davidson family was no doubt motivated by further economies that could be realized by following traditional ways.[26] A desire to construct a house that preserved the appearance of a traditional dwelling seems consistent with the conservative practice of economy and efficiency in building. After the transition from old to new had occurred, ell- or T-plan farmhouses became the typical dwelling for the family farm, or "Grandma's house." It was also called the "prairie house" because it became the most prevalent on the farmlands and grasslands of the Upper Midwest.[27]

This fourfold basis for a vernacular aesthetics is predominantly practical and lacks the theoretical basis of professional systems of aesthetics. The nature of beauty, abstract systems of measurement and proportion, the social role of architecture, and the moral effect of a domestic environment upon members of the family were expressed concerns of professional architects, social reformers, and clergymen during the second half of the nineteenth century. Vernacular builders dealt with these questions in practical ways, rather than through theories expounded in sermons or published in stylebooks. Although they practiced an aesthetics, it was an aesthetics based on expediency, not luxury.

Andrew Jackson Downing's aesthetics of domestic architecture in America in *The Architecture of Country Houses* is indebted to Pugin and Ruskin and the stylebooks of Loudon. These Englishmen worked from theory to practice, blended aesthetic and moral issues, and assumed an Anglo-Saxon superiority about matters pertaining to the values upon which civilized life is based. Downing initiated his work with the assertions that a good house was "a powerful means of civilization" and that each home had social, moral, and religious value.[28] He established a relation between the physical environment of the *house* and the human environment of the *home*, which he used as the basis for advising in matters of taste and for dictating a program for a particular lifestyle "where the family hearth is made a central point of the Beautiful and the Good."[29]

Downing's approach toward defining the nature of "the Beautiful and the Good" was authoritative and subtly arrogant. Making an initial distinction between the useful and the beautiful, he claimed that each appeals to a different aspect of human nature. He suggested, however, that some humans are beneath the apprehension of the beautiful and by implication are shut off from a vision of the good. "There are many," wrote Downing, "to whose undeveloped natures the Useful is sufficient; but there are also not a few who yearn, with an instinct as strong as life itself, for the manifestation of a higher attribute of matter—the Beautiful."[30] He further characterized the yearning for the beautiful as a sentiment akin to the religious that endows its possessor with purity and nobility. By implication, those without this yearning or sentiment would be ignoble, impure, undeveloped, and perhaps ignorant and immoral. Since the concerns of vernacular builders were primarily focused upon the useful, or the practical, they would fall into this state without grace or taste.

Downing distinguished between what he called absolute beauty and relative beauty. The former he described in customary abstract categories of proportion, symmetry, variety, harmony, and unity. His treatment of relative beauty was more germane because he related it to "the expression of elevated and refined ideas of man's life" in architecture—in domestic architecture as well as in civil architecture.

It [a dwelling] plainly shows by its various apartments, that it is intended not only for the physical wants of man, but for his moral, social, and intellectual existence; if hospitality smiles in ample parlors; if home virtues dwell in cosy, fireside family-rooms; if love of the beautiful is seen in picture or statue galleries; intellectuality, in well-stocked libraries; and even a dignified love of leisure and repose, in cool and spacious verandas; we feel, at a glance, that here we have reached the highest beauty of which Domestic Architecture is capable—that of individual expression.[31]

This beauty of expression, Downing explained, is based upon educated feeling because "it is obscure and imperceptible to the majority of those who have never sought for it, as the beauty of clouds or aerial perspective in landscape is to the most ignorant ploughman in the fields."[32] Further, a house that is without this expression of virtue can become an expression of vice; for if a dwelling is built to serve only the animal wants of eating and drinking, the house will express sensuality instead of hospitality. Such a statement, coming as it does immediately after reference in *Country Houses* to the ignorant ploughman, suggests that Downing may have had a simple, expedient form of vernacular farmhouse in mind as a model for a house lacking moral qualities. Writing just before the middle of the century, he could not predict the shape of things to come in the advent of balloon frame farmhouses in the Upper Midwest a generation or more in the future. Had that prophetic vision been given to him, he would have written even more urgently and evangelically to ward off the architectural depravity of the future that he already perceived in the transgressions of his own time.[33] These new homes in the West were built by "utterly practical people" who knew and cared little for theoretical approaches to prescribed patterns of behavior and methods of accomplishing tasks.

Figure 5.17. The Osten Pladson farmhouse, Griggs County, North Dakota, 1887. From Artha Nordbo, ed., *Torgo Midboe Family History* (Griggs County, North Dakota, n.d.).

A comparison of the exteriors of two ample, "homemade" versions of ell-plan farmhouses will illustrate the aesthetic qualities that practical people brought to vernacular building. One dwelling in Griggs County, North Dakota (Figure 5.17), is exemplary of the picturesque; the other in Douglas County, Minnesota (Figure 5.18), is representative of the plain and simple. Photographs made of the structures shortly after each was completed will be the basis of the analysis. These vintage images document the houses in their original state as works that embodied the meaning their designers and builders intended to communicate.

The structural and decorative embellishments of the Pladson farmhouse distinguish it from the simple appearance of the Douglas County dwelling.[34] The roof line of the former is varied by a series of gables. The molding on the eave of the roof is divided into three zones and accented with variations in color. The front porch is set forward as a major architectural element, emphasizing the symmetry of the principle view of the house but also adding a pronounced interruption to the surface of the broad façade. The porch columns compose an aggregate of four slender verticals supported by a base divided into three horizontal zones. The thick brackets attached to each column exude a patterned energy of plant forms. Windows are crowned with complex, double-pediment shapes projecting far enough from the wall to cast strong shadows. Dark shutters flank each window,

Figure 5.18. Farmhouse type 3, Douglas County, Minnesota, ca. 1880 (Minnesota State Historical Society)

widening their proportions and creating a pronounced rhythm along the first and second stories of the major wing of the house. That rhythm appears to miss a beat at the stretched accent point of the window on the side porch enclosure where it is a greater distance from any other similar accent and tucked in and touching the band of ornament beneath the eave of the porch. The ascents of the end boards at each corner of the house have three horizontal projections near the eave, making them appear as extremely elongated columns. The decorative treatment of the panel set in the gable of the side porch is carried over to the patterns in which the roof shingles are cut and laid. The three corbeled chimneys and the lightning rods add vertical accents of varying weights to the ridge of the roof. Osten Pladson was a skilled carpenter and cabinetmaker who created elaborate wooden altars for area churches. He lavished this kind of fine work on his house in a combination of sophisticated Victorian Gothic elements and untutored forms from folk tradition.

Those features that add variety, complexity, and elements of applied style to the Pladson farmhouse create qualities that are inconsistent with the fundamental nature of a balloon frame structure and an aesthetics based upon vernacular principles of building. The Douglas County farmhouse lacks the added features of the Pladson house but is no less finished as a dwelling. Because of its simplicity, one can clearly perceive the proportions of each unit of the structure and their relation to one another. The unbroken lines of the end boards on each corner of the house aid one in gauging the proportions between the height and width of each wing. The unbroken line of the roof describes a 45-degree angle forming the broad reach of the gables. The porch roof built at the intersection of the wings casts a shadow that accents the porch columns and their decorative brackets. The steps to the front and back porches are put together with simple directness. They are ascending platforms, not treads. The steady rhythmic accent created by the regular placement of windows is strengthened by the way the second-story windows align at the middle with the bottom of the roof line and by the way the first-story windows align with the porch eave. A more subtle structural relation is observed in the way the clapboard siding is aligned to the top and the bottom of each window. The continuous horizontal bands of thin shadow that each board etches on the surface of the house help the eye to proportion the scale of the windows to the walls.

It is evident that special care was taken to situate every feature of the structure carefully and clearly in its proper place. This care constitutes more than attention to detail; it is a quality of mind and spirit that finds meaning, satisfaction, and delight in making things in the best-crafted manner as possible. Whatever looks "right" and good is done properly with the least expenditure of materials, time, and energy. It is impossible to separate the structural and decorative features of this farmhouse because they are essentially the same elements of the design. Every feature of the house is framed and accented in a way that reveals a marvelous clarity of planning and construction. Those qualities instruct and please the eye and the mind. One is able to simultaneously perceive, understand, and appreciate the unity of the entire building as well as the way various parts of the design relate to the whole.

Osten Pladson was captivated by the Victorian ornament he used to embellish the surface of his farmhouse. Rather than add to the beauty of the dwelling, those decorations make it difficult to perceive the underlying integrity of the balloon frame structure. In viewing the Douglas County farmhouse, the eye is not entangled with surface complexities. Planar geometry prevails in every aspect of this farmhouse. The linear and planar qualities of the balloon frame construction become the expressive qualities of the structure. The house is a simple sheath enclosing proportioned rectangular spaces—a monument to the values of economy, efficiency, adaptability, and individuality that underlie vernacular aesthetics.

It would seem appropriate at this point to continue to sing the praises of vernacular builders and to argue for establishing this tradition in American architecture as true grass-roots creativity embodying the experience of the good and wise farmer. Such efforts would, however, lead to needless debate about the virtues of vernacular building versus those of professional architectural practice. It should suffice to recognize the existence and qualities of each as major contributors to American arts and culture. Selection of one or the other tradition of building in American history would be based upon personal taste. Of taste there is no disputing, except to realize that it should be informed and educated to include all viable evidence on which to make aesthetic judgments of quality. Andrew Jackson Downing would have agreed to that, as would farmer-builders, local carpenters, and contractors. The differences between the activities of these two classes, between professional and vernacular practices in building, should provide sufficient means to sharpen one's perceptions and refine one's judgments to appreciate and enjoy the best of each tradition.

6. FARMHOUSE TYPES 5 AND 6: STYLE, SUBSTANCE, AND COMMUNITY

The large number and wide variety of ell- and T-plan farmhouses in the Upper Midwest allow one to compare and judge levels of performance in vernacular building. Farmhouses of types 5 and 6 are fewer in number but are of such commanding scale, exhibit such classical balance, and display such appropriate use of ornament that most merit judgment as high-quality performances. Their ample proportions and commodious interior spaces sheltered large families and welcomed many guests for significant community events. These double-wing dwellings were built to impress the viewer and to communicate the substantial position their owners and occupants had attained in rural society.

Farmhouse types 5 and 6 consist of a central gabled rectangular unit joined at right angles to two gabled rectangular wings. The configuration of the three units in the two house types varies. In some structures, the central unit is bisected by the plane defined by the two lateral wings of the house, creating a cross or cruciform plan. In other examples, the central wing projects from the front of the two lateral wings, but the back exterior wall of the house is continuous and unbroken. The wings on both farmhouse types are usually identical to one another, as doors, windows, and ornamental motifs are usually symmetrically composed; sometimes they are arranged to generate some imbalance in the broad façade of the house. Farmhouse type 5 is composed of units that are one-and-a-half stories high; all units of type 6 rise to a full two-story elevation. Of the many variations in actual examples of these two farmhouse types, there seem to be no combinations of number of stories in the three basic units of the structure. The actual heights of the lateral wings may be slightly different from each other, but the number of stories in each is determined by the number of stories in the central gabled rectangular unit.

Minnesota Valley Lutheran church, Lac Qui Parle County, Minnesota

Figure 6.1. The Fronas farmhouse, Pope County, Minnesota, ca. 1912 (above and opposite)

The Fronas farmhouse (Figure 6.1) is an example of type 5; the Smaagaard farmhouse (Figure 6.2) is a representative of type 6. The dimensions and the majority of features of the Fronas farmhouse create a symmetrical effect on the principal façade, but the treatment of the roof on the right wing differs from that on the left. All of the aspects of the Smaagaard house present a formal balance. Both farmhouses were realized in one phase of construction, resulting in a deliberate equilibrium of the major architectural volumes of the structures. The principal façade was designed to impress the visitor approaching from the farmyard lane or the county road. There are not now, nor is there historical evidence that there ever were, picturesque plantings of trees and shrubs that would obscure full view of the façade. The lateral extension of the wings of both houses is best viewed in an unobstructed space as one approaches the dwellings from a distance. These house types are characteristically and appropriately rural in form and composition insofar as they require the broad, deep space of the countryside to best display their formal presence.

The designs of the Fronas and Smaagaard farmhouses manifest classical qualities of symmetry and balance. These balloon frame structures were, however, embellished with late nineteenth-century Victorian American ornament. They are manors realized in a democratic mode of construction and decorated with fashionable architectural motifs. Both structures were

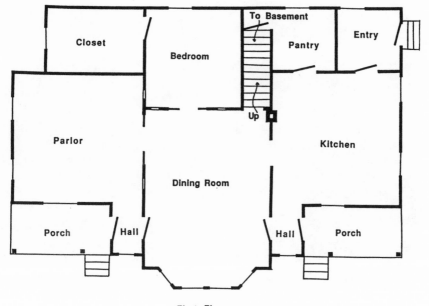

First Floor

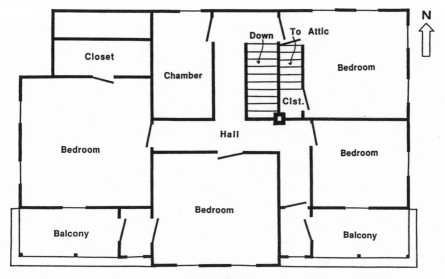

Second Floor

Figure 6.2. The Peder Smaagaard farmhouse, Lac Qui Parle County, Minnesota, 1901 (above and opposite)

built by local carpenters to satisfy their clients' desire to communicate their position in the rural community. By the 1890s, when these farmhouses were constructed, many farm families were replacing smaller dwellings with larger, more ostentatious ones. In some situations, such as the Fronas farmhouse, the need for a new building was based primarily on a desire "to keep up with the Joneses." The Fronas couple were in their sixties when they began to enjoy their new house and were assured that it was as large and stylish as other farmhouses recently built by their neighbors.

The floor plans for both farmhouses illustrate that their designs enclose a series of interior spaces intended for specific practical domestic operations with an emphasis on the social functions of the home. The wing on the right contains a culinary complex of kitchen, pantry, and convenient access to either the farmyard through the back entry or the food-storage areas in the cellar through the pantry. The central unit encloses a formal dining room that is extended and illuminated by a bay window. A doorway from the front porch allows direct access to this room. A bedroom at the back of the central unit was reserved for overnight visitors or for members of the family who were sick and needed care during the day. The parlor occupies the left wing of the house and has a separate entry for formal occasions.

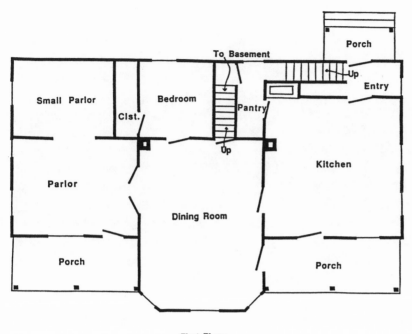

First Floor

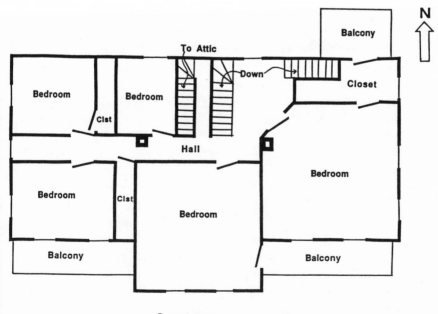

Second Floor

Figure 6.3. The Peter Martinson farmhouse, Grant County, Minnesota, ca. 1880
(Grant County Historical Society, Elbow Lake, Minnesota)

The second floor of each house contains four to five bedrooms and some closets.

Not all farmhouses classified as types 5 and 6 achieve the kind of classical balance and symmetry evident in the Fronas and Smaagaard dwellings. Some are more casual in plan and appearance because they were the product of an additive method of building—for example, the Martinson and Hintz farmhouses (Figures 6.3 and 6.4). The reason for enlarging the ell-plan Martinson farmhouse is evident from the size of the family in front of the final form of their home. The linear arrangement of parents with thirteen children parallels the extension of the structure behind them. In this case the longer wing on the right was the last unit added to the structure, which provided space for a large parlor and two upstairs bedrooms. Two photographs, one from 1899 and another from 1908, provide a two-phase record of the growing Hintz family and home. The completed house is a hybrid of a T plan with a kitchen wing and a cross-gable structure. The size and gable window of the large wing on the left side destroys any formal symmetry. The completed structure does resemble type 5 farmhouses.

The search for historic prototypes or precedents for farmhouse types 5 and 6 turns up a variety of related candidates and points of origin. It is possible to trace a history of the house types to classical revival styles of the seventeenth century. The pedigree for this kind of house may begin with examples as magnificent as Versailles, but in more realistic and local terms

Figure 6.4. The Louis Hintz farmhouse, Filmore County, Minnesota, 1899 and 1908
(Minnesota State Historical Society)

it originates with some eighteenth-century American colonial houses in the classical revival style. The Semple house of Williamsburg, Virginia, or Monticello at Charlottesville were both designed by Thomas Jefferson as cruciform manorial houses in the classical style.[1] These and other colonial examples were, however, composed of a two-story central block joined to one-story wings and identified as *temple-form* houses.[2] If a relationship exists between these structures and farmhouse types 5 and 6, it is in the emphasis upon architectural symmetry achieved in part through accenting the central unit of the structure. Another possible source for farmhouse types 5 and 6 originates in a vernacular tradition of building. A variation of the I-house has been suggested as the genesis of a cruciform plan that results in a *cross-house* type. This house type, which originated in the Chesapeake Bay area, displays the front of the center wing as an enclosed porch and the rear of the unit as a stair tower.[3]

The balance and formality of the temple-form house were not well suited to satisfying the Victorian taste for picturesque asymmetry. Few examples of this house type are found in nineteenth-century stylebooks.[4] Woodward's *Victorian Architecture and Rural Art* (1867) contained two designs for cruciform-plan dwellings. By comparing Downing's Design XXIII (Figure 6.5) with Woodward's Design No. 25 (Figure 6.6), "a very neat and pretty home," it is evident how the house type changed from classical to picturesque.[5] Downing's villa shows symmetry and classical simplicity. Woodward's design uses decorated porches, a bay window, a bracketed canopy, and extended eaves over exterior walls that create strong shadow patterns, making a picturesque statement. In addition, roof shapes are rusticated and ornament elaborates the ridge of the roof on either side of the pair of elaborate chimneys. Underneath all of this is a cruciform plan that consists of four equal parts.

A double-wing design that was specifically identified as a farmhouse appeared in S. B. Reed's *House Plans for Everybody* in 1886 (Figure 6.7). Reed noted that "opportunities abound for 'spreading out' as in the country" and that this plan was particularly adapted for rural purposes because it provided much valuable space as well as "pleasing and symmetrical outlines."[6] The elevation of the house indicates that it was an unusual combination of a two-and-a-half-story central unit with two one-and-a-half-story wings. Reed explained that "the form and arrangement of this plan admit of its execution in section."[7] The central part of the house could be the first section for a farm family and the wings added later. The floor plan for the design is similar to actual farmhouses of this type except for the large areas specified for corridor and hall.

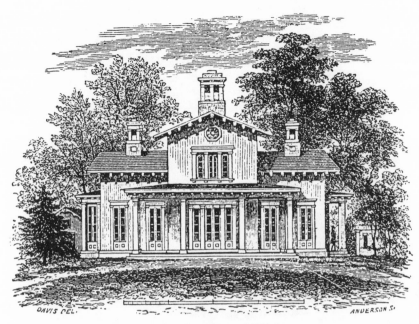

[Fig. 125. Small Classical Villa.]

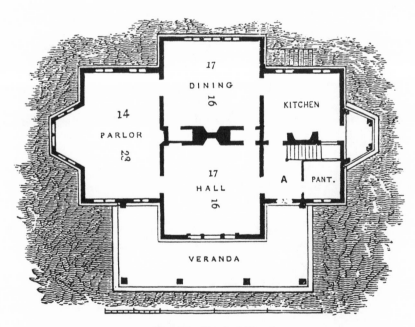

[Fig. 126. Principal Floor.]

Figure 6.5. "Design XXIII: A Small Villa in the Classical Style," 1850. From Andrew Jackson Downing, *The Architecture of Country Houses* (New York: D. Appleton, 1850), 293.

FIG. 76.

FIG. 77.—CELLAR PLAN.

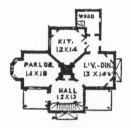

FIG. 78.—FIRST FLOOR.

FIG. 79.—SECOND FLOOR.

Figure 6.6. "Design No. 25," 1867. From George E. Woodward, *Woodward's Architecture and Rural Art, No. 1—1867* (New York: George E. Woodward, 1867), 62.

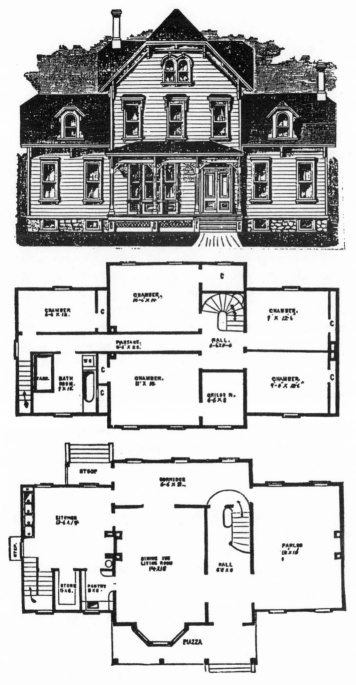

Figure 6.7. "Design XXVI: A Farm-House Costing $2,900," 1886.
From S. B. Reed, *House Plans for Everybody* (New York: Orange Judd,
1886), 153.

Representatives of farmhouse types 5 and 6 can be appropriately interpreted in the context of rural community. For the purposes of this study, a
community is defined as a group of people in a particular locale who share
common beliefs, values, and activities. Identification and analysis of such
communities is accomplished with some ease and clarity in studies of many
areas of Europe and of the eastern seaboard colonies of America. In these
places, families lived in villages and their farmland adjoined the settlement
within a well-defined geographic area. In the Upper Midwest, people settled in a pattern of dispersed farmsteads of about 160 or more acres within
the grid system of the federal land survey. The dispersion and separation
make it more difficult to discern the boundaries of rural communities in
the region. Patterns of life in the Upper Midwest have been likened to a
crazy quilt insofar as geographic areas within the region are characterized
by varying qualities resulting from human interaction with the natural habitat. What is true for one area in terms of soil condition, rainfall, and potential for agriculture may be different for neighboring areas. Several townships within a single county may vary in the composition of ethnic groups
that settled them and the consequent social and religious life of those rural
neighborhoods. Community studies in the Midwest have been limited to a
single county, township, or rural church parish.

Two important considerations must be made in defining a rural community. The first is the locale in which groups of people center their activities
on common institutions such as schools, churches, and businesses. The
second is the shared beliefs and values that create the social dimensions in
which people in the locale interact.[8] For the purposes of this study, the locale of rural community can initially be focused upon one county in western Minnesota, Lac Qui Parle County, and next upon similar church parishes in two townships. Scandinavian immigrants of a pietistic Lutheran
faith settled these areas and established well-defined cultural identities
based on the church as a religious and social focal point in their lives. More
than an average number of large farmhouses were built in the county from
the 1890s to about 1910, many of which were one-and-a-half- or two-story
double-wing dwellings. The significance of these farm homes can be interpreted by considering the nature of the families who planned them and occupied them, the rural communities in which those families built, and the
church parishes they served.

Lac Qui Parle County is located in west-central Minnesota, bordered on
the east by the Minnesota River and Lac Qui Parle Lake, on the west by
the Minnesota–South Dakota border and the Dakota coteau, and on the
south by a county line. The area contained open prairie except where trees

grew along the Lac Qui Parle River and Lake and the Minnesota River. Black topsoil 1 to 2 feet deep lay under the original belt of prairie grasses, giving the area excellent growing potential for small grains and corn. Trappers and fur traders worked the area from about 1835 to the early 1860s. In 1862 a band of renegade Sioux Indians swept through the central and western parts of Minnesota, killing some settlers and frightening many more. This conflict discouraged settlement of Lac Qui Parle County until 1868, when some Yankee families and a large group of Norwegian immigrants established themselves in the southeastern section. The Norwegians who had come from northern Iowa eventually sent word to their countrymen there and along the migrant path of these people into Wisconsin that good land was available in Lac Qui Parle County. Eventually the message reached Norway and immigrants began to arrive on the Minnesota frontier from all of these locations. By 1905 Norwegians constituted the major ethnic group in every township of the county except four. One of those townships was predominantly Swedish and the remaining three, in the northwestern corner of the county, were German. From the time of settlement to the present, the persistence of families on the "home place" has been extremely strong. Land ownership is firm and occupancy is enduring. The elements necessary for rural community are present.

Wheat, oats, and corn were the crops initially grown. Wheat, at 15 to 20 bushels per acre, was the largest cash crop. Two railroad lines had been built through the county by 1884. Although they brought many benefits to the area, they also generated serious conflict between the monopoly powers of the grain elevator owners and wheat farmers who believed that their grain was consistently graded below its real quality and not weighed accurately. Many joined the Farmers' Alliance to more effectively fight railroad and elevator control over their farm produce and economy. A greater diversification of agriculture in the county resulted from this conflict. Farmers planted less wheat and cultivated more forage and feed crops for larger herds of dairy cows, cattle, and swine. By 1890 virtually every farm in the county was a well-established, diversified operation as a second generation of farm families began to carry on what their pioneer parents had established. Agriculture had clearly passed from a subsistence phase to one of commercial enterprise based upon experience, hard labor, and good fiscal management.

An immigration convention, held in the county at Dawson in 1896, was the occasion for a presentation by O. G. Dale. The content and tone of his speech expressed a restrained Scandinavian boosterism. Dale claimed,

In seeking a new home the thoughtful and prudent man finds it necessary to make careful inquiry in regard to many matters connected with
the community he is inspecting. Cheap lands, productive soil, healthful
climate, convenient markets, suitable social and educational advantages,
and immunity from excessive taxation—these are some of the most important advantages to be sought. Few localities can offer a better combination of these than Lac Qui Parle County and its neighboring counties.[9]

The speech was printed and accompanied by a map of the county, pro-
nouncements from various state notables about the advantages of the
county, statistics about land value crop yields, and human as well as livestock population figures. The inevitable conclusion from all the positive
facts and figures was, "If with united efforts we set about promoting diversified farming and incidentally let the world at large know the unrivaled opportunities that are at hand for the settler about to engage in diversified
farming, our population is sure to increase and our lands cannot fail to
double in value inside of ten years."[10]

In 1899 the *Madison* (Minn.) *Independent Press* published a special edition
celebrating life in the county at the end of the century. A major article
written by George T. Williams framed an account of life in the county in
the context of the myth of the Garden. After Williams had painted a sub-
lime picture of the land and explained how the early settlers had fulfilled a
God-given destiny by coming to Lac Qui Parle County, he ascended into
ecstatic prose:

Our eyes wander over the valley. Where is the land made of the desert?
Gone forever! The barrenness of a thousand years clothed in unuttera-
ble beauty during a few short decades. For miles it presents a mammoth
garden. We pause in ecstasy at the sight. Our eyes can contain no
more. . . . From hundreds of happy homes spread out before us, grati-
tude and thanksgiving are ascending to Him who wrought the miracle
in the desert, and see: the glorious sun has also climbed to view the
splendor of the scene and now fills the valley to its brim with golden
light, a fitting emblem of God's benediction upon the work of the
pioneer.[11]

However inspired this statement may seem, other sections of this special
edition offered sober facts that helped substantiate the rhetoric. In a full-

page advertisement, A. J. Skolba's Land Agency printed photographs of three large farmhouses recently built in the county and claimed that Lac Qui Parle "is the greatest county in the Northwest to build a home."[12]

The development of farm sites through the construction of houses and outbuildings did, of course, parallel the establishment and growth of the population, agriculture, and economy of the county. Log cabins had been built by the earliest settlers who claimed land along the Lac Qui Parle River and Lake and the Minnesota River where some trees grew. Those who settled on the open prairie constructed sod houses. The nearest railroad line and lumberyard were in Benson, Minnesota, about 30 miles from the eastern border of the county. Early building projects with milled lumber necessitated extended journeys to and from this point of supply. Modest frame structures began to replace original subsistence shelters and outbuildings began to serve special functions of the farm. The number of building projects naturally increased after railroad lines created new trade centers and made lumber immediately accessible, bolstering the pioneers' ambitions to improve their farms. Evidence for this exists in the farmhouses that were built in the county in the mid-1880s and especially from 1890 to 1910.

A local building boom began in 1892 when Hans Dahl hired Claus Hoff, a Norwegian carpenter and contractor, to construct a large farmhouse in Cerro Gordo township (Figure 6.8). The completed structure is not a double-wing house but rather a large square unit covered by a truncated pyramid roof with a large two-story kitchen ell. Dormers, porches, a bay window, and metal work along the roof lines are ornamental features applied to the surface of an essentially simple balloon frame shell. Through their occupancy of this new farmhouse, the Dahl family heralded their arrival at a position of importance in the rural community. Others soon followed their example. By 1908 approximately twenty large farmhouses—many modeled after the Dahl house—had been built in a four-township area around Cerro Gordo. Others were type 6 farmhouses such as the Smaagaard farmhouse (Figure 6.2), built by Hoff in 1901, and the Holtan farmhouse (Figure 6.9), built by Hoff in 1903. As a local carpenter in high demand, Hoff was able to get at least a couple "plans in the head" and build them with slight variations to satisfy his rural clients with a dwelling as large and stylish as their neighbors' but sufficiently different to be individually distinguished.

Another surge in building activity began in the southern part of the county in 1898 when the Ness family decided to enlarge their 12 × 14 foot house to a fully appointed one-and-a-half-story double-wing structure. The

Figure 6.8. The Hans Dahl farmhouse, Lac Qui Parle County, Minnesota, 1892. (Minnesota State Historical Society)

Figure 6.9. The Ole and Maren Holtan farmhouse, Lac Qui Parle County, Minnesota, 1903 (above and opposite) (Minnesota State Historical Society)

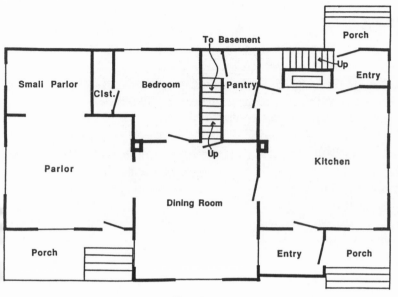

To Basement

Porch

Small Parlor

Clst.

Bedroom

Pantry

Up

Entry

Up

Parlor

Kitchen

Dining Room

Porch

Entry

Porch

First Floor

Down

Bedroom

Clst.

Closet

Down

Hall

Bath

To Attic

Hall

Bedroom

Clst.

Bedroom

Bedroom

Balcony

Balcony

N

Second Floor

Carlson brothers from nearby Dawson were the carpenters for this project (Figure 6.10). In 1900 in the bordering township, the Landerdahls built a slightly larger version of the Ness house. Meanwhile, about 15 to 20 miles to the north in townships where large farmhouses were already being built, a number of smaller one-and-a-half-story double-wing dwellings were constructed (Figure 6.11).

The Ness and Holtan farmhouses are representative of the many other farmhouses that came into being during the Lac Qui Parle building boom. They will be analyzed and interpreted in the context of the rural communities in which they functioned to explain the ways in which the structures satisfied family needs, how the scale and style of the houses communicated socioeconomic position in the rural community, and how the farmhouses and families served the social and spiritual life of their respective rural church parishes.

Almost all the large Lac Qui Parle farmhouses were constructed to shelter large families. Both census data and family photographs document large families in the county. The family farm was conceived of as an economic enterprise that necessitated a full roster of male and female workers. Sons and daughters were integral members of a labor force that directly contributed time and energy to the farm operation and to the well-being of the extended family. Families of twelve children were not unusual. Hired men, grandparents, relatives, and guests either permanently or occasionally increased the number of household members seated at the table. Ole and Maren Holtan had eleven children at home, one grandmother, a hired man, the township school teacher, and frequent overnight visitors.[13] The Ness family consisted of parents and nine children. Because of the hospitality of Andrew and Ingeborg, their home was known as the "Providence Hotel." They welcomed all kinds of travelers and visitors to share shelter and meals in their home.[14]

The size and plan of the Ness and Holtan farmhouses were in part determined by family needs and the open-door policy for guests. The Ness farmhouse contains five bedrooms and the Holtan house four. The sons and daughters were assigned large bedrooms in which they slept dormitory style. The parents and grandparents used the smaller chambers. A bedroom on the first floor functioned as a room for guests or for an ailing member of the family who needed nursing. The kitchen-pantry complex with easy access to the root cellar or basement was essential in each house to prepare meals for family and guests. The Holtans used the kitchen for family meals and reserved the dining room for entertaining guests. The dining room and central dining room–living room in the Ness house provided a set of spaces that seated either the immediate family group or larger gatherings on special occasions. A small separate structure that functioned as a cook shanty or summer kitchen is near the kitchen entrances of each house (Figure 6.12). During large outdoor gatherings it became a workplace, and during harvest it served as a place for processing and preserving foods.

It is difficult to pinpiont the exact date each large farmhouse was constructed in Lac Qui Parle County. The possibility of tracing patterns of formal influence from one structure to another is equally complex and hypothetical. The editor of the *Madison Independent Press* noted receiving a small architectural plan book in an 1890 winter issue of the newspaper. That book was published in Chicago by George W. Ogilvie in 1885 and entitled *Architecture Simplified, or How to Build a House.* The plans and elevations in this book appeared in 1884 under the title *Rural Architecture* by the Adams-Horr Company and published by Northwestern Lumberman Print in Chicago. Ogilvie, like other entrepreneurs, apparently "borrowed" these designs because he knew them to be popular. Most of the house designs in the book are simple vernacular models for dwellings that would be appreciated and used on the local lumberyard level of architectural patronage. Ogilvie, however, also included some plans for more elaborate houses designed by Palliser, Palliser, and Company. Design No. 30 in *Architecture Simplified* presents a Palliser plan for a six- or eight-room house that is similar to the large houses built in Lac Qui Parle County (Figure 6.13). A plan such as this could have been the original model that Hoff's clients modified until those variations became established practices of the local contractor. The pattern of adapting a locally available plan for building was not unusual in rural building practices.

What is clear from the increased investment of time and money in new construction is that neighbors were competing with one another for architectural distinction. Norwegian-American farmers have been characterized as self-assertive, self-conscious, and competitive. They measured personal success in terms of ownership of land and property. The acquisition and display of an educated and cultured lifestyle was also perceived as important.[15] Ness and Holtan were considered successful farmers, owning 470 and 560 acres, respectively. Both immigrated to America in the late 1860s, homesteaded in Lac Qui Parle County in the early 1870s, and continued to enlarge their farm operations. The biography of Andrew O. Ness was included in a history of the region, and his life was characterized in the context of the heroic values of Jefferson's virtuous yeoman. "The prosperity of the republic has always been regarded as resting on the hard working and

Figure 6.10. The Andrew O. and Ingeborg Ness farmhouse, Lac Qui Parle County, Minnesota, 1898 (above and opposite)

prudent farmer, and the men who dig things out of the soil, and grow things out of the soil, are the real producers of riches the world over. This country owes much to its farmers, and much to the men who have made the Northwest a garden instead of a wilderness. Mr. Ness is one of these solid and substantial citizens of Providence township, and has done much for Lac Qui Parle County."[16]

The stages through which each family passed to attain this success were documented in the various houses they inhabited on the homestead. From 1886 to 1893, Ole and Maren Holtan lived in a log cabin as tenants. A small frame house was their shelter when they acquired land in 1893. An addition was built to this house to accommodate their growing family. The large house was finished in 1901.[17] The original Ness farmhouse was built about 1874 from lumber hauled 30 miles from Benson, Minnesota. This 12 × 14 foot structure served as the kitchen after the new house was finished in 1898. These farm families experienced either a gradual or a sudden expansion of space into their new homes. Occupying and owning such grand houses was an affirmation of the place they had earned in their rural communities.[18]

Like other families in the region the Nesses and Holtans endured the

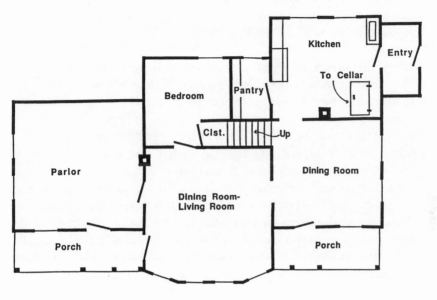

First Floor

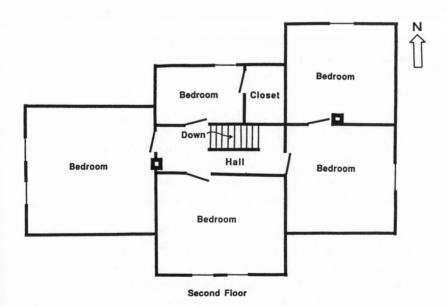

Second Floor

Figure 6.11. The O. K. Olson farmhouse, Lac Qui Parle County, Minnesota, 1905 (above and opposite)

hardships of the frontier and suffered from local and national catastrophes during the years they labored to secure their economic positions as substantial households in the county. In 1873 and 1874 a severe crisis crippled the U.S. economy and for almost a decade directly affected the prices farmers received for their crops. In 1876 the first devastating wave of locusts came from the western mountains, descending on farmlands and devouring everything remotely edible. The grasshopper plague returned with varying intensity for approximately six years, ruining crops and living conditions on many farms in the county. Droughts, floods, hail, tornadoes, and blizzards were the climatic extremes that could set a farm back for a year or more when crops failed, livestock were killed, or buildings were destroyed. Injuries and illness frequently resulted in permanent impairment or death of family members since medical treatment was scarce and crude. Successful farming in the county depended not only upon persistent labor but also upon a beneficence beyond human control.

When the Ness family arrived in Lac Qui Parle County and when the Holtans were married, both households were virtually penniless. Ingeborg Ness remained on the homestead and cared for livestock and crops during the early years because Andrew hired himself out for wages to an estab-

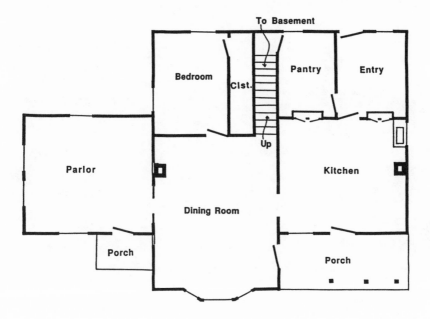

To Basement

Bedroom

Clst.

Pantry

Entry

Up

Parlor

Kitchen

Dining Room

Porch

Porch

First Floor

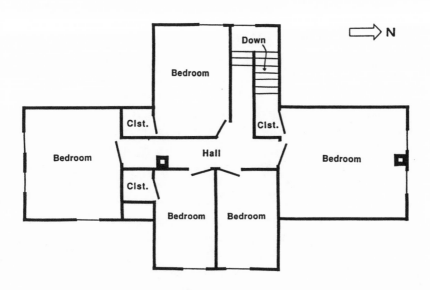

Down

N

Bedroom

Clst.

Clst.

Bedroom

Hall

Bedroom

Clst.

Bedroom

Bedroom

Second Floor

Figure 6.12. The summer kitchen on the Andrew O. and Ingeborg Ness farm, Lac Qui Parle County, Minnesota, 1898

lished farmer in the next township. Ole and Maren Holtan worked the farm of Ole's father while they were buying it from him. After seven years they were able to increase their landholdings and begin to enjoy some of the results of their work together. Like Ingeborg, Maren contributed directly and consistently to the establishment and enlargement of the farm. Each wife and mother performed the numerous and varied tasks related to the running of a household and raising of a family and helped with the farmyard chores. Maren walked 7 miles to the county seat each week to sell eggs and butter. There are no special or unique experiences to distinguish the efforts of these families from others trying to become established in the new land. It is important, however, to remember that they began with very little and that every member of the family worked for the success of the venture they shared. When their large farmhouses were planned, each family could afford the major expenditure. Approximate costs for the Ness farmhouse were $1,000 to $1,100. The Holtan farmhouse cost about $1,200 to $1,300.[19] Although these were relatively high figures in the budget of the farm, they could be paid through the sale of one cash crop raised in a single season. An important factor that permitted such seasonal largess in the accounts of these farms was the period in which they were developed in the history of American agriculture. Wheat farming on the new lands in the Upper Midwest was quite profitable during the 1860s to 1890s. Despite difficulties with grain elevator lines and railroad monopolies, farmers were able to earn considerable amounts of money.[20]

The houses that appeared on the Ness and Holtan farms communicated the substantial socioeconomic status that their owners had achieved. The principal façade of each farmhouse faces the lane that brings visitors to the yard. In this setting, the extension of the double wings of the houses creates an impressive, formal view of each structure seen against the grove of trees behind them. The two-story elevation of the Holtan farmhouse generates a more monumental effect than the Ness house. Ornament on porches and eaves goes beyond vernacular economies to indicate an extra flourish of refined taste. Separate doorways to either the dining room or the parlor introduce guests to the houses from the front porches. Both dwellings qualify as manorial settings for the lives of the farm families and the social activities that were held there.

Strong community bonds were generated and maintained through basic social patterns in Lac Qui Parle County from the late 1860s to the 1890s. Because almost all the settlers were Scandinavian, they shared the same or similar language.[21] From the time of their exodus from Scandinavia and from one area to another in America, families or groups of families moved and settled together. The pattern of social interaction that the immigrants had learned and practiced in Norway equipped them to work well with each other in the New World. In rural Norway neighborhoods were established on the basis of self-help and social obligation. The smallest social group was the *granne*, comprising the families of adjacent farms. The *granne* operated like an extended family. A larger social entity was the *bedlag*, based on collective labor and participation in important social events. The *grend* was the largest entity, usually defined by geographic boundaries and named after a prominent farm in the district. In this context, weddings, funerals, and multiday festivals were shared.[22]

When immigrants arrived in Lac Qui Parle County, relatives, friends, or other settlers housed the newcomers until a cabin or sod house was built through a group effort. When the first sod was broken to initiate farming on the homestead, many neighbors gave time and energy at "plowing bees." By the mid-1880s, when farms were better established, it was not unusual for a group of farmers to cooperatively purchase, use, and maintain expensive machinery such as threshers. When a thresher was hired out, the threshing crew consisted of able-bodied males from neighboring farms. Each farm family shared in the lives and labors of neighbors. Local-history

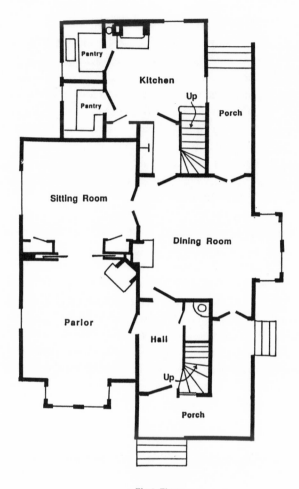

First Floor

Figure 6.13. "No. 30—Floor Plans of Modern Eight Room Cottage," 1885 (above and opposite). Floor plans drawn by author from Palliser, Palliser, and Company, original as printed in George W. Ogilvie, *Architecture Simplified, or How to Build a House* (Chicago: George W. Ogilvie, 1885), 43.

accounts describe the way farm families cooperated with one another in the social structure of their rural neighborhoods. A member of the Holtan family describes this aspect of life in the rural community. "People were very neighborly and friendly and found time to visit each other and help each other in any emergency. I remember my mother would go somewhere

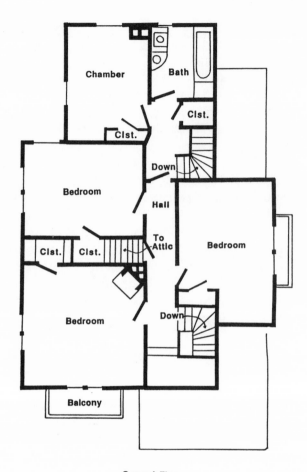

Second Floor

to assist at the birth of a baby, or at a funeral, etc. And the neighbors would help us in return."[23]

Being a visitor or receiving visitors were important parts of rural social life. From an outsider's point of view, farms in the countryside appeared widely separated. One could infer that life in these places was isolated and lonely.[24] However, the network and number of visitors received at farmhouses effectively worked against isolation and did much to perpetuate family ties and social relationships outside the family and beyond the farms. Records in diaries and recollections of individuals relate how a steady stream of visitors passed through the doors of the farmhouse each day and week. The most frequent guests were members of the extended family. Distant relatives, friends, or travelers also visited. The duration of a visit varied from a few hours to several months. Those who stayed for a while and who were capable were expected to share in the work of the farm. Visits that involved larger groups of neighbors were inspired by particular social events such as birthdays, anniversaries, or national holidays. Whenever work was involved in these gatherings they were called "bees"— for example, quilting bees and husking bees.[25]

The geographic space in which individuals and families interacted in rural Lac Qui Parle County was relatively small. Travel to and from a farm was measured by the speed and endurance of the horse that one rode or that pulled a wagon or carriage. Roads were not "improved" until the 1920s, when automobile transportation necessitated safety and maintenance. Before automobile transportation, a round trip of 15 to 20 miles would be a full day's journey. The pace of life was slow and the scope of one's concrete personal experience was limited by the immediate environment. Subscribers to local newspapers were informed of state, national, and world events, but just as much print was devoted to local happenings. In a single issue of the *Dawson Sentinel* or the *Madison Independent Press*, one could read about the war in the Philippines, about the grain market in New York City, and about folks in the next township who were redecorating their home with wallpaper, having relatives visit from Iowa, or raising a newborn baby named Lars. Bad news as well as good news was announced in these "Farm and Fireside" and "Local and Personal" columns. Accidental injuries and deaths, illnesses, and tragic family events were briefly and stoically described. News about people in the community was shared because it was considered valuable and interesting. It was not thought to be malicious gossip. News consisted of real stories about people who shared the same beliefs and values, experiences, and space.

The rural community in Lac Qui Parle County was focused primarily upon small church parishes in the countryside within reasonable travel time of all parishioners. Both the Holtan and the Ness families lived in church parishes that were small Scandinavian-American enclaves. The Holtans lived in a settlement that was 75 to 100 percent Norwegian. Half of the Nesses' neighbors in the Providence township were Norwegian and the other half were Swedes.[26] Each farm was located in a church parish that was about 16 miles in diameter. Approximately one hundred and fifty people—children and adults—constituted the membership of each church. The map of Providence township locating the Ness farm in the context of the parish of the Providence Valley Lutheran Church illustrates the geographic scale of the religious community.[27]

The Hauge Synod of the Lutheran church in America was strongly represented in Lac Qui Parle County. The congregations who shared this faith were characterized as "low church" and evangelical. The Lac Qui Parle Lutheran Church to which the Holtans belonged was the place of the national synodical conference in 1878. Members of county parishes demonstrated the strength of their identification with the synod by dispatching teams and wagons to carry convention visitors from area towns at which railroads ended.[28] Families opened up their homes to lodge convention participants. Synod members devalued formal liturgy in worship, the authority of the ordained clergy, and the use of clerical vestments. According to their beliefs, lay ministers could lead worship services in appropriate places other than the church. The practice of one's piety could be carried out within the wider community through one's daily vocation. There was no sharp distinction made between worship on the Sabbath and the worship a believer could perform through daily devotions at home, daily chores on the farm, or service and work within the parish community.[29] As they worked to form and maintain their religious community, members of a parish were each considered responsible for the others in their circle of faith. Members of the congregation were to either encourage or rebuke one another for good or wrongdoing, respectively. When put into practice, praise and rebuke contributed to overcoming any long-standing hostility or misunderstanding among parish members. Issues so resolved maintained and strengthened the religious community.

Members of the Lac Qui Parle Lutheran and the Providence Valley Lutheran churches learned these precepts and practices throughout their lives. Each was required to attend at least two years of religious instruction before he or she was confirmed in the faith. Children and young adults received weekly religious training at Sunday school. Sermons from the pulpit continued to instruct and edify members of the congregation. In addition to these institutional forms of education, daily devotions at home led by the father extended the religious dimension into domestic and work environments. Both Ole Holtan and Andrew Ness owned copies of a book of sermons written by Martin Luther. This *House-Postil* was the source of individual and group devotional reading in the family. When winter storms or flooded roads prevented the family from attending the Sunday service at church, the head of the household read an entire sermon from the *House-Postil*. The Holtans and the Nesses could hear the words of Luther: "And everywhere God may be served, not merely in church, but also at home, in the kitchen and cellar, in the workshop and in the field, by people in cities and in the country, if we all heed and understand. For God has not merely ordained the government in Church and State, but also in the family; this also He wants to support."[30] Through a belief in a calling or vocation from God, the believer was to perceive that all work could be sacred.

Faith and piety overlapped and transformed the secular spaces of work and social life in the home and in the rural community. Sunday worship and religious festivals remained paramount, but frequent meetings at the homes of parishioners contributed to the blurring of boundaries between worship at church and worship at home. These church-related events filled everyone's social calendar. Opportunities to host these were shared by members of the parish, and responsibility for readying the house and preparing the refreshments was passed among the households.

An inventory of the socioreligious functions that the Holtans and Nesses hosted documents the importance of their farmhouses in their parishes. Basket socials, ice cream socials, lawn socials, revival meetings, temperance meetings, and the annual Fourth of July picnic were held during the spring and summer. In the fall and winter there were church handkerchief parties, church suppers at which oyster stew was a featured favorite, a ladies' sewing circle, ladies' aid meetings, and young people's socials. Throughout the year church bridal showers, wedding receptions, wakes, and funerals might be held at these farmhouses. The church choir and vocal and instrumental ensembles practiced at the Ness farmhouse because they had a pump organ in their dining room–living room. School picnics and programs were difficult to distinguish from church meetings because virtually every child in the township's public school was a member of the church congregation.

The program for the annual Fourth of July picnic celebrated by each parish exemplifies the blending of church and state, the sacred and the secular. A participant describes a typical day at the festivity.

> The summer church festival was the outstanding event of the summer. It was held on a farm where there was a big house and a large grove. After readying the grove, a long table, benches, and a speaker's table was set up. It was a must that all attend. We always made an early afternoon start, carrying with us a washtub or boiler filled with good food. The older women on arrival began preparing the food and setting the tables. A hot dinner was served free to all. In due time all gathered about the platform to hear the minister's sermon and the singing of the choir, also congregation singing of psalms. This was followed by an auctioneering of the fancy articles made by the women of the Ladies Aid. The church activities closed with the Benediction. The rest of the day and evening was spent in fun making by both old and young. Supper was served and all who found it necessary to go home for chores, left in a hurry, soon to be

back to join the playing or visiting and enjoying the get together. No doubt there was a bit of matchmaking too. The whole affair usually broke up at midnight.[31]

It is clear that the farmyard and grove were important environments in which events took place. Both the Holtan and the Ness farms had summer kitchens (Figure 6.12). These structures were essential for preparing food for the large church-related gatherings, such as the summer picnic, wedding receptions, and temperance meetings.

Large houses in the county like the Holtan and Ness farmhouses were not primarily intended as ostentatious displays of success and style. Farmhouses of this scale were meant to serve the rural religious community. They were large enough to host the various gatherings that blended together the worship one performed in the sanctuary of the church and the faith one lived in one's vocation as wife and mother, father and farmer, obedient son and daughter, or servant. As already noted, the large kitchens of the Holtan and Ness farmhouses could serve the extended families as well as meet the demands of even larger meals spread on long dining room tables for guests numbering over twenty. Should a formal occasion such as hosting a visiting clergyman or politician arise, the parlors were proper places to assemble. Deceased members of the family and sometimes of the congregation were laid out in the parlors of these farmhouses for wakes and funerals. The smaller parlor in the Holtan house served this special purpose as well as being the place where family photographs and memorabilia were displayed. The downstairs bedroom was the extra room that frequently sheltered overnight guests in comfort.

A daughter of the Holtans explains the orientation of her parents toward such community service. "Father and mother were both willing and enthusiastic church workers. We children used to say that our home was a station where all the ministers and evangelists that visited our congregation stayed, 'Prestestation' in Norwegian. Our parents were devout Christians and Father never failed to read God's Word morning and evening."[32] By reading and listening to sermons from Luther's *House-Postil*, the Holtan and Ness families learned:

Our daily experience teaches this. If a man and wife live together, their Lord their God will abundantly bless their industry, so that they earn much more than they imagine. . . . [T]here is a secret blessing of God connected with all this: we earn a penny today and one tomorrow, and economize accordingly, so that the blessing of God is experienced in quiet economy. In this way, Christ, our Lord, still continues to change water into wine in my house and in thine, if we are but faithful and pious. . . . If we but open our eyes, our experience would compel us to exclaim: Lord in thee do we trust in the performance of our domestic labors, they are also of thy institution, thou didst honor and bless them and still continuest to bless them. Therefore I will cherish my calling and be industrious in it.[33]

Although each structure can be characterized as an American Victorian home, each also exhibits ethnic qualities translated from Norway to the New World. A family resemblance exists between the Ness and Holtan farmhouses and manors in rural Norway. From the 1780s to the 1870s, neoclassical styles dominated Norwegian architectural taste and practice. Public and residential buildings exhibited a three-bay division with emphasis placed upon the central section to strengthen the balance and symmetry of the classical designs. This tendency toward symmetry and balance in the façade of a house was also evident in folk building in Norway. In this case a projected porch or accented major portal frequently marked and emphasized the center of the principal façade of a dwelling. In addition to these classical qualities in both professional and folk architecture of the nation, a Swiss style became popular from 1860 to 1910. The construction of the railroad through Norway introduced and spread this fashion in domestic building. Wood-frame train stations featured two-story decorative porches on the broad façades of central two-story gabled rectangular units. Elaborately cut and turned wood ornament was used on the porch and along the eaves of the roof. A variety of exterior wallboards, shingles, and roof coverings added surface patterns and textures for a picturesque effect.[34]

The Swiss style spread to domestic architecture in Norway and was manifested especially in large manors in the countryside. These *Herregaarden* were impressive structures that marked the presence of a large farm and the seat of an important person in the area. Many of these country homes were built when the Swiss style was popular in Norway and some were adaptations of older, traditional folk dwellings by the addition of the characteristic two-story porch and other decorative elements (Figure 6.14). However they came into being, they were perceived as architectural expressions of the class system that characterized rural Norway in the nineteenth century. Although the population of Norway was made up primarily of yeomen, with no aristocracy, there existed clearly defined classes that framed one's position in society. In terms of rural social classes, there were small landowners (*Bonde*) and the landed and leisure gentry (*Godseier*) and the mer-

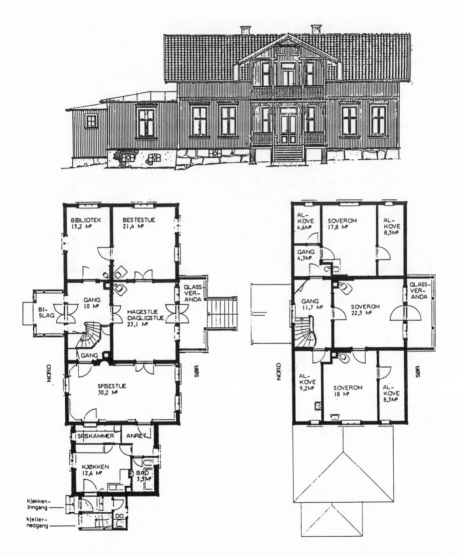

Figure 6.14. A Norwegian house in the Swiss style, Solbakken, Maridalsun, Oslo. From Arne E. Oldem, *Sveitserstil—1800-Arenes Byggestil* [The Swiss style—Nineteenth-century building style] (Oslo: Institut for Ethnologi, Universitet, 1984), 188, 190–91.

chants (*Herr Grosseser*). The former were able to keep bonded farmers (*Hus-mand*) on their estates and provide them with a small house and plot of land. A ploughman (*Plodsmand*) was also in the service of the *Godseier* but owned his own house and land except that he hired out as a farm laborer on the larger farm (*Gaard*) of the country lord.[35]

Andrew and Ingeborg Ness and Ole and Maren Holtan were young adults when they emigrated from Norway. They had experienced the social hierarchy of their homeland as well as appropriate ways to behave and communicate one's station in life there. The *Herregaard* of the *Godseier* was one of those prominent features of the physical and social environment that they admired and envied. After they became established on their farms in America and were able to build farmhouses that reflected the scale of their rural estates, it seems reasonable that they would remember these Norwegian *Herregaarden* and desire to emulate the domestic monumentality of that fashionable house type. The Ness and Holtan farmhouses reflect the formal symmetry of the neoclassical architecture of Norway and specifically the picturesque qualities of the manors built in the Swiss style. The balanced, neoclassical composition of the units and the Swiss-style two-story porch parallel the central unit of farmhouse types 5 and 6. Porches on *Herregaarden* were frequently capped by broad dormers similar to the central gables of the Ness and Holtan farmhouses. When a Norwegian Swiss-style house rose to a two stories, a band of ornamental woodwork marked the division of the stories. The curvature halfway up the exterior wall on the Holtan house and the decorative frieze under the porch eave on the Ness dwelling serve a similar purpose. Other Swiss-style qualities of the Holtan house include ornamental woodwork on the porch, balcony, and gable as well as shingles of various colors and shapes on the porch roof and central gable.

The floor plans of large and moderate-size houses built in the Swiss style in Norway are also similar to those of the Lac Qui Parle farmhouses. These similarities may, however, be just coincidence or an international dispersion of a typical nineteenth-century layout for a house in both Victorian America and Europe. It is doubtful that any of the Norwegian-American farmers in Minnesota ever saw or studied the interiors of specific manors in Norway; if they did, they could not have remembered them in any detail.

Traditional ways to decorate the interior of important rooms were, however, transmitted from Norway to America. Dating from the eighteenth century *rosemaling* was the direct painting of decorative motifs on walls and ceilings. This traditional folk art paved the way in the nineteenth century to stenciled walls and ceilings. The popularity of stenciling and of wood graining pine doors to make them look like oak, walnut, or birch increased in Norway with the advent of the neo-Gothic style in the 1840s and the Swiss style in 1860s.[36] Most of the large farmhouses built in Lac Qui Parle County between 1890 and 1910 had one or more rooms that were stenciled and that had pine woodwork painted in oak graining. A Danish painter known as Maaler Johnson did the work in these interiors. It was he who finished the dining room and parlors in the Holtan house and the parlor in the Ness dwelling. Wallpaper could be purchased in Lac Qui Parle County and was available through mail-order catalogues, but these Norwegian-American farmers choose decorative techniques that were meaningful and popular in their homeland. The similarity of these houses to *Herregaarden* in Norway, the full complement of specified rooms arranged in the extended floor plan, and the decoration of important rooms all qualify these dwellings as translations of Norwegian traditions and styles to the American prairies.[37]

The stencil decorations of the Ness parlor are a significant feature of the farmhouse (Figure 6.15). The walls are covered with an abstract representation of a garden. A star-filled sky spreads across the ceiling. The historical-cultural context in which these themes can be interpreted suggest two levels of meaning. The garden was both the Eden that Andrew and Ingeborg Ness labored so hard to realize from the wilderness of the prairie and the Paradise that awaited them at the end of their earthly pilgrimage. The starry sky suggests the expansive space that acted as a motivational force on the frontier but also symbolizes the Heaven in which the believer hoped to find a new and everlasting home. This duality of meaning seems possible insofar as it is consistent with the blending of the secular and the sacred in the lives of these people.[38]

The Scandinavian immigrants who established farms on the frontier in western Minnesota were accustomed to making decisions that shaped their lives and the lives of those close to them. They also learned, through the repetitive daily and seasonal chores they did to build and maintain a farm, the most direct and effective ways to accomplish tasks and achieve long-range goals. The planning and the realization of their farmhouses must be included in this kind of thinking and action. Within two months of his death, family members recall Andrew Ness saying that "it takes a lifetime to build a home and then one is ready for the grave."[39] The inscription on Andrew's tombstone in the cemetery of the Providence Valley Lutheran Church reads: "Viss er Doden, Unviss dens Time" [Death is certain, uncertain is the hour]. The statement is brief and aphoristic, but it does reveal a mindset and mode of living that moved toward establishing a home and working within one's time to create a house that was suitable for that home. The Ness and Holtan farmhouses, like others in their parishes, were more than a display of social and economic achievement. These houses were places that bore testimony to the faith of their builders and occupants and to the ceaseless service they gave their religious communities.

Figure 6.15. The parlor of the Andrew O. and Ingeborg Ness farmhouse, Lac Qui Parle County, Minnesota, 1898

Another inscription that appears on many of the tombstones of these pious Lutherans of Lac Qui Parle County is also appropriate to cite. It reads, "Jeg fundet harr at bedre hjem det evige Jerusalem" [I have found a better home in everlasting Jerusalem]. The Ness farmhouse as it stands now, abandoned and decaying, ironically bears testimony to such faith and hope. According to the belief of the faithful, the manors of Lac Qui Parle County were only temporary places where one could serve God before living in his mansions in heaven.

7. FARMHOUSE TYPES 8 AND 9: CONSOLIDATION AND STANDARDIZATION

The simple monumental shape and utilitarian floor plan of one- and two-story foursquare houses embodied values related to major national trends from the 1890s to the 1920s. After generations of expansion and growth, the nation turned toward consolidating natural and human resources. Means to process raw materials and manufacture products became standardized. The conveyor belt, piecework, and mass production of uniform-quality goods developed. At this time the two-story foursquare farmhouse became the most commonly built because it offered labor-saving efficiencies at the lowest cost. The foursquare was a popular dwelling that prospective home owners could choose from a catalogue featuring precut, ready-to-assemble houses. During this period, features related to the local rural community and Old World ethnic qualities began to disappear. The foursquare became associated with the modern American farm.

The simple architectural components that describe farmhouse types 8 and 9—the one- to one-and-a-half-story foursquare and the two-story foursquare, respectively—are the square or almost square enclosure and its pyramidal roof.[1] The low profile of farmhouse type 8 harmoniously parallels the low, broad horizons of the upper midwestern prairies but limits the interior space of the house. The addition of a kitchen wing to the basic square of the design was a customary way to gain more room. A one-story dwelling in Hamlin County, South Dakota (Figure 7.1), presents a simple foursquare façade toward the road and extends a one-and-a-half-story gabled rectangular kitchen wing toward the farmyard. The 24-foot-square section of the house is divided into four almost equal spaces, with the chimney placed inevitably at the center of the unit. The kitchen wing includes a

Hart-Parr tractor and plow, Stevens County, Minnesota, 1917 (Stevens County Historical Society, Morris, Minnesota)

pantry and a staircase to the half-story chamber above it. Additional storage space in the cellar is accessible through a trap door immediately outside the kitchen door. Two side entrances lead directly to the kitchen and to the dining room, and a front door opens into the living room and dining room that function together as one space. The compactness and centrality of the plan of this house type facilitated this merger of interior spaces. Some privacy is obtained for two small bedrooms by placing them off a narrow lateral corridor. One other small bedroom is managed from the half-story space above the kitchen. Planners and architects suggested that the house type provided "snug" quarters. It is more accurate to describe it as cramped.

A one-and-a-half-story foursquare in Wright County, Iowa (Figure 7.2), illustrates how living conditions in this house type are indeed cramped. The steep pyramidal roof has three dormers that give light and ventilation to the upstairs chamber. A 4-foot-high perimeter high wall is necessary in the half story to provide enough height to place furniture around the room. Over one-fourth of the total floor space of this level is lost under the slope of the roof. Only one other bedroom is provided on the first floor. Despite the addition of a kitchen wing and entrance hall, the dwelling is

Figure 7.1. Farmhouse type 8, Hamlin County, South Dakota, ca. 1900

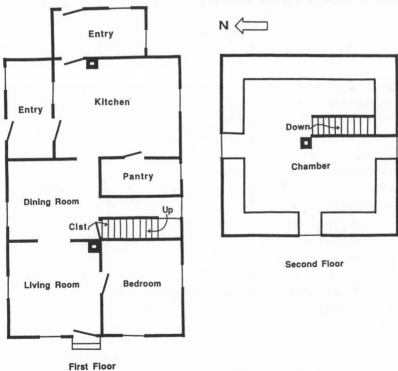

Entry

Entry

Kitchen

Pantry

Dining Room

Cist.

Up

Living Room

Bedroom

First Floor

N ⇐

Down

Chamber

Second Floor

Figure 7.2. Farmhouse type 8, Wright County, Iowa, ca. 1915

not big enough to serve even a moderate-size family whose sons and daughters are old enough to need separate bedrooms. The survey of farmhouse types documents that families chose to build two-story foursquare houses far more frequently than the one- to one-and-a-half-story foursquare. For a reasonable additional cost, a structure could be built that enclosed two full stories with 75 to 100 percent more space.

Designs of farmhouse type 8 from stylebooks described it as small and economical. Palliser, Palliser, and Company suggested that their design (Figure 7.3) would "fill the wants of a large class of people who want their own home, no matter how small it is." Fred Hodgson labeled his model (Figure 7.4) the Workingman, suggesting that it was intended for the low-income laborer. *Modern American Homes* presented one model as a "little house" and another as "a very charming nest for newlyweds." The small scale and low cost of this house type identified it as a dwelling that would fit a family's budget at a particular stage in its socioeconomic rise in American society. It is implied that one would continue to "step up," that one might eventually be able to obtain a larger dwelling, and that once the newlyweds began to raise a family, the "charming nest" would prove to be insufficient.[2] This house type provided many owners and occupants an opportunity to live in what is now called a starter home. The type was a practical option for more than three generations of rural and urban Americans, underwent changes in fashion, and was identified during the Victorian period as a cottage and during the Progressive Era as a bungalow. The Sears, Roebuck, and Company model incorporates the best of both worlds by naming Design No. 106 (Figure 7.5) a One-Story Cottage and decorating it with the bungalow features of front porch and dormer.[3]

Like ell- or T-plan farmhouses popular in the rural Upper Midwest from the 1860s to the 1880s, the two-story foursquare farmhouse is the kind of dwelling that can be identified with a specific period in the history of American agriculture from the mid-1890s to the 1920s. The extended wings of ell- or T-plan farmhouses and the stages in which they were built reflect the expansion that was typical during the 1860s and 1870s. The square perimeter and centrally designed roof of two-story foursquare farmhouses architecturally symbolize a move toward consolidation and standardization that occurred after the American frontier was "closed," the population of the rural United States began to decrease markedly, and the practice of agriculture became increasingly similar to industrial and commercial enterprises in management, specialization, and cost effectiveness.

Many of the families that remained on upper midwestern farms and successfully adapted to the greater complexities of agricultural operations and

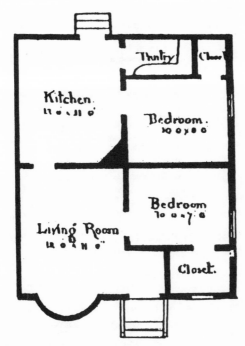

Figure 7.3. "Design 124: A One-Story Cottage," 1887. From Palliser, Palliser, and Company, *Palliser's New Cottage Homes and Details* (New York: Palliser, Palliser, and Company, 1887), plate 40.

"The Workingman"

Price of Plans and
Specifications

$5.00

Full and complete working plans and specifications of this house will be furnished for $5.00.
Cost of this house is from $400 to $500, according to the locality in which it is built.

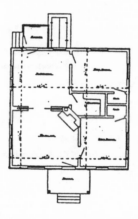

Figure 7.4. "The Workingman," 1902. From Fred T. Hodgson, *Modern Carpentry: A Practical Manual* (Chicago: Frederick J. Drake, 1902), n.p.

economics experienced the need to replace their old and/or small dwellings with larger, more updated structures. At this point, farm families apparently came to prefer a house that would comfortably shelter a grown family and make possible some of the modern technological conveniences. Paralleling a fashion for suburban bungalows, the two-story foursquare farmhouse was designed and built as a structure that directly expressed simplic-

No. 106

A one-story cottage with attic finished into one large room. This home has two good-sized windows in each room on the first floor and four sash in the room in the attic. Outside cellar entrance.

. . . .

Details and features: Five rooms and no bath. Front porch with hipped roof; hipped dormer in front.

Years and catalog numbers: 1908 (106); 1911 (106); 1912 (106); *1913* (106)

Price: $498 to $1,190

Figure 7.5. "No. 106: A One-Story Cottage," 1908. From Katherine Cole Stevenson and H. Ward Jandl, *Houses by Mail: A Guide to Houses by Sears, Roebuck, and Company* (Washington, D.C.: Preservation Press, 1986), 239.

ity. The taste for Victorian complexities in plan, elevation, and ornament never strongly manifested on farms in the Upper Midwest was clearly something of the past by the close of the century. The broadly proportioned, symmetrical façade of the two-story foursquare farmhouse communicates a clarity and crispness of design that supplanted gingerbread ornament. This house type incorporated more living space for less cost because it was easy and economical to build in a balloon frame construction that had become increasingly standardized, efficient, and economical.

The inventiveness of popular pattern-book designs and the achievements of local carpenters and farmer-builders, however, worked a surprising number of variations upon the basic geometric volumes and appearance of the two-story foursquare. Two initial examples of the type illustrate the basic shape to which changes could be made and ornament could be added. Whether square or slightly rectangular, the roof on farmhouses of this type is either a fully pointed pyramid, a truncated pyramid, or a hipped roof.

The Adrian van Amstel farmhouse in Pope County, Minnesota (Figure

Figure 7.6. The Adrian van Amstel farmhouse, Pope County, Minnesota, ca. 1910 (above and opposite)

7.6), is exactly 28 feet square and 28 feet from the foundation line to the point of the pyramid roof. That symmetry is repeated in the division of interior spaces, especially the second-floor chambers. The enclosed entry and bay window on the south wall and the simple porch on the east are the only extensions that add variety to the compact mass of the structure. The large kitchen wing extending from the Henry Lee farmhouse in Walsh County, North Dakota (Figure 7.7), is a feature that is a basis for a subtype of the two-story foursquare. The unit usually contains a kitchen, pantry, and at least one bedroom on the half story. A wing such as this was planned and constructed when the house was built. It was not an add-on project characteristic of the ell- or T-plan farmhouse type.

Virtually every farmhouse of type 9 was built with a large porch that spanned the principal living room façade. The style of the porch varied from classical revival to a bungalow design consistent with the simplicity of the entire structure (Figures 7.8 and 7.9). Another typical addition that modified the profile of the structure's elevation was the incorporation of roof dormers of various designs, number, and scale. In some instances a single triangular dormer identified the front elevation of the house, drawing attention to the porch below and to the house's orientation toward the county road (Figure 7.10). When the farmhouse was at a rural intersection,

N

Entry

Kitchen

Pantry

To
Basement

Up

Living Room

Bedroom

Porch

First Floor

Bedroom

Clst

Clst

Bedroom

Down

Bedroom

Clst

Clst

Bedroom

Second Floor

Figure 7.7. The Henry Lee farmhouse, Walsh County, North Dakota, ca. 1915 (State Historical Society of North Dakota)

Figure 7.8. Farmhouse type 9, Iowa County, Iowa, ca. 1915

Figure 7.9. Farmhouse type 9, Poweshiek County, Iowa, ca. 1900

the dormers faced both means of access; sometimes three to four dormers with multiple windows supplied a half story that functioned as a fully illuminated attic or as finished chambers (Figure 7.11). Bay windows, enclosed entries, a "widow's walk" on a truncated roof, or an extended two-story porch with monumental orders continue the list of ways that planners and builders endeavored to individualize a simple, symmetrical house type. Despite all of these variations and complexities, specific examples of this farmhouse are readily identifiable in the rural landscape. Because of their full two-story elevation and broad proportions, these white cubical structures appear as monumental presences whether viewed in the open space of the prairie or the wooded hills of a river valley. The fundamental elements of walls, roof, porch, and dormers extending vertically and horizontally into the space of the farm site impress one with the stability and position of the structure. Although the house type is economical in construction and cost, it communicates a manorial quality derived from its classic form and qualities.

Eighteenth-century Georgian mansions or nineteenth-century southern plantation houses suggest some historic precedents for the two-story four-square.[4] Some late nineteenth-century Italianate dwellings indicate sources that are closer in time and space to the actual origins of farmhouse type 9.

Figure 7.10. Farmhouse type 9, Clark County, Wisconsin, ca. 1910

A wide, squat Italianate farmhouse in Columbia County, Wisconsin (Figure 7.12), is a regional example of this historical model. Italianate houses usually had flat or low, sloping roofs that seldom had dormers. The basic cubical mass crowned by a central peaked roof is the essential architectural form that relates the Italianate house to the two-story foursquare.

Designs for the two-story foursquare house type appeared in architectural stylebooks as early as the 1850s. Henry W. Cleaveland and Samuel Backus, for instance, offered Design No. 16 (Figure 7.13) as a two-story frame house that was essentially a square plan except for two projecting bay windows on the major façade. The symmetry of plan and elevation consistently led to a division of space on both floors into equal or almost equal chambers. George E. Woodward's 1867 variation on this house type (Figure 7.14) has a more Italianate exterior and an interior with spaces laid out in a typical balanced and symmetrical fashion. Woodward's design is a traditional full Georgian plan adapted as a fashionable stylebook model.

Design No. 7 (Figure 7.15) from the *American Lumberman* is an example of a no-nonsense project that was available at local lumberyards. This model is described as "almost square, in which respect it furnishes the

Figure 7.II. Farmhouse type 9, Dodge County, Wisconsin, ca. 1900.

greatest amount of floor space in proportion to the outside walls. It may not be strong in point of beauty, but it is 'long' on utility."[5] The plans and front elevation of the house are given with an explanation of the practical aspects of the layout of rooms. A bill of materials is provided that lists the quantity and sizes of the lumber necessary to build the structure. The rhet-oric of earlier stylebooks about the social and moral values of the home is absent. The house design is presented on a purely economic, practical basis,

Figure 7.12. Farmhouse type 9, Columbia County, Wisconsin, ca. 1870

a manifestation of the quality of life on farms in the rural Upper Midwest from about 1895 until the 1920s.

A description of some national developments that effected changes in agriculture in the Upper Midwest during the second half of the nineteenth century is necessary to explain how the two-story foursquare farmhouse became a popular and significant house type from the 1890s to the 1920s. Major factors contributing to a transformation of agriculture from subsistence labor to a commercial enterprise were an increasing mechanization of farming, indigenous and governmental organization of farmers' roles in politics and society, growing emphasis upon the management of farm operations as businesses, and new and increased means of communication between rural and urban segments of the nation.

The cultivation of tens of thousands of acres of land in the Upper Midwest constituted an enormous struggle that tested the strength, skills, and endurance of every farm family member against the forces of nature. That transformation of the frontier wilderness was, of course, aided by the development of machines that enabled the farmer to increase his energies and efficiencies in every aspect of farming. Changes in the design of and materials for the plow were fundamental to these mechanical improvements. The invention and rapid development of the McCormick reaper was even more indicative of the increasing mechanization of agriculture. Introduced to the

FIRST STORY PLAN.

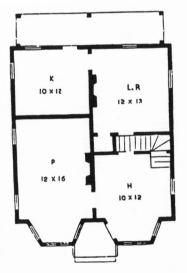

SECOND FLOOR PLAN.

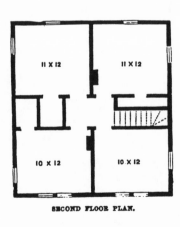

Figure 7.13. "Design No. 16," 1856. From Henry W. Cleaveland, William Backus, and Samuel D. Backus, *Village and Farm Cottages* (New York: D. Appleton, 1856), 103.

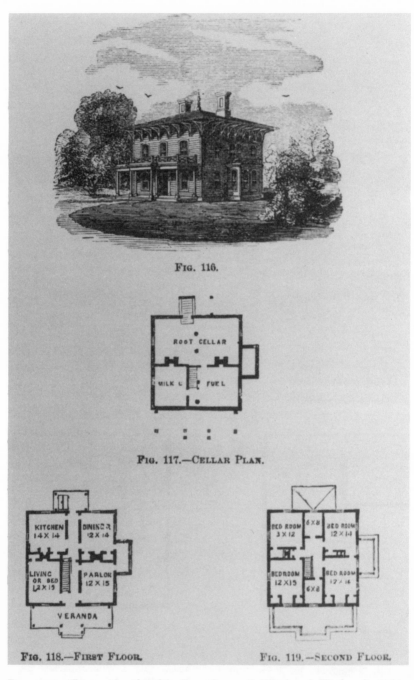

Fig. 116.

Fig. 117.—Cellar Plan.

Fig. 118.—First Floor.

Fig. 119.—Second Floor.

Figure 7.14. "Design No. 38," 1867. From George E. Woodward, *Woodward's Architecture and Rural Art, No. 1—1867* (New York: George E. Woodward, 1867), 84.

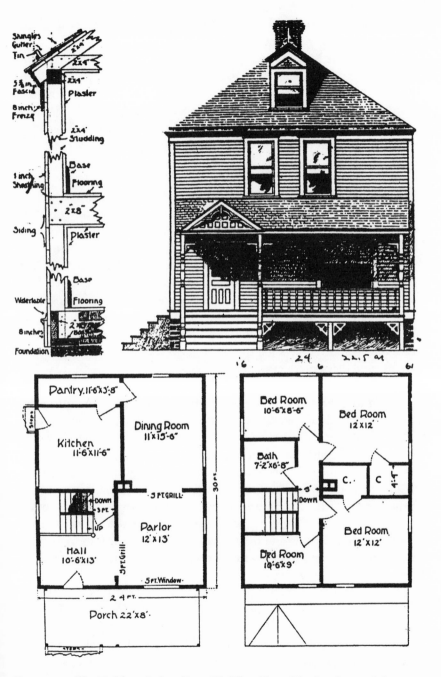

Figure 7.15. "Design No. 7," 1899. From "Building Plans: The Lumberman's Low Priced Houses," *American Lumberman* I (May 1899): 17.

market in 1858, the reaper was soon in great demand, so much so that sales doubled every other year during the 1860s.

By the 1880s the McCormick reaper and similar devices had been developed to be harvesters—machines that could cut, bundle, and bind the grain in one continuous operation. One machine was able to do the work for which five men were needed when hand tools were used to harvest grain, and the machine could do it faster and more efficiently. A report in the *U.S. Department of Agriculture Yearbook, 1899* characterized the nature of the changes that mechanization had brought to farming.

> The most prominent feature in the development of American agriculture is the immense improvement that has taken place in agricultural methods and machines—indeed, the word improvement is not adequate to express the change that has taken place in the methods of agriculture in this country, because implements and machines are creations rather than improvements, and their mission has been radical and far-reaching. They have reduced the amount of human labor required to produce a given quantity of crops and to cultivate given areas of land, and they have been largely, if not chiefly, instrumental in converting local markets into world markets for the principal cereals, cotton, tobacco, and animal and dairy products.[6]

In addition to improvements in plows, reapers, and harvesters, the author reported similar developments in planters, cultivators, harrowers, cornhuskers and shellers, seeders, and mowers. Further, he cited significant improvements in the varieties of seeds for cultivation crops, in the prevention and control of illnesses of livestock and poultry, and in increased knowledge about soil types, fertilizers, and anticipated crop yields.

Farmers organized cooperatives at broader levels in order to confront powers in the industrial and business world that, like the forces of nature, seemed sometimes hostile and beyond control. The Granger movement began in Minnesota, and the Non-Partisan League came into being in North Dakota. Another, lesser known farmers' organization was the American Society of Equity in Wisconsin, Minnesota, and North Dakota. The formation of these groups and their successes in addressing the problems of their members helped to convince many farmers that organization was an effective way to relate to issues in the world beyond the rural community. When the National Farmers' Union was formed in 1902, it was again in the Upper Midwest and based on the principles and practices of other regional farmers' organizations.

An immediate foe was the grain elevator line, which worked in collusion with the railroad and was sometimes owned by the railroad. Company workers at the local elevator often graded farmers' grain below its actual quality and paid them prices lower than its real worth. The same elevator also charged a farmer to store his grain until it was shipped to market. When it was shipped, the railroad lines extorted high rates. In each step toward the market, farmers lost a percentage of their profits and an honest return for their labor. Local groups formed to confront this issue laid the basis for future organizations that represented the farmer at state legislatures and in Congress. Farmers joined together to work for changes in their immediate environment with the faith that they could improve their positions as members of the national economic community in a capitalist society.

While many farmers were gathering together to speak for their interests more effectively through a collective voice, federal legislation was introduced and passed into law that furthered involvement of farmers in national and world economics and in scientific and informed practices in agriculture. The Land Grant Act, passed by Congress in 1862, ensured that large tracts of federal land would be used to establish colleges offering curricula in agriculture and the mechanical arts for improvement of the farmer's work and life and for the well-being of the nation. In 1887 the Hatch Act enabled the creation of agricultural experiment stations throughout the nation to research better methods of animal husbandry and plant culture in circumstances that were applicable to farmers in specific growing areas. By 1909, agricultural extension courses were being offered in rural areas beyond agricultural college campuses. The Smith-Sever Act in 1914 established county agricultural agents to further governmental involvement in and organization of the life and labors of the modern commercial farmer.

Beginning in the 1870s, the fluctuations of the national and world markets made it difficult to know what price per bushel would be paid for various grain crops and other raw materials farmers could cultivate. Some farmers started to learn business practices so they could successfully forecast the grain market and more wisely choose the right crop to plant to bring a high price on the future market. These business-oriented farmers recognized that agriculture was not a self-sufficient life on the homestead but, instead, a large and complicated working relationship with many aspects of the commercial and industrial society.[7]

By the beginning of the twentieth century, successful farming in the Upper Midwest and in other regions of the nation required that one bring the operation under a formal system of management and specialize in one type

of farming. It was too expensive to purchase and maintain all the equipment and technology necessary to run a diversified operation that included
livestock, dairy cows, poultry, grain, and special crops. Such diversification
also led to market complexities too great to predict and control. The *U.S.
Department of Agriculture Yearbook, 1902* offered some advice:

> The most successful system of farming is that which gives the largest
> profit, leaves the soil in a condition to yield maximum crops, and brings
> to the farmer and those dependent upon him the largest measure of hap-
> piness. . . . Here and there in all parts of the country farmers can be
> found who are highly successful. True their success is generally due to an
> unusual executive ability; but this is simply saying that they have an-
> swered the questions propounded in the above definition of farm man-
> agement and answered them correctly for their conditions.[8]

Some of the questions to be asked and accurately answered involved
what, when, and where to plant; where, when, and at what profit products
should be sold; what was the best way to care for a crop until harvest; and
what was the best way to ensure continued fertility of the soil. Agriculture
had become a complicated business in which the farmer now had to be
knowledgeable in scientific agriculture, finance, and business. He also had
to be his own mechanic to repair machinery. And as a manager he had to
know the principles of organization and efficiency to maximize his labors
for the greatest profits.

It was the economic depression of 1893 that signaled the "closing" of the
American frontier and the end of agricultural expansion into new fertile
lands. The depression caused thousands of farm foreclosures and increased
farm tenancy, but it also permitted some economically secure farmers to enlarge their landholdings. After homestead tracts were no longer available,
the land values in the region increased, sometimes as much as 300 percent,
providing collateral with which secure farmers could purchase more machinery and acquire more land. Greater and greater efficiencies were
achieved with the use of farm machinery. The number of men needed to
farm a given number of acres steadily decreased, as did the rural population
of the Upper Midwest.

Beginning in the mid-1890s, crop yields in the region began to be consistently good and the market for those crops increased. Fewer farmers were
competing in the market, and food consumption increased significantly because of the growth in urban populations. New markets opened up as industries developed uses for some fiber crops. Farm income rose and re-

mained stable in the rural economy. A comfortable balance occurred between the prices farmers received for their produce and the prices they had to pay for nonfarm goods. Although farmers enjoyed a "golden age of agriculture" that lasted from about 1897 to 1917, none became wealthy by national standards; by this time the millionaire had become the new measure of success and power in American economics and society.[9]

As farmers were better able to cope with commercial and industrial powers because of the rise in and stabilization of the farm economy, they also became more closely connected with some aspects of the urban lifestyle. Free rural mail delivery greatly increased communication between isolated rural areas and urban commercial centers. Mail-order houses used the new delivery service to sell their wares to customers everywhere. The variety and number of periodicals increased with the enlarged market of mail subscribers. City newspapers could eventually reach the most distant agrarian outposts. Some areas within the region established and operated telephone co-ops, electronically linking themselves together on a party line and eventually hooking up to the world outside. Automobile transportation became an affordable option in the rural Upper Midwest about 1910, especially when improved township and county roads ensured better travel and commerce conditions. These developments appeared at a time most farmers felt economically secure to enjoy them.

For many farm families it also seemed to be a time to build a new house. Lumber prices were reasonable, local contractors and carpenters had become experienced and reliable builders, and a new and wider range of houses was available in plan books at the local lumberyard, in magazines like the Ladies Home Journal, and through mail-order firms. Pioneers who had settled in sections of northwestern Minnesota, North Dakota, and South Dakota during the 1880s were just getting into a position to move from their homestead log cabins and shanties into large modern houses. Imagine the change in lifestyle when some of these large families left their subsistence shelters to live in a two-story foursquare farmhouse that provided some of the conveniences of a contemporary urban dwelling! Farmers in older, more-established areas of Iowa, Wisconsin, and Minnesota began to replace dwellings built in the 1850s and 1860s with updated farmhouses. The two-story foursquare house began to appear on more and more farms in the region.

Many two-story foursquare farmhouses built in the first decades of the twentieth century were based entirely on or derived from plans furnished by specialists in house design. These plans were supplied by local lumber companies, available through mail-order sources such as W. A. Radford's

Book on Farm Improvements, or delivered as precut, ready-to-assemble houses from Sears, Roebuck, and Company and other regional suppliers such as Aladdin Homes of Bay City, Michigan, and Gordon Van Tine of Davenport, Iowa. Precut houses were the culmination of the logic and standardization inherent in balloon frame construction and the mass-production approach to house design that stylebooks had fostered in America from the mid-nineteenth century. To make houses available through catalogue sales and to deliver them as precut structures to sites for local carpenters to assemble, professional designers and businessmen began coordinating the lumber and transportation industries of the nation. The changes in the American economy and society that had brought the housing industry to this level of organization were similar to those that had transformed the life of the yeoman from subsistence labor to diversified farming and finally to specialized operations in scientific agriculture.

Merchandising houses through the mail had begun in 1877 when the architectural firm of Palliser, Palliser, and Company of New York City had offered a custom service for house planning and construction. The firm advertised that it would draw up plans and specifications for houses upon request. The steps of selecting and refining a floor plan of the prospective house were to be handled through the mail. The client could, however, order a "clerk of works," who would be sent to the construction site to supervise the building of the house after a Palliser, Palliser design was purchased. A 2.5 percent charge of the total cost of the house was made for plans and specifications. The clerk cost an additional 1 percent plus travel and living expenses for the duration of the project. The architectural firm listed fourteen areas of information needed to plan a house for a specific customer. The most important of these was the dollar amount the prospective client wished to spend, local costs of materials and labor, and the nature of the site and its surroundings. Palliser, Palliser, and Company did, of course, illustrate more than one hundred plans and elevations in their *Model Homes* of 1878. These plans and all the services of the company were available to clients anywhere in the nation according to the schedule of charges. All houses were specified to be built in balloon frame construction using standardized dimension lumber, which was available in the United States wherever railroad transport delivered it to local lumberyards.[10]

The T. W. Harvey Lumber Company of Chicago was a major supplier of dimension materials that further developed the sale of houses through correspondence. An 1889 catalogue from the company's yards explained that it owned its own forested land, cut and kiln-dried its own lumber, and could deliver these goods to its clients without the costs of a middleman.

We claim that by our plans of construction, we can erect buildings far superior to those built in the ordinary way, in strength, warmth, and quality of work, and guarantee satisfaction in style and design. . . . It is generally conceded that work done by machinery is more uniform and exact and that *fine work can be done at less cost* than by the old method of hand labor. . . . Our facilities for doing *good work at a minimum cost* are unsurpassed.[11]

The phrases italicized in the catalogue emphasized the quality one could expect to receive for less money. It is also important to note that these savings were to be achieved through mass production of materials with machinery. The exact and uniform dimensions of the lumber were not only to ensure the quality of structure but also to ensure speed and efficiency of construction. Using a photograph of a two-story gabled rectangular design to illustrate one of their houses under construction, the T. W. Harvey Lumber Company explained that in just fourteen hours after the sills were laid the house was completely framed and had one coat of paint on the exterior, the kitchen walls were plastered, and the main roof of the house was ready to be put on. The house was completely finished in twenty days. There was no explicit statement in the catalogue that the parts of these balloon frame houses were precut before they were loaded on railroad cars to be sent to the site of construction. The speed of construction and the fact that the exterior siding was already given a coat of primer paint before leaving the yard suggest that the structures were to be assembled from precut pieces. In order to ensure a quality job, the company claimed that it would send a trained person to supervise the construction of the first home in any community. After that, the local carpenters would presumably understand the new system and be able to build for future clients of the T. W. Harvey Lumber Company.

By 1893 another firm with the dubious name of the Chicago House Wrecking Company was in the business of selling mail-order houses. The company was apparently searching for a new name to replace the one it had assumed when it had been established to dismantle most of the buildings of the Chicago International Exposition of 1893. Like the T. W. Harvey Lumber Company, the Chicago House Wrecking Company advertised houses of a type popular during the period. House Design No. 130 offered for only $720 is a good example of a two-story foursquare structure that appeared on many farms in the region (Figure 7.16). The design did, in fact, appear many times in full-page advertisements in farm journals such as *Wallace's Farmer*. The company also advertised designs and materials for

$720

HOUSE DESIGN No. 130.

Here is a handsome eight-room house. Size 25 ft. 20 in. by 29 ft. 6 in. Large front porch. Reception hall, living room, dining room and pantry on first floor. Front and rear vestibules. Second floor, four good sized bed rooms, bath room, closet in each room. A modern plan. Can be built at a minimum cost.

Figure 7.16. "House Design No. 130," 1910. From Chicago House Wrecking Company advertisement in *Wallace's Farmer* 35 (1910): 36.

barn construction as well as all kinds of building materials, bathroom fixtures, furnaces, floor and wall coverings, and even clothing. Every item, including all the materials to build a house, were said to be available to the customer at a 30 to 50 percent savings because the middleman and the trusts were eliminated from the transaction. A free general catalogue and a book of house and barn plans could be ordered through the mail. Should one choose House Design No. 130, all the lumber needed to build the structure would be shipped on rail to the town closest to the construction site. The lumber was not precut to be assembled but would be worked by local carpenters. Like other mail-order contracts, materials for the foundation and chimney were not included in the shipment.

The publishers of the *Lumberman's Gazette* of Bay City, Michigan, printed an article in 1883 entitled "Ready Made Houses," in which they advocated a manufactory of such dwellings for the city.[12] Near the northern forests at an inland seaport, the place seemed ideal for such a development. The article stated that "at certain eastern and Canadian points" such manufacturing had already gained considerable prominence. Quoting a local journal about the Kennebec Framing Company of Bangor, Maine, the article asserted, "Dwelling houses are made like boots and shoes—in any quantity or of any size or style, and for any market in the wide world." The article continued to stress the market potential for such houses.

> The great prairie lands of the west yet unpopulated must have buildings to shelter the people as well as the stock, and owing to the lack of lumber, it is almost impossible to obtain lumber except at a very exorbitant price. Transportation is a very important item, and the saving in this direction alone will insure demand for these buildings. The least calculation and consideration will demonstrate that it will cost more than double to transport the lumber in the rough for a desired building than it would to send the building, complete in every department on arrival at its destination.[13]

This kind of potential and level of organization began to be realized with the founding of the North American Construction Company in Bay City, Michigan, in 1902.[14] Later renamed Aladdin Homes, to imply the magic through which dream homes could materialize, the firm incorporated the essential elements of cost-effective mass production. By delivering an "Aladdin Readi-Cut Home" to the building site, the company claimed that it was eliminating the costs normally incurred by hiring an architect and contractor. Most of the work of a carpenter was also made obsolete. The costs of the big timber jobber, the lumber wholesaler, and the local lumber-yard were also subtracted from the cost of the house because Aladdin bought timber directly from the forest, then milled, cut, and shipped it. The plans, specifications, and complete precut materials were shipped directly to the purchaser at the lowest freight costs.

Catalogues of Aladdin Homes explained to prospective clients that the standards and processes of the company had reduced waste from 18 percent to just 2 percent. Resultant savings were passed on to the customer. Further, it was asserted that "Aladdin's Famous Board of Seven" was composed of professionals who checked each plan for accuracy, practicability, strength, and structural harmony. As long as factory experts maintained a standardized cutting of lumber and moved to higher efficiencies, the company would maintain its economy of costs. The lumber and members of the house frame were cut by machines that would guarantee accuracy and time/labor efficiencies. More building material, it was claimed, could be realized from board feet of lumber because machines were guided by principles and practices devised by experts who discovered ways to continue to get the most out of time, energy, and raw materials. The structural system that was illustrated in Aladdin Homes catalogues was a platform frame and not a balloon frame. Cutting and shipping efficiencies may have indicated that shorter lengths of 2×4 inch studding, used in a platform system of construction, were cost effective.[15]

Aladdin Homes catalogues presented a wide range of house types and costs as well as advertisements for barn designs and various ways to finish the interior of the new house with lighting fixtures, built-in conveniences, indoor plumbing, and central heating. Prices ranged from about $300 for a small one-story end-gable house to almost $2,000 for a colonial revival home. The Hudson (Figure 7.17) was moderately priced at about $1,000 and like other houses of its type was supposed to give the greatest amount of space in the most convenient arrangement at the lowest cost. A two-story foursquare was, in fact, the kind of house most frequently characterized in this way because the plan and two-story elevation allowed both designer and client to achieve values believed to be most important at the time. These values were those inherent in the precut balloon frame construction and merchandising of the house—economy, simplicity, utility, and efficiency.

Houses like the American Lumberman's Design No. 7 (Figure 7.15) or Aladdin Homes's Hudson (Figure 7.17) were, therefore, advertised as best suited for the modern American family at the beginning of the new century. These two-story foursquare houses were offered in two basic interior

The Hudson $1,098.20

Price. $1.156.00
Cash discount, 5%
Net price, $1,098.20

C AN you imagine a better utilization of space than is obtained in the plan
of the Hudson? The constant thought of Aladdin designers is toward
giving a maximum of convenience and comfort for the lowest possible cost.
It is doubtful if this result has been exceeded by any other Aladdin house. The
exterior will please you, we are sure, as this home has a greater number of admirers.

The Design
is practical
and conserva-
tive with no
sign of over-
trimming be-
ing evident.
Simple lines
in the porch
construc-
tion, heavy
overhead
boxing, and
roof are in
perfect har-
mony with
the balance
of the home.
The windows
of both first

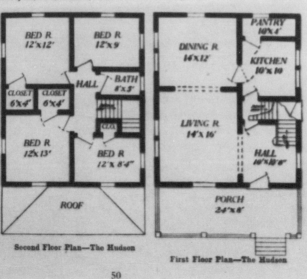

50

Figure 7.17. "The Hudson," 1917. From Aladdin Homes Company, *Aladdin Homes:
Catalogue #29* (Bay City, Mich.: By the company, 1917), 50.

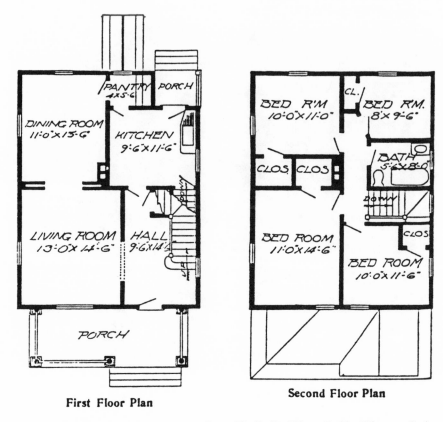

First Floor Plan

Second Floor Plan

Figure 7.18. "Design No. 2009," 1909. From *The Radford Home Builder* (Chicago: Radford Architecture, 1909), 42.

layouts. One common arrangement of first-floor space comprised a front entry staircase and passage that was immediately adjacent to the kitchen-pantry complex. On the other side of the first floor, the living room and dining room were spatially related by means of wide portals or double sliding doors. The front hall was also open to the living room space (Figure 7.18). Another popular first-floor arrangement eliminated the reception hall so that entry at the front door brought one immediately into a living room or sitting room (Figure 7.19). The second floors of these plans were similar, providing four bedrooms with closets and a bathroom that included a tub, sink, and toilet stool. It is evident in every floor plan that the interior spaces were arranged by function and grouped accordingly into spatial zones of the house—kitchen to front hall to upstairs traffic was direct, as was movement from kitchen to dining room or from front hall to

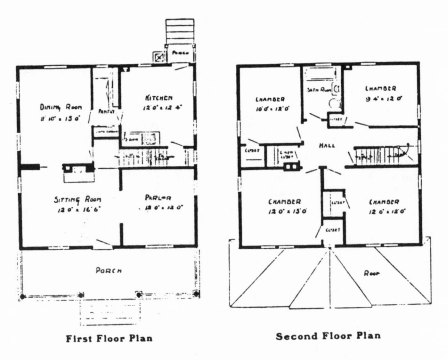

First Floor Plan   **Second Floor Plan**

Figure 7.19. "Design No. 126," 1903. From *The Radford Ideal Homes* (Chicago: Radford Architecture, 1903), 102–3.

living room. Because these spaces were cohesively organized in a square plan, it seemed natural, if not inevitable, that interior space would be used more effectively and that housework would be accomplished more efficiently. The consolidation of space in these houses also increased the effectiveness of a central-heating furnace installed in the basement of the house to warm all rooms equally by forced air or hot-water radiators.[16]

Although some farmhouses were constructed according to these plans, most locally built two-story foursquare dwellings document only a partial use of these new ideas and technologies. In many instances, the new domestic heating and plumbing systems were judged to be too difficult to build and operate or too costly to purchase. If many of these supposedly "modern" farmhouses were still infused with traditional ways of dividing and using domestic space, it does not follow that a conservative outlook on building prevailed in the region from the 1890s to the 1920s. When new features or updated amenities were not included in these farmhouses, it was because there was no viable way to do so. In some instances, the traditional way of planning a house was judged to be acceptable because those ways worked as well as any of the new procedures available. A stasis existed in which there was neither an active move to protect and preserve the traditional ways nor much real motivation to adopt the new ways of planning and finishing a home. In short, the exciting choice for modernity that was real for most urban home owners was not an urgent decision confronting many farm families.

The Adrian van Amstel farmhouse (Figure 7.6) documents this situation. The farmhouse was built on the site of a gabled rectangular farmhouse that had burned down in the winter of 1909–10. The foundation of the old house was saved and doubled in size to provide the base for the new foursquare house. The first-floor layout incorporates a side entrance and living-room entrance common to plan-book models, but the Van Amstels were aware that these portals were exits and added one more at the kitchen and a fourth on the west wall of the house. Fearful of being trapped by another fire, they planned exits to the structure toward all points of the compass.[17] The house was built without central heating. A kitchen range and a wood- or coal-burning space heater in the living room warmed those parts of the house. No indoor plumbing was initially included. The door on the west originally led to an outdoor privy. Sometime after 1920 a bathroom was installed in the upstairs northwestern chamber and later moved to the room directly below it. Pipes and drains and a septic tank with a field tank for waste processing were necessary to make the new bathroom operational and hygienic. A cistern was built in the northwestern corner of the basement so that soft water could be collected from the gutters and downspouts on the house and pumped to the kitchen above and later to the bathroom sink and tub.[18]

The Van Amstels chose a popular house type to replace their first house and continued to think of the larger space of the second farmhouse in terms of adaptability of chambers. The history of the structure indicates that the farm family did not always think in terms of one ideal floor plan that would provide once and for all for greater efficiencies. Indoor plumbing and central heating were not options to include in the original plan but were added when it was possible. A central heating system was not installed in the Van Amstel house until the 1950s.

Another two-story foursquare farmhouse located in Day County, South Dakota (Figure 7.20), provides further evidence that qualities inherent in the house type were utilized; however, individual variations in the plan indicate that it was tailormade by a local carpenter. Its present condition accentuates the simple cubical mass of the structure. A porch originally stretched the entire 28-foot width of the house, marking the major façade.

A rear entry leads to either the basement or the kitchen, but not to both. A typical arrangement of kitchen, dining room, and living room is present on the first floor, but a back bedroom with a toilet stool in a small cubicle and a tiny closet depart from professional plans. A staircase at the rear of the house is accessible from the dining room. The first flight of stairs is 40 inches wide; on the second flight it narrows to 30 inches. The staircase at the rear of the house and its deviation in regular measurement resulted in some tricky maneuvers in the entry below, where three doors swing open and closed in syncopated movements. The second floor of the house contains the usual four bedrooms reached from a central hall. Space ordinarily designated for a bathroom was used for closets. A 6 × 8 foot walk-in closet serves one bedroom. In alignment and proportion with that space, the two closets on the other side of the hall are each 6 feet square. Ample space is provided to hang the outfits one could order from Sears, Roebuck, and Company or Montgomery Ward and plan to wear for a Saturday night's trip to town in the Model A.

The builder of this house studied lumberyard floor plans and actual structures of this house type and then built this foursquare in an intuitive manner. He knew how to build a house of this kind and worked out room divisions according to the preferences of the farm family that was to inhabit it and to the dictates of balloon frame construction. This practical carpenter aligned the first-story load-bearing walls over supports in the foundation of the house and divided the second-story space so walls on this level would be positioned above those on the first floor. The division of space and placement of walls in turn depends upon the regular intervals of joists and studs placed 16 inches on center in the frame. Although the South Dakota design deviates from model-house floor plans, the structure reveals a logic of spatial division that is derived as much from balloon frame construction as it is from the builder's practical wisdom.

A comparison of three other floor plans of two-story foursquare farmhouses built between 1895 and about 1910 provides further evidence that Upper Midwest farm families tended to adapt the house type to meet their own needs in their rural situation. The wide second-story hall, a separate staircase to the kitchen, and two laterally placed chimneys in the Fegland farmhouse (Figure 7.21) are explained by the fact that the dwelling was designed for two families. The use of second-floor chambers was equally divided between the two families and all shared the space and conveniences of the first story of the dwelling. The fourfold division of space on both stories of the Thorsgaard (Figure 7.22) and Enderson (Figure 7.23) farmhouses is closer to model-house plans from mail-order catalogues, but neither fol-

Figure 7.20. Farmhouse type 9, Day County, South Dakota, ca. 1910 (above and opposite)

lows the standardized arrangement and designation of rooms that one finds in the prepackaged versions of the house type. Each house included a traditional downstairs bedroom. In the Enderson house, the dining room and parlor were separated and enclosed as they would have been in earlier Victorian houses. Without central heating, these rooms were difficult to keep warm during Minnesota winters and hence it was more practical to keep them closed up then. These farmhouses did not have central heating. Costs for the system were probably judged to be too high, and it would have been difficult and expensive to haul a sufficient amount of fuel across dirt roads to the farm site.

Although both the Thorsgaard and Enderson farmhouses incorporate large kitchens with built-in cabinet conveniences, neither dwelling includes indoor plumbing for the kitchen or for a second-floor bathroom. Like cen-

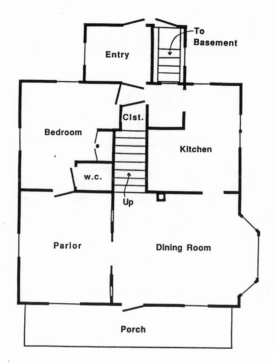

To Basement

Entry

Clst.

Bedroom

Kitchen

w.c.

Up

Parlor

Dining Room

Porch

First Floor

N

Bedroom

Down

Bedroom

Closet

Closet

Hall

Closet

Bedroom

Clst.

Bedroom

Clst.

Second Floor

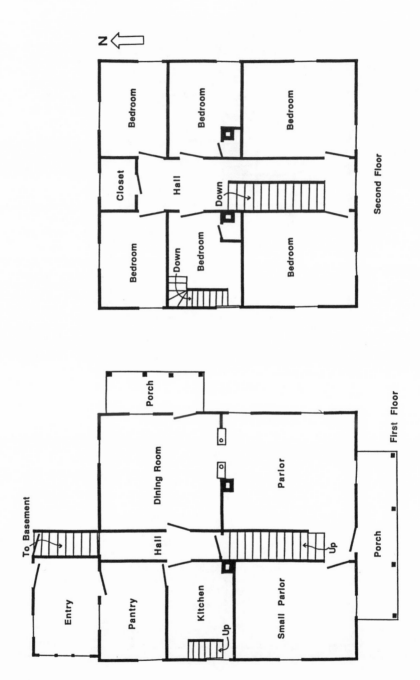

Figure 7.21. The Fegland farmhouse, Poweshiek County, Iowa, ca. 1890

Figure 7.22. The Thorsgaard farmhouse, Traill County, North Dakota, ca. 1905

Figure 7.23. The Enderson farmhouse, Lac Qui Parle County, Minnesota, ca. 1915

tral heating, plumbing for hot and cold running water was costly. Each farm had to be equipped with a complete water and sewage system in order to make such a convenience possible. A water system would include a source of supply (a spring, a well, and/or a cistern); a hand pump, windmill, or small gasoline motor; storage capacity in a gravity tank (either a water tower or an attic tank); and piping to carry the water to designated places in the farmyard and in the house. Water used for washing dishes, bathing, processing foods, or caring for livestock had to be channeled to a septic tank some distance from the yard so that waste materials could be safely eliminated in bacterial decay and seepage. The diagram that appeared in *Carpentry and Building* with an article entitled "Plumbing in a Farmhouse" (Figure 7.24) illustrates the basic network of pipes joining various appliances that made the whole system work for the farm family.[19] The Thorsgaard and Enderson farmhouses cost no more than $900 when they were built at the beginning of the century. The complete system that would provide an indoor bathroom would have cost an additional $400 to $500. It is easy to understand why farmers decided such an expenditure was unnecessary until the new technology became more economical.[20]

Farm families in the Upper Midwest as well as in other parts of the nation benefited economically during the golden age of agriculture from about 1895 to 1917. Higher levels of efficiency were possible through improved machinery and greater mechanical horsepower. Farm management principles furthered specialization of agricultural operations and both farmer-originated and federal governmental organizations offered more order and direction to the farmers' role in national policies controlling farm production and prices. Linked more closely with the rapid growth of the urban sector and the commercial elements of the nation, farm families were open to new ideas and the influence of urban lifestyles. The popularity of the two-story foursquare farmhouse during this period generally reflects these trends toward efficiency, consolidation, control, and convenience; but closer investigation of representative farmhouses indicates that farm families adapted the ideal model house to their own circumstances and values. The plan-book models for the two-story foursquare were intended primarily for an urban environment, where indoor bathroom facilities were enforced by law and where water was supplied under pressure from city mains. The electrification of houses occurred much earlier in cities than in rural areas. The urban housewife could enjoy electrically powered gadgets long before her rural counterpart. The farm wife who could read about these time- and labor-saving devices in periodicals or study them in mail-order catalogues had to forego their use until a rural electrification program

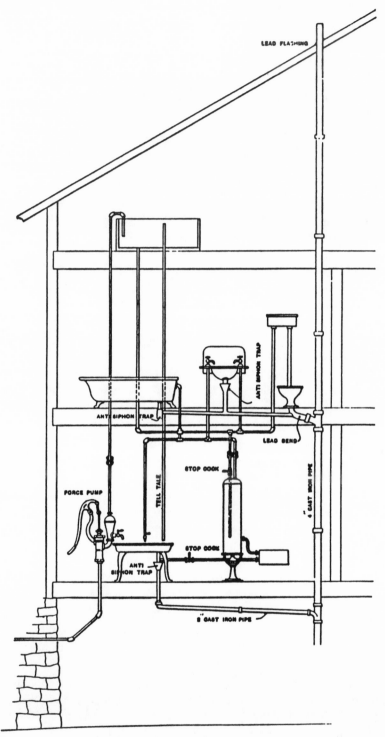

Figure 7.24. A diagram for plumbing in a farmhouse. From "Plumbing in a Farmhouse," *Carpentry and Building* 29 (January 1907): 25.

was initiated in the 1930s. Somehow the simple, efficient appointments of the new modern house as pictured in plan books seemed incomplete and ineffective unless the entire energy-driven operation could be obtained. In the meantime, farm families adopted as much as they could and made adaptations and allowances for what they could not yet acquire and enjoy.

Two-story foursquare farmhouses do, however, communicate in their simple planar walls and their adaptable, efficient interior spaces a standardized and utilitarian approach to life and labors on farms in the region. Each foursquare farmhouse communicates the attainment of a solid, stable, and well-managed place in the rural and national economy. Their symmetric, stately monumentality clearly expresses that these were the manors of the new agriculture. The balloon frame that by this time had become a standardized method of construction was the perfect means to realize these kinds of houses by and for upper midwestern farm families.

8. FARMHOUSE TYPE 10: RURAL IMAGES OF SUCCESS

A significant way in which farmers signaled their success was the planning and construction of houses that were evidence of their prosperity. Houses of this type would approximate the high style mansions one could admire in towns and cities. Most farmers' mansions, however, only approximated these urban models in scale, asymmetrical plans and irregular elevations, finishing touches of elaborate ornament, and complete furnishings for every room. In comparison with other farmhouse types, relatively few of the "large, irregular" kind exist in the region. Some two-story farmhouses have already been characterized as manorial (Figures 4.13, 5.8, 6.9, and 6.10). When these examples are considered as a group with type 10 farmhouses, they provide an adequate basis to understand how upper midwestern farmers realized residences that communicated their position of importance in the rural community.

A survey of any area in the Upper Midwest indicates that most families were content with farmhouses that were small and economical. In addition to the generally held belief that being frugal was being virtuous, two factors help explain the relatively small number of large and fashionably finished balloon frame farmhouses. First, the structure that resulted from the balloon frame method of building with lightweight members of wood was regarded as flimsy and ephemeral. The advice in every architectural stylebook to prospective home owners was that large houses should be constructed of brick or stone. These were deemed the appropriate building materials for communicating substantial and lasting achievement in architecture. Second, if a wealthy farmer did choose balloon frame construction for a large and stylish house, he might have encountered difficulty finding rural contractors and carpenters capable of accomplishing the complex cutting and joining of members involved in such a project. A saddle or pyra-

Mr. and Mrs. Henry Cotner, Hettinger County, North Dakota (State Historical Society of North Dakota)

mid roof is based on a series of rafters simple to cut and set at regular intervals on the plate atop the vertical studs of the structure. Roofs with many and varying gables, dormers, and towers demand considerable ability in reading blueprints and practical skill in calculating and carrying out the cutting and assembly of parts. Most carpenters in the rural Upper Midwest would not have had the training and experience to accomplish such construction. Large, complex houses were built according to revival styles in many upper midwestern towns, indicating that some skilled workmen were present and able to build structures that involved complicated cutting and joining.

If a family did plan and build a large and ornate house, the choice and means to do so were affected by where and when the farm was established in the region. If the family had arrived early and settled in southern Wisconsin, eastern Iowa, or southeastern Minnesota, they obviously would have had more time to establish the farm and benefit by the economic development of the region agriculturally. Investment of time and labor tended to bring good dividends to a farmer-entrepreneur who was included in the local economic infrastructure, acquiring land, buying stock in local businesses, or becoming a trustee of a local bank. In addition to the length of time in an area, the nature of the environment and the quality of the soil were important determining factors for success and security. Although the Red River valley area in Minnesota and North Dakota was settled as late as the 1870s and 1880s, its rich soil brought farmers consistently good yields and profits in No. 1 Hard Wheat. Railroads were built in the valley before or soon after settlement so that the means of commerce increased a farmer's chances of success in the area. Many large farmhouses were built in the Red River valley from the 1890s to the 1920s.

Obviously the time when a family planned to build a large and substantial dwelling influenced the house design. In most cases, larger houses were not built until the working elements of the farm enterprise were well established. By that time, the Gothic revival, Italianate, Second Empire, and neo-Romanesque styles had passed their respective decades of popularity, and choices remained from the eclectic fancies of the 1880s or some of the more elaborate designs of mail-order houses available by the 1890s and early 1900s.

Four examples of farmhouse type 10 will be discussed here to illustrate how successful farmers of different ethnic groups expressed their attainment of wealth and prestige at different times and places in the history of the region. First, the prevalent Victorian image of success will be used to compare relative qualities of four Upper Midwest examples of a successful farmer's house. The four structures are the work of a Yankee farmer in Iowa, a Norwegian immigrant to North Dakota, and a German dairyman in Minnesota. The fourth farmhouse embodies values of the future rather than of the past. It is a fashionable mail-order house of 1914 furnished with the latest household conveniences, making it a palatial paradise realized through modern technology.

Regardless of ethnic background, farmers in the Upper Midwest were pervasively influenced by the dominant Victorian values that framed the American image of success. Hard working, intelligent, and persevering were qualities a farmer needed to succeed and to provide himself and his family with a large and stylish house. Both the images (Figures 8.1 and 8.2) and the words in a classic Horatio Alger saga of the farmer that appeared in an 1879 issue of the *Independent Farmer and Fireside Companion* featured these traits. The text that accompanied the illustrations is presented here at some length because it focuses on the farmhouse as an emblem of success, a metaphor for an individual's lifework and purpose.

The picture before us presents a familiar scene of the early pioneer farmer. He has entered the woods, with but very little money. Camping

Figure 8.1. "The Pioneer Farm." From "The Pioneer Farm," *Independent Farmer and Fireside Companion* 1 (1879): 160.

out with his young wife and little ones, he has, with his own hands, cut, hewed, and built the cabin you see and the barn and shed for his cattle. A year or two later he has broken and cultivated several acres; he has added to his stock; patched up his house; gathered together some necessary agricultural implements, and is really in a comfortable condition. . . . Up in the morning before the sun, he toils day after day, not for a week steady, or a month, but for a season, aye, even for a year. He is shut out from society—from books—from social intercourse with the human family. He tugs and toils, and economizes; saves and plants and gathers. Loses one year what he made the year before; is imposed upon by designing men; cheated in the weight of his store goods, he toils on unmurmuringly until, perhaps, a good crop . . . lifts him on to a plane of comparative ease.

. . .

Could anything be more beautiful, more attractive? Mark the elegant grounds! See the beautiful house—the capacious barn and sheds, and the grand wheat fields, stretching off in the distance. You enter the gate and pass up winding walks by the cooling spray of the fountain. Symmetrical evergreens confront you, and the soft green velvety grass yields

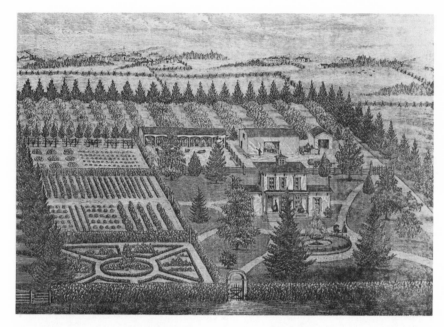

Figure 8.2. "The Prosperous Farm." From "The Prosperous Farm," *Independent Farmer and Fireside Companion* 1 (1879): 164.

to your tread, while the fragrance of flowers steals upon your senses. The garden invites you to its well-cared beds; the trees beckon you to repose under their shade; all nature is calm, while the farmer and his wife pursue the even tenor of their way, assisted by such help as money can provide. . . . He has had his Struggle; he reaps his Reward.[1]

This view of labor and achievement attributes Promethean powers to the farmer that enable him to transform chaos into order, change wilderness into a garden, move one from danger to safety, bring gentleness in place of harshness, and, like the Creator, institute repose after his labors were accomplished. The power to make these transformations, to issue positive change into one's experience and into the world at large, comes through work and toil, discipline of mind and spirit, and temporary deprivation.

Figure 8.1 ("The Pioneer Farm") presents the scene from a relatively detached perspective so that the farmer, his family, and their rough environment can all be seen when their struggles to make a homestead began. The representation of the log cabin is somewhat distorted because the illustrator tried to compact one and a half stories into the small structure. The façade of the cabin is classically symmetrical and even displays a neoclassical front portal with side lights. Figure 8.2 ("The Prosperous Farm") presents the scene from an elevated perspective to obtain the big picture of what the farmer had wrought. It is as if one were assuming a God's-eye view of the miracle shown below. Geometry and symmetry prevail in the design and elevation of the farmhouse as well as all of its surrounding outbuildings, gardens, and fields. This portrayal of abundance and plenty focuses upon the waters pouring forth from the fountain in front of the farmhouse—the symbol and source of all the fertility and life that abound. The life-giving and sustaining labors of the farmer are seen as the boon of food, nourishment, abundance, health, and well-being that he brings to the world—to the other houses and the village shown in the distance.

Although this investment of superhuman power and exemplary values in the farmer is not unusual for the rhetoric of the time, it certainly did not fit the realities.[2] Economic resources were necessary for any accomplishment. In the conclusion of "The Prosperous Farm," the writer claims that one should "have some idea of what a farmer's home should be, and can be, with care and taste, and culture, but of course not without money." In another place in the text, one learns almost parenthetically that the farmer and his wife have been "assisted by such help as money can provide."

Throughout the second half of the nineteenth and into the twentieth century, the growing importance placed upon money and the means of labor, industry, and commerce to make profits generated conflict with what have been identified as the "classical village values" of Victorian America. These values are "equal opportunity for each man; a test of individual merit; wealth as a reward for virtue; credit for hard work; frugality and dedication; a premium upon efficiency; a government that minds its own business; a belief in society's progressive improvement."[3] These beliefs and values are at the core of the pioneer-prosperous farm epic. The saga also includes recognition of the cash economy in which the practical realization of "the Reward" was effected. With the development of industry and the growth of cities in America as centers of business, commerce, and banking, the realities of life on the farm and the rewards of that life to the farmer and his family were progressively adapted to the new economic situation. The development of the national economy meant that farming had to change from a Jeffersonian self-sufficient subsistence operation to a specialized commercial venture operating under the same principles of management as other businesses. If a farmer were to succeed and realize his reward of a secure farm and impressive home, he had to be "assisted by such help that money can provide" and earn that money by wisely following the best business policies at his disposal. A fully appointed and stylish house on the farm indicated more than reward for virtue. These kinds of farmhouses documented the success of the farmer in his practice of entrepreneurial skills in agriculture, in the market, and possibly in financial investments that ensured long-term dividends.

A chronic conflict was experienced by farmers who believed in the virtuous yeoman defined by Jefferson and who also acknowledged the realities of a capitalist, industrial economy. Most farmers who settled in the region seemed never to have thought of themselves as subsistence operators. Farmers eagerly sought markets for their surplus crops, especially wheat as a cash crop.[4] When a farmer did realize success and a large farmhouse, the good fortune was frequently described in terms of the two-act drama of "Pioneer Farm" and "Prosperous Farm." When families apparently failed to achieve this goal, one could fall back on a rhetoric that eulogized the good life on the farm. Dark images of life in the new American cities were used as foils to brighten conditions on a smaller, supposedly unsuccessful farm. "The poorest farmer," claimed one farm wife, "in the poorest hovel ever called a farmhouse has kingly quarters compared to the inmates of the swarming tenement house, for all around him are light and air and sunshine. He knows the scent of wildflowers, and the color of the June sky. Scavengers may clean city streets of their filth every night, but the springing turf upon which the farmer walks, wet with evening dew, is fresh each morn and sparkling with a myriad of gems."[5] This kind of justification of rural poverty over and against rural wealth began to appear more frequently in farm journals in the late 1880s and the 1890s, a time when many larger farmhouses were being built in the region while most other farmhouses remained expediently small dwellings. A moderating voice of the time claimed, "The truth is that while farming pursued with diligence and success will certainly give the farmer and his family a very comfortable home, free from many of the anxieties which harass his equals in other kinds of business, it will seldom make him very rich."[6]

The need to explain or reconcile differences between the grand and the small to moderate-size farmhouse in rural America became more pressing as the nineteenth century drew to a close. By this time the emergence of millionaires of banking and industry and the notoriety of their great houses had created a national controversy about the house as "the most visible and potent symbol of property." On the one hand, the mansions of the Vanderbilts and the Morgans could be seen as signs of national prosperity and indicators of achievement in culture and taste in the arts. On the other hand, they could be viewed as the ostentatious show of excessive wealth in the hands of the few.[7] Success began to be interpreted in the context of social Darwinist theories that attributed abilities to acquire wealth and power to inherited traits. The traditional values of equal opportunity, individual merit, and wealth as rewards for virtue shifted to biologically inherited strengths and potentials such as superior intelligence and strong physical constitution resistant to illness and psychological stress. Learning the proper habits and disciplining oneself to maintain those habits were, of course, viewed as important.

The serious implication of this social Darwinian view was its condemnation of the poor. It was asserted that if one were not born with the proper mental and physical powers, one would be fated to failure. Failure of this kind would be evident in a lower station in life and by uncivilized and immoral behavior. The domestic environment in which one lived would naturally reflect one's fortune or fate. Those born unfit to succeed would never have palatial dwellings; rather, they would spend their miserable lives in tenements and slums—or in small vernacular farmhouses.[8]

This kind of moral judgment is implicit in rural clean-up campaigns that appeared in agricultural journals from the 1850s through the 1890s. Contrasts between "Old Slovenly" and "President Thrifty" (Figure 8.3) delivered the message that virtue is visible in the way that one acquired property as well as the way it was maintained. Laziness, drunkenness, and insensitivity to the beauties of nature were given as causes for a place like Old Slovenly's den. President Thrifty was introduced as the president of the town agricultural club and characterized as "a gentleman of high intelligence, and a farmer of enterprise and high ambition." All aspects of his life, work, environment, and family were described as attaining perfection. Slovenly was portrayed as a foul-mouthed old tyrant who lived in visual and verbal squalor. Nothing of worth was noted in a life such as his, which was apparently judged to be destined by genetic ("half-human") defect.[9] Similar verbal and visual essays were directed toward urban slums, but they seemed especially pointed when focused upon rural America. Farm families did not usually rent or buy a house that was already constructed. Either a local carpenter was hired to build their house or they built it themselves. Identification of the family with the farmhouse was, therefore, immediate and direct and expressive of the specific conditions in which the family lived and the values that shaped that environment.

The construction of large, ornate farmhouses in the Upper Midwest can be interpreted from the varying perspectives and changing values of the time in which they were built. The meaning of these architectural assertions of success should be understood as a complex of aesthetic, economic,

PRESIDENT THRIFTY'S HOME.

OLD SLOVENLY'S "DEN."

Figure 8.3. President Thrifty's home and Old Slovenly's den. From "Thrifty's Home, Old Slovenly's 'Den,'" *Wisconsin Farmer* 10 (August 1858): 294–95 (above and opposite).

Figure 8.4. "Residence of D. M. Flinn, Boone T[ownship], Dallas Co[unty], Iowa."
From Alfred T. Andreas, *Illustrated Historical Atlas of the State of Iowa* (Chicago: Andreas Atlas, 1875), 255.

social, and moral values. Whether built of stone, brick, or wood, whether
finished in Gothic or Queen Anne features, the large and impressive farmhouse said something about the occupants and their relationship to others
in their rural community in quite a different manner from the moderate expression of an average farmhouse. The following examples of larger-than-
average farmhouses are intended to present a spectrum of buildings that
were considered a show of success by the farmer and his family to the rural
community in the context of both monetary and ethnic values.

D. M. Flinn of Dallas County, Iowa, projected an image of himself as a
gentleman farmer within the context of mainstream Victorian values of the
time. He worked to create this image by owning and operating a certain
kind of farm, by building a farmhouse befitting an English country estate,
and by paying for a half-page engraved illustration of his farm in the 1875
Andreas *Illustrated Historical Atlas of the State of Iowa* (Figure 8.4). As portrayed, Flinn's farmhouse is advantageously situated on a rise of land above
a little valley through which a creek flows. From this elevation the house
presents an impressive, formal façade visible for some distance from many
perspectives. The house and the site announce Flinn's importance as a
farmer in the rural community, just as the engraved image of his farm pub-
lishes his success to the entire state.

Flinn had this house built in 1863. He had immigrated from southern Indiana to the frontier in central Iowa as early as 1846. By 1875, Flinn was

identified as a farmer and stock raiser. His land was well situated for this kind of operation. His farm had good tillage acreage, good pasturage, and a water supply. He was just 2½ miles from Booneville, through which the Chicago and Pacific Railroad operated. He was also one day's journey from the state capital, Des Moines, 14 miles to the east. Advantageously situated for commerce and culture, farming good land, and able to buy and breed good livestock, Flinn had every quality of the successful farmer. It is Flinn we see in Figure 8.4 wearing a tall hat and standing just outside the gate to his farm. He is truly a country gentleman.

The Flinn farmhouse is a three-story structure built into a hill that was graded to create a level area for the foundation (Figure 8.5). The structure is a heavy braced balloon frame, using 2½ × 6 inch milled lumber for the vertical studs. The foundation-basement constitutes a basement level that contains a kitchen–dining room and a living room for everyday family use, workrooms for food preparation and laundry, food-storage areas, and a furnace room. The house was progressive in design because it was to incorporate the technological luxury of central heating. On the first floor, Flinn planned a formal dining room, living room, parlor, and two oddly spaced bedrooms. It is evident from the greater height of rooms on this floor that these spaces were to be the more impressive chambers used for social functions. The second floor has four bedrooms and an access to the half-story attic. The design is that of a central-hall, double-pile Georgian house of New England origins.[10] Flinn, however, updated the older house type with fashionable Gothic revival features such as the steep, projecting gable decorated with an elaborate bargeboard. A central porch on the first story is extended by the banister that stretches across the entire façade. The areas enclosed by the banister were not used as balconies, but the feature nicely embellishes the façade at a place where it is quite effective. A hint of a classical feature is given in the second-story central portal where side lights flank two simple columns. If one can trust the accuracy of the Andreas depiction of the house, its roof line was broken by two chimneys, lightning rods, and a tall weather vane. All of these features decorate an essentially simple house with fashionable touches of applied style.

The success of area farmers was sometimes celebrated by local newspapers and regional agricultural publications. Editors of these works wrote articles describing the virtues of the hero of agriculture and printed photographs of his large and substantial farmhouse with an inset image of the farmer's first log cabin, sod house, or shanty. Farmers neither commissioned these stories of success nor protested the recognition they gave. A North Dakota farmer of local fame can be presented in this before-and-after format—from the pioneer to the prosperous farmer. The log cabin of pioneer Fingal Enger has already been illustrated and briefly discussed as a subsistence shelter (Figure 3.5). Another perspective of that early dwelling is provided in a 1910 photograph (Figure 8.6) illustrating the success story told in *The Norwegian Farmers in the United States*. What this image lacks in photographic clarity is made up for in rhetorical brilliance.[11]

A brief biography of Fingal Enger and a critical evaluation of his life will yield a more objective assessment of the farmer's success.[12] In 1869, at the age of twenty-three, Enger migrated from Norway to Mitchell County, Iowa. Immigrants like Enger were not totally self-reliant. They depended upon countrymen who had gone before them and had established farmsteads in the New World. In this way, Enger hired out to Norwegian farmers in Iowa and later in Minnesota so that he could become accustomed to the new way of life, learn the language of the land (as well as continue to practice his Norwegian), and acquire some knowledge of and skills in the agriculture of the Upper Midwest. So purposeful was Enger that he attended a rural school near Albert Lea, Minnesota, one winter so he could learn English better. By 1871 he had ventured to the edge of the frontier in the region and was working for the Northern Pacific Railroad, which was building a line into the yet unsettled areas of northern Minnesota and North Dakota beyond Fargo. In the spring of 1872 he and two other Norwegian pioneers set out on foot farther north in search of good farmland available under the homestead law. It was in what was to become Steele County, North Dakota, that Enger staked his claim to 160 acres of land. By the time he died in 1913 he owned and operated 11,520 acres. His landholdings had been reduced to this amount because he had earlier given two sons 160 acres each to farm and had sold an additional 5,540 acres. In the context of any economic system, Fingal Enger had become a successful farmer.

Some of the factors that helped Enger attain this position have already been noted. He was one of the first to settle in an area that had exceptionally rich topsoil. He conscientiously learned the language and the ways of the New World and was prepared to become a "culture broker" as well as a financial broker to his countrymen who later immigrated to the area. By the 1880s, when there was a new wave of immigration to North Dakota, Enger's expanding farm operation and financial situation enabled him to lend money to many newcomers and to buy land from others who, for various reasons, quit farming and left the area. Enger's accumulated capital also qualified him to become a vice president of a local bank and earned him terms as president of a hospital, seminary, and farmers' grain elevator

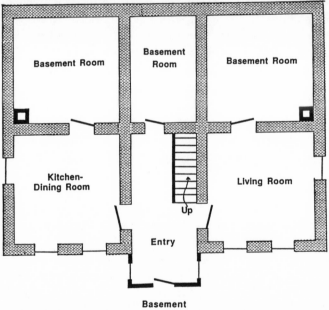

Basement

Basement Room

Basement Room

Basement Room

Kitchen-Dining Room

Living Room

Up

Entry

Figure 8.5. The D. M. Flinn farmhouse, Dallas County, Iowa, 1863. Specifications for the floor plan from James S. Cook, "A Mid-Nineteenth Century Iowa Farmhouse," the Wolf Collection, State Historical Society of Iowa Archives (above and opposite).

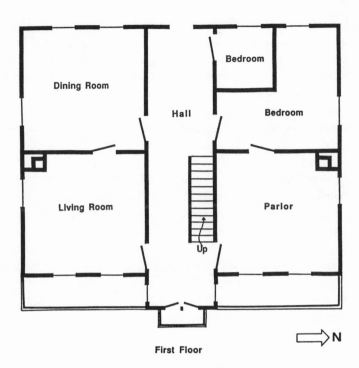

Dining Room

Bedroom

Hall

Bedroom

Living Room

Parlor

Up

N

First Floor

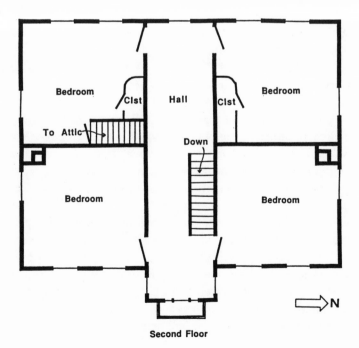

Bedroom

Clst

Hall

Clst

Bedroom

To Attic

Down

Bedroom

Bedroom

N

Second Floor

corporation. He owned one grain elevator and held stock in another, providing him with the advantage of storing and holding grain until he could sell the commodity on the market at the highest price. In recognition of his role in the public life of his community and state, he was elected as a senator to the North Dakota legislature from 1890 to 1899.

It was immediately before he was elected to the state senate that Enger built the sixteen-room farmhouse, perhaps as a seal upon his past accomplishments and as a prophetic sign of an anticipated public station in life. Until this time he, his wife, eight sons, and one daughter had inhabited their original log house. Although a wing had been added to accommodate the large family, it was not a proper place for people such as Enger and his family to live.[13] The new and larger house was not the most elaborate and costly mansion that Enger could have afforded. The farmhouse cost approximately $4,000 in 1889. It was neither overly ornate and complex in its elevation nor immoderately appointed and finished. It did, however, architecturally announce Fingal Enger's success in the fashion of the rural Upper Midwest.[14]

The Enger farmhouse is a large, almost square volume with a rectangular kitchen wing integrated into the structure on its northwest corner (Figure 8.7). A two-story front porch (originally screened in on both levels), an open porch at the kitchen entrance, and a bay window on the south side of the house add some interesting but not elaborate variations to the simple masses of the structure. The foundation of the house is made of dressed and evenly sized blocks of granite 18 inches thick. A full basement includes a furnace for central steam heat, a space for a supply of fuel for the furnace, a cistern under the kitchen for an ample supply of fresh soft water, and a long chamber beneath the entire width of the front of the house for the storage of produce and canned goods. The basement is reached directly from the kitchen and from the outside through a trap door near the back kitchen door. The kitchen complex includes a large pantry with a pass-through serving buffet between the pantry and the dining room, a washroom for the men to clean themselves before meals, and a room where milk was stored and processed. A maid's or servant's room completes the wing. The remainder of the first floor contains traditional front and rear parlors, a dining room, and a bedroom. Sliding doors between the two parlors and between the back parlor and dining room allowed flexibility in the use of these rooms as related spaces. The central front hall is graced by a slightly curving and rather steep staircase. Two halls on the second floor provide spacious access to the two sets of bedrooms on this level. Another asymmetrical space serves as a passage or hall from one side of the house to the

Figure 8.6. "Fingal Enger's Farm, Hatton, N.D." From T. A. Hoverstad, *The Norwegian Farmers in the United States* (Fargo, N.D.: Hans Jervell, 1915).

other, except it leads through a small back bedroom to the other side of the house. This seems to be the only defect in a dwelling that was planned to serve the entire Enger family, servants, and hired men. The Enger home is one of the largest and most fully appointed frame farmhouses in the region.

Enger became an important entrepreneur more specifically identified as a Red River valley bonanza farmer. In order to run his large operation, he had fifteen hired men year-round. That number more than doubled during harvest. He owned fifteen grain cutters and binders to bring in the harvest that, after expenses, realized profits in tens of thousands of dollars. Consistent with the facts of his life or the rhetoric of American success or both, Enger's physical and personal character were described in his biography and obituary as profiles of strength and virtue. It was said that he could work longer hours than most other men and in that time do the work of two. "Enger was blessed with good health and fired with tremendous energy, ambition, and drive, and kept advancing each year. Although not well educated, he was astute in business matters and had a sharp foresight."[15] He was described as a deeply religious man, firm in his own beliefs yet tolerant of others. He was said to have been kind and patient and always helpful to those in need. One reason that Enger was so well known and admired was that he was a resident farmer. His bonanza operation was not run by eastern interests like others in the area. The absentee powers that owned and operated these large agricultural ventures generated mistrust and hostility toward outside interests in the local community. Enger

Figure 8.7. The Fingal Enger farmhouse, Steele County, North Dakota, 1889 (above, opposite, and following page)

doubly excelled because he was a bonanza farmer and someone who was present and active in the community.

The farmhouses of D. M. Flinn and Fingal Enger display the secure position they had achieved as farmers at two different times and places within their respective communities. Flinn was Anglo-American. The form, function, and style of his farmhouse can clearly be traced to Yankee sources in the eastern United States and ultimately to England. The manner in which he subscribed to the Andreas Atlas by underwriting a half-page illustration of his farm seems consistent with a Yankee desire to underline and make permanent one's station in life, implying one was a member of the landed aristocracy. Enger's farmhouse in North Dakota was also modeled after an Old World prototype. Many of the large farmhouses built in this area by Norwegian-American farmers present broad two-story façades with central two-story porches, characteristics of the Norwegian *Herregaard*, or manor. Fingal Enger could have remembered these kinds of Old World mansions from his youth in Norway. His memory was refreshed when he returned to his homeland the year before he built his great house. He seemed eager to follow the precedent of his neighbors and build a house that reflected that prestigious Norwegian model. Here the frame of reference was not a heredi-

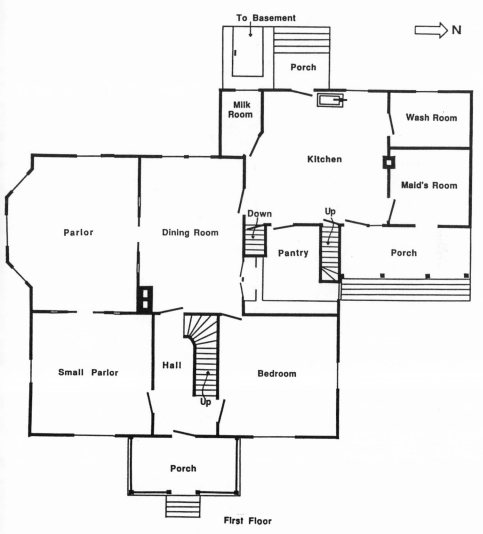

First Floor

tary title but the socioeconomic rank of a privileged class of wealthy and powerful farmers, "the Quality," as they required others to address them in Norway.[16]

Upon initial inspection, the home of Peter Schoemaker in Stearns County, Minnesota (Figure 8.8), should not be included here as a large farmhouse discussed under type 10. However, this farmhouse is a display of substance and success, the biggest and best frame dwelling one will find in its rural community. The structure is obviously a two-story foursquare house, a type 9 farmhouse. It may not compete with either the Flinn or the

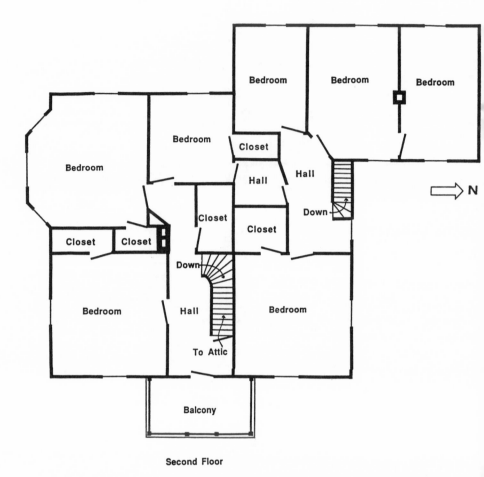

Second Floor

Enger houses for size and style, but it was not built to be compared on a scale that grand. It was planned and realized in the context of a German-American community that expressed achievement in more moderate terms than other ethnic groups in the rural Upper Midwest. Schoemaker's success should be evaluated in the context of his own group. He did not preempt or purchase 160 to 320 acres as Flinn did, and he certainly did not amass the fortune in farmland as Enger did. Schoemaker, in fact, realized his secure position on only 80 acres of land. The farm was not big enough for raising cattle or growing cash crops, but it was certainly adequate for a herd of dairy cows that brought a steady income.

Stearns County began to be settled in the 1850s as an effort of the Roman Catholic Church in Germany and America to relocate poor farmers from the homeland to what seemed to be a promising situation for agricul-

ture in central Minnesota. From the beginning of settlement, these German immigrants established a subsistence lifestyle that depended upon one
or two dairy cows for milk and all its by-products. The slaughtered cattle
provided meat and leather for clothing, straps, thongs, and other practical
articles. In comparing their poverty in Europe with their ownership of a
quarter section of land (or less) and one or two cows, they judged themselves to be wealthy citizens of the New World. By the mid-1880s, dairy
farming in the county had changed from subsistence to a commercial operation. Dairy cooperatives were formed, providing opportunities for farmers
to pool their resources and commercially produce butter and cheeses for expanding markets now linked by rail commerce. Improvements through
breeding dairy cows also increased the quantity and quality of milk.[17]

Dairy farming necessitates an unchanging, unending round of chores because the cows must be milked twice each day during season. The same
rhythm of work is involved in feeding, watering, and bedding the cattle
and in cleaning the dairy barn and cow yard. Because these tasks must be
done every day, one does not think of leaving home for any duration unless elaborate preparations for the care of the herd have been made. The
processing and use of the milk must also follow soon upon its production
so that it does not spoil. Butter and cheese making, whether done on the
farm or in a cooperative, must proceed in an orderly manner. Dairy farming requires a consistent, disciplined frame of mind. There exists a positive
reciprocity in the art of dairy farming in Stearns County because it seems
that the solid character of German-American farm families was well suited
for this kind of work and that the work in turn was satisfying and fulfilling
for these people.

Peter Schoemaker and his family acquired their land in Stearns County
in the early 1880s. By about 1890, they had built the house that stands on
the site today. The dairy barn, no doubt, was built before the large house
was completed. The farm was not only identified in the 1896 Stearns
County plat book as belonging to Peter Schoemaker, it was also called
"Spring Knoll Farm." This designation seems to indicate that Schoemaker
was especially proud of his achievement as a dairy farmer and wanted a special name for his farm. The house was built on a rise that overlooks the
surrounding rolling countryside and also the nearby village of Freeport. On
its site the broad cubical structure and its wide front porch communicate
an established, enduring presence. The only way that Schoemaker could
have architecturally expressed this message better would have been to build
his house of brick. Many German-American farm families in the area did
just that, but this balloon frame structure sufficiently realizes the impres-

Figure 8.8. The Peter Schoemaker farmhouse, Stearns County, Minnesota, ca. 1890 (above and opposite).

sion of permanence. It is 32 feet square, approximately 4 to 6 feet wider and deeper than most two-story foursquare farmhouses in the region. The overall dimensions and the placement of the doors and windows in the house reveal that the builder thoroughly understood balloon frame construction and planned this dwelling so that the regular spacing of studs and joists at 16 inches on center was uninterrupted throughout the entire structure. The foursquare simplicity of the house is not so much an all-American design as it is a German-American grasp of essentials and a thorough practical application of them in a building project. If the farmhouse can be evaluated as a "moderate" show of success, the genius of its design and construction can be characterized as lacking any ostentation. The integration of design and construction is present as a significant contribution to the certain and subtle way the structure communicates its place in the rural community.[18]

Finally, the house of Halvor P. Iverson in Yellow Medicine County, Minnesota (Figure 8.9), is an example of a fashionably complex and up-to-date dwelling of a successful farmer in the Upper Midwest in the early twentieth century. As is evident from its elevation and from the floor plan, this structure is similar to an elaborate mail-order design of the period: Sears, Roe-

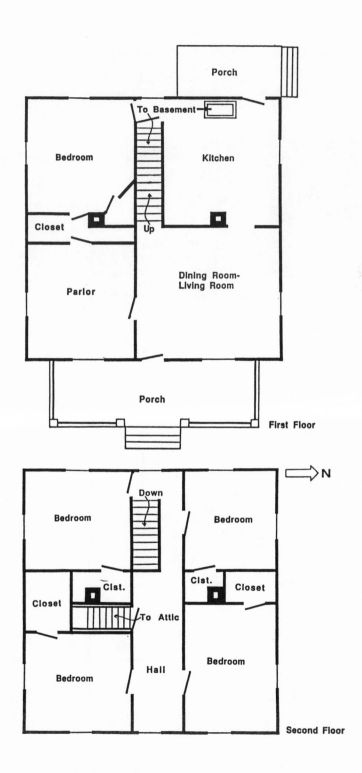

Porch

To Basement

Bedroom

Kitchen

Closet

Up

Parlor

Dining Room-
Living Room

Porch

First Floor

N

Down

Bedroom

Bedroom

Cist.

Closet

Cist.

Closet

To Attic

Bedroom

Hall

Bedroom

Second Floor

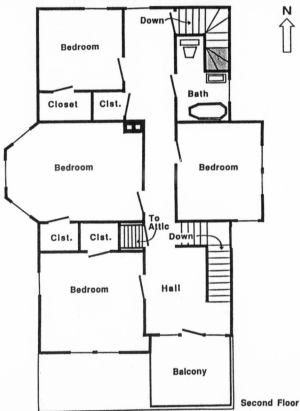

Figure 8.9. The Halvor P. Iverson farmhouse, Yellow Medicine County, Minnesota, 1914 (above and opposite)

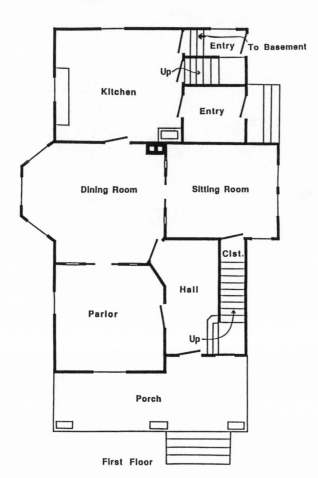

buck, and Company's Design No. 119 (Figure 8.10). Like the elevation for the house in the catalogue, the Iverson farmhouse originally had a first-floor porch railing and the balcony enclosed with a banister on a portion of the front porch roof. The mail-order floor plan was modified to suit the particular needs and preferences of the Iversons. These alterations eliminated the front vestibule and enlarged the reception hall, reversed the arrangement of entry and stairs in the rear kitchen area, eliminated the pantry, and also reversed and reordered the second floor at the rear of the house.

This is a good substantial design, constructed with a view to economy and affording a great deal of room. It has a large front porch with a balcony over part of it. It is built on a concrete block foundation, sided with narrow beveled-edge cypress siding and has a cedar shingle roof.

. . . .

Details and features: Nine rooms and one bath. Full-width front porch with partial balcony above; paired columns; bay window in sitting room; front door with leaded art glass. Corner fireplace in parlor; open stairs.

Years and catalog numbers: 1911 (119); 1912 (119); *1913* (119); 1916 (119); 1917 (C119)

Price: $1,518 to $1,731

Location: Hereford, Tex.

Figure 8.10. "Design No. 119." From Katherine Cole Stevenson and H. Ward Jandl, *Houses by Mail: A Guide to Houses by Sears, Roebuck, and Company* (Washington, D.C.: Preservation Press, 1986), 232.

Iverson and his family included every new convenience and comfort in their farmhouse. The structure was built with central steam heat to warm the rooms and halls. In addition, a complete hot- and cold-water indoor bathroom was included on the second floor. Although small, the bathroom was truly a large expense because it involved considerable technology.[19] In this case, gutters on the sides of the house's complex roof channeled rain water and melting snow to a cistern built at the rear of the house. From this storage unit, the soft water was pressured by a hand pump to pipes that ran through the kitchen range. Here the water was heated before it was piped upstairs to a water reservoir built into the stairwell next to the bathroom. From this elevated position, hot water could flow into the sink or the tub. Cold water was pumped directly from the cistern by a hand pump. A septic tank and field-drainage tank completed the plumbing system.

Halvor's father, Iver Iverson, was one of the first to homestead land in the township, and by the time Halvor inherited the farm at his father's death, the place was about 230 acres. That was 1914, the same year that the house was built. The Iverson farmhouse is not unusually large or elaborate for the area of rich land where farmers' probabilities for success were high. Because of the added features of central heating and indoor plumbing, the cost of the house was said to be about $6,000. That estimate may be too high, but even at $4,000 the house can be ranked with a top-of-the-line structure for the period in any area where it would have been built. Halvor's inheritance of the farm may have seemed to him a proper occasion to make his mark on the homestead by building a large house that would not only announce his and Iver's success in farming but also be the envy of neighbors who did not enjoy the modern technological conveniences that the Iversons did in their truly new home.

In this instance, the story of the attainment of the American dream seems well documented. The transition from the pioneer farm to the prosperous farm was achieved by the Iversons in just two generations of working the land. When the family staked their claim in Minnesota, Halvor was already three years old. He lived in the subsistence shelter first erected on the farm, and he caused the farmhouse to be built that marked the completion of the process of change from a pioneer existence to civilization. The transformation of the prairie wilderness into the Garden was accomplished. When Eden was prophesied in the rhetoric of nineteenth-century politicians, reformers, and boosters, a habitation with evenly heated rooms, hot baths, and a flush toilet was not envisaged to be a part of that glory. These features of Paradise were, however, the technological extras that came to be identified as the realization of the good life. The move from Iron Age conditions to those of the modern technological world that occurred on this and many other farms in the Upper Midwest became the pattern and pace of change that radically reshaped the lives of farmers and their families in the region.

Halvor P. Iverson was nicknamed "H.P.," for "Horsepower." Were his family and friends referring to the steady determined energy of a work horse or were they comparing Halvor's capacity for labor to a machine, a gas engine tractor, perhaps? In this instance the frame of reference was probably to both sources of power. Iverson was born in 1870 and he died in 1964. His ninety-four years of life attest to the appropriateness of his nickname.

The Iverson farmhouse is large in scale and irregular in elevation and exemplifies farmhouses of type 10 quite well. Its elaborations are not, however, those found in costly stylebook designs. These Vernacular Villas still stand today and are easily identified as manorial homes finished in the various fashions of the period. The other examples of farmhouses discussed in this chapter decidedly cause confusion in the nature of farmhouse type 10 because some of these structures could more accurately be classified as other farmhouse types. As noted earlier, however, all of these dwellings become candidates for discussion here in the context of an interpretation of the farmhouse as an architectural communication of success. What has been considered the mark of success varies greatly from one area to another in the region. It seems appropriate and ironically accurate, therefore, to define farmhouse type 10 less precisely than the other farmhouse types in this study. Anything more would suggest that the study of these dwellings is now clearly delineated and complete, which would be untrue. Much remains to be done before the "successful" completion of an inquiry so broad and complex is reached.

9. CONCLUSION: BRICKS, BALLOON FRAMES, AND HI-TECH

Builders adopted balloon frame construction in the rural areas of the Upper Midwest as an economical, adaptable, and easy method of building that met the demands of rapid growth in settlement and population that had resulted in an unprecedented need for domestic and commercial structures. Factors that facilitated using this new method of construction were the ready availability of materials and the technology necessary for its application—milled lumber from the great pineries of Minnesota and Wisconsin, mass production of nails, the means to transport building materials to or near virtually every construction site in the region, and the presence of inexpensive skilled and unskilled labor. Balloon frame construction appears as the logical outcome of this time and place.

Builders often used balloon frame construction to perpetuate the past by erecting modified versions of traditional house types. In other instances they adapted patterns available from the large number of professional architectural stylebooks whose authors offered projects based on traditional models as well as popular Victorian designs. In this interchange between traditional practice and popular taste, carpenters and farmer-builders established a grammar of forms based upon balloon frame construction and developed a limited number of house types.

An analysis of those structures according to categories of shape, scale, and style is an approach that suits an understanding of farmhouse types in the Upper Midwest. The shape that any individual farmhouse assumed resulted from the geometry inherent in balloon frame construction. The shapes of balloon frame farmhouse types are characterized by the simple three-dimensional volumes that the planar wall enclosures and the roof surfaces present as the exterior of the structure. A relatively simple grammar of forms determined the basic shapes of these structures. The square, rectan-

241

Abandoned farmhouse, Ottertail County, Minnesota.

gle, and triangle became the basic geometry upon which the overall shape of structures was based. Obviously, this architectural geometry is not unique to balloon frame structures, but it is a necessary result of this method of construction, that is, the members of milled lumber and the system and method of joining them together logically resulted in this grammar of forms. The planar walls and roof surfaces are most effectively and efficiently joined at angles measuring 90, 45, or 30 degrees. Octagonal and circular volumes can be created in frame construction, but the complexities of methods to realize these shapes go beyond the simple principles and practices of the balloon frame.

Farmhouse types 1 through 6 are based upon the rectangle or the consistent combination of two to three rectangular shapes and covered with a triangular saddle roof on the one or more units that compose the type. Farmhouse types 8 and 9 are based upon the square or almost square shape covered with a triangular roof spanning the symmetrical substructure. The shapes of houses that appeared as consistent applications of balloon frame construction were few in number. The ability to create a great number of variations within each type was, however, quickly realized as farmhouses with different dimensions and proportions were built.

The limited number of fundamental shapes of houses was more than compensated for in the range of scale that balloon frame houses provided. Traditional methods of building and traditional house types imposed more limitations on the scale and floor plan of a dwelling. One could build a moderate-size balloon frame house of adaptable floor plan on a small budget. With ample funds one could stretch one's architectural ambitions to realize a residence of palatial scale, proportions, and complexity. Each builder-occupant could readily vary the floor plan of a balloon frame structure to express preferences in design and function, offering a way of building that paralleled the democratic ideals of the nation.

Balloon frame construction adequately met the need for houses varying in size from two-room shelters to complex, monumental structures with elevations up to two and a half stories. Carpenters became assured that the new building materials and method were structurally sound. The extension of a house on its site could be determined by multiplying the number of studs, joists, and rafters that could be joined in the exterior walls, floors, and ceilings of the structure. Posts and girders or stone or cement walls could be added in the foundation at appropriate intervals needed to support joists where wider spaces were spanned. A module proportion system inherent in balloon frame construction provided the basis for the proper and regular placement of these structural reinforcements in large houses. Theoretically, a balloon frame structure could extend indefinitely into space as long as each section was adequately tied in with the adjacent units and each unit sufficiently supported within itself. Scale was determined by economic, aesthetic, and moral values, but not by restrictions of the building method itself.

The concept of style as a tool to analyze characteristic formal elements of a structure or group of structures allows one to infer the intention of the builder or class of builders. Evidence from stylistic analysis of balloon frame farmhouses indicates the presence and vitality of a vernacular taste. Decided preferences for economy, efficiency, and adaptability in the process of building and in the completed structure were consistently embodied in the nature of balloon frame farmhouses. These practical values were channeled through changing style preferences influenced by the various architectural revival fashions of the period. The values of this vernacular taste in architecture placed a premium on practicality and expedience, with special appreciation for results manifested in a simple and direct form. The goal was to achieve with the least means, time, and energy what looks "right" and works well. The persistence of traditional designs for houses and the persuasive fashions of model houses in architectural stylebooks was the framework in which the shape, scale, and style of balloon frame farmhouses developed as a significant feature of the Upper Midwest. It is the combination of these values that has so influenced the appearance of this rural landscape.

Analyses of balloon frame farmhouses provide the bases for a clearer understanding of what these structures are. The process of understanding can be furthered to include interpretations of what these structures mean. To that end it has been necessary to perceive types of balloon frame farmhouses and individual dwellings in a complex network of relationships. How farm families acted and reacted to national and local events during the settlement and development of the Upper Midwest has been of fundamental importance in interpreting the meaning of the houses they made their homes. Studies of particular aspects of rural homes lead one to focus upon functions of interior spaces and changes in furnishings, utensils, and appliances that established and promoted a characteristic lifestyle in farmhouses. Another point of focus is the relation of the farmhouse and family to the local rural and national societies of which both were a part. The domestic life of the family and the home as well as their relationship with the outside world is the context in which questions of value can be investigated. Social and ethnic, economic and commercial, industrial and technological, religious and moral factors, define and determine issues that compose a broad framework in which the meaning of vernacular building can be more fully understood. Issues of artistic style, aesthetic quality, financial success, moral integrity, personal worth, individual rights, and social responsibility are all within the purview of one interpreting a form of expression and communication as complex as domestic architecture. The multifaceted aspects of change experienced by the individuals and groups that created the farmhouses of the region are significant factors that must be constantly acknowledged. In only three generations, the residence of the farmer changed from a minimal, improvised shelter to one offering modern amenities in a standardized form. This transformation is the pattern of change in which the meaning of farmhouses should be interpreted.

Balloon frame construction is more than a predictable result of circumstances in one region of the country. It is a creative expression of national trends that developed from the 1860s to the early 1900s. After the Civil War, the northern states led the nation toward increased industrialization. The means and methods of mechanical power to process the country's raw materials were being put into operation. The emergence of an ethic that justified the role of the machine in the development of "the Garden" of yet unsettled territories furthered the acceptance of increasing mechanization of production and the nature of the products themselves.[1]

The balloon frame structural system developed as part of a larger trend toward processing raw materials into units that could be assembled into a functioning entity. Values of economy, practicality, and adaptability guided the process and characterized the product. Efficiency and standardization of machine production were other values that were soon closely related to this production process. These values came to be perceived as desirable in products as well as in people—from functional structures to candidates for public office. Many Americans believed that difficult and complex situations were best addressed and solved through the power these values appeared to invest in people, places, and things. The benefits Americans perceived as originating from technology and industry furthered their belief in rational, positive change from a difficult past to an abundant future.

The profound changes that industry and technology effected in every aspect of American life are especially evident in balloon frame farmhouses of the Upper Midwest. In the earliest settled areas of southern and eastern Wisconsin and Iowa and at outposts along water routes, house-building techniques were transplants of traditional forms using traditional materials and methods. Box frame, brick, and stone versions of I-houses, upright and wing houses, and Georgian-plan houses were some of the old domestic forms built in the first decades after the region had opened for settlement in the early 1830s. By the time the first generation of settlement had passed, balloon frame construction had appeared and virtually monopolized the way people thought about and built houses and many other kinds of frame structures.

A comparison of the Daniel Nelson and Lars Hanse farmhouses (Figures 9.1 and 9.2) will indicate the extent and nature of the changes in the ways people thought and labored to realize a house when balloon frame construction supplanted traditional ways of building. Nelson inherited and learned the design of his I-house dwelling from the previous generation and from the kinds of houses he saw as he migrated from the settled areas of Ohio to the frontier in Iowa. The floor plan and elevation of his Iowa farmhouse were determined by tradition, as were its materials and methods of construction. Nelson had preempted land in Mahaska County, Iowa, in 1844, had built a log cabin to shelter his family of seven, and had begun to establish himself as a farmer-entrepreneur consistent with his Scotch-Irish ancestry. In 1849 he purchased and began to operate a steam-powered sawmill, cutting trees for his own use and for neighbors who hauled logs to the mill. In 1852 he purchased a local grain mill recently ruined by floods, rebuilt it with his lumber, and sold it for $1,500. In the fall of that year he began to construct the foundation of his house with limestone blocks quarried from the banks of a nearby river. Materials for quicklime also came from that quarry.

Construction resumed in the spring of 1853 after the foundation had settled. Bricks made from clay dug on the Nelson farm and fired on the site composed the outer walls of the house. Timbers, joists, laths, floor boards,

Figure 9.1. The Daniel Nelson farmhouse, Mahaska County, Iowa, 1852-53 (above and opposite)

roof shingles, and all the woodwork were from Nelson's wood lot and were cut in his sawmill. All cabinets, doors, and trim were fashioned with hand tools. Hand-forged iron nails joined sheathing and shingles to the roof rafters. The plaster that surfaced interior walls and ceilings was mixed from locally obtained lime and sand and strengthened by hair from Nelson's herd of cattle.[2] Traditional symmetry is expressed in the central hall flanked by chambers of equal size on both floors. The substantial nature of the house and its reflection of traditional values are indicators of Nelson's position in the community. The perpetuation of the house type underscored and symbolized the equilibrium of Nelson's life.

Nelson was fortunate to have all the raw materials available on or near his land. Although the design was traditional, utilizing those materials provided the dwelling with some individuality and a little innovation. The external dimensions of the main section of the house measure approximately 17 × 40 feet. However, because of the varying dimensions of the homemade bricks, distances between windows are not regular. Elm, walnut, butternut, basswood, ash, and cherry were used selectively throughout the house. The door to the parlor from the hall was sufficiently wide for a coffin to pass

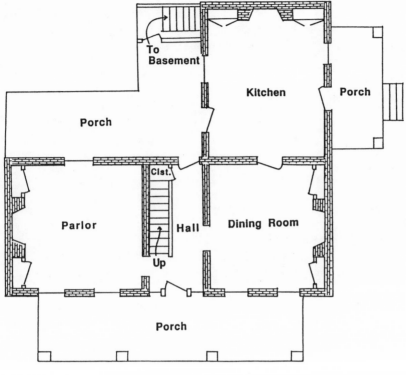

First Floor

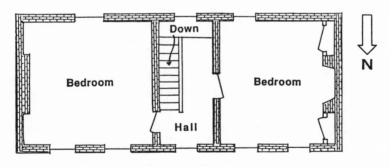

Second Floor

through for wakes and funerals. These features represent some diversity within the traditional form of the house. After the house was completed, however, its design and construction offered hardly any potential for change. The only changes made to the original house were the addition of front, side, and back porches in the early 1890s and the use of wood- and

Figure 9.2. The Lars Hanse farmhouse, Stevens County, Minnesota, 1878–1940 (above and opposite)

coal-burning heating stoves in some chambers of the house. Electricity was never introduced to the dwelling.

The Hanse farmhouse began without a traditional form as a model; it originated as a minimum shelter that had potential for growth. The first balloon frame unit, measuring 16 feet square, was made of lumber hauled from a town 6 miles from the farm. The Great Northern Railroad created this prairie community when the line was built through its site in 1871. Hanse began his house in 1878, after the town's commercial lumberyard had been established. The members of the frame were purchased in standard dimensions and lengths. Nails could be bought by the pound. Clapboard, shingles, windows, and doors were all made in standardized sizes. Rolls of tar paper and bags of plaster were sold at stated widths, lengths, and weights. Hanse could calculate fairly easily and accurately the quantities and costs of materials he needed from the lumberyard.

Hanse had to have a conception of the building method and a practical knowledge of how to proceed. The small, square shelter he built was his primer in balloon frame construction. His only personal touch in structural details was the use of an excessive number of nails at every joint to secure the frame. By 1879 he had added a unit almost identical to the original.

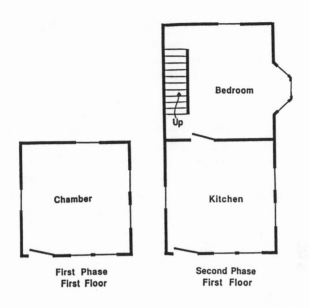

Bedroom

Up

Chamber

Kitchen

First Phase
First Floor

Second Phase
First Floor

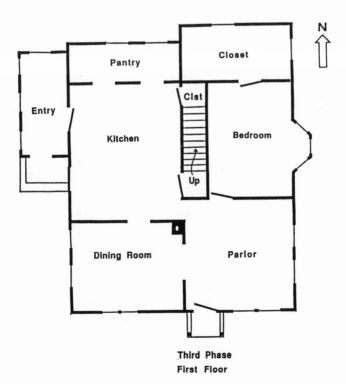

N

Pantry

Closet

Clst

Entry

Kitchen

Bedroom

Up

Dining Room

Parlor

Third Phase
First Floor

That addition doubled the first-story space and provided chambers on the half story, which were accessed by a steep, narrow staircase tucked away on the west side of the house, a placement that conserved space in the back room. A small bay window added extra light, ventilation, and some style to the enlarged dwelling. About ten years later the house again almost doubled in size with the addition of a wing that contained a new kitchen and dining room and an upstairs bedroom. The same centrally located chimney served the house through all of these alterations. The closet at the north end of the second unit was added before the new kitchen and dining room were built. The pantry was constructed some years after the kitchen was completed. The original entrance to the house was on the east side of the first unit and later was moved to its southern wall. The stairway to the upstairs chambers was relocated in the kitchen after the latter room was completed. The enclosed porch at the kitchen entrance was built as late as 1940, when the entire half story of the structure had to be rebuilt after a fire destroyed much of the original superstructure. By that time a neo-colonial look was popular, so the current generation of Hanses designed the roof as a saddle type with two balanced dormers.[3]

The flexibility and adaptability documented in the history of this balloon frame structure makes it difficult to establish its identity. It was and is a result of its history. Although its exterior has assumed a specifically dated appearance, its interior provides clear evidence of the way spaces spun out, up, and around the central chimney as the source of warmth and food preparation.

The Nelson farmhouse served its occupants well and clearly heralded the owner's attainment of a permanent position in rural society. Nelson's house makes a statement about the necessity to preserve forms from the past in order to ensure a secure and lasting situation in the present and future. Hanse built his house primarily to serve the needs of his growing family and farm. Its evolving plan had a central focus, but it did not follow a pattern that necessarily reached a preordained form. Balloon frame construction became the suitable means to make the house in stages. Hanse not only learned how to build in this new way but also assimilated qualities of the method into the way he thought. This new way of thinking is evident in the multitude of changes in housekeeping, farming, travel, communication, commerce, and economy experienced by Hanse and his contemporaries. Unlike the Nelson farmhouse, the Hanse dwelling was able to accommodate various kinds of stoves for cooking and heating, was modified for indoor plumbing, and was wired for electricity.

The flood of "new and improved" products entering the market during the second half of the nineteenth century implied a progression to a better way of life eventually to be experienced by all sectors of the nation. Some changes in household technology did effect such improvements. In two generations of farming in the region, the traditional fireplace was supplanted by the manufactured iron cooking range and the potbelly heating stove. These appliances eventually gave way to shining white porcelain ranges and central furnaces that maintained comfortable temperatures throughout the house. During the third generation of farming in the region, hot and cold running water and indoor bathrooms became affordable through the development of economical mass production techniques that manufactured sinks, tubs, and toilet stools.

As new appliances, fixtures, and machines created more conveniences and comforts, people changed their way of thinking about the quality of life a house could provide. New amenities such as metal screens for doors and windows were easily affordable necessities that improved ventilation and protected the interior of the house from hosts of marauding insects. There were other, more costly labor-saving appliances. Sewing machines and washing machines were two such items that were initially viewed as luxuries. These too eventually were perceived to be essential to the good life.

Services such as free rural mail delivery, telephones, mail-order supply houses, and automobile transportation facilitated the farm family's integration into a national and international network of communication and commerce. These kinds of choices marked the farm family's entrance into a modern industrial, commercial world in which the values fostering specialization, standardization, and efficiency influenced their attitudes, values and behavior. The process of planning and building a farmhouse in balloon frame construction was consistent with these directions in national history.[4]

Nostalgia for this period of national growth and for the era of the family farm can color our perception and understanding of the times. One prefers to see the past as comfortably different from the present—a time and place simpler, more secure, less troubled, less threatening, and less challenging. The cozy, picturesque qualities of Grandma's ell- or T-plan farmhouse or the central stability of a two-story foursquare farmhouse can act for some as architectural symbols of a better time. We have invested in these farmhouses the qualities of home, family, and community. We have, perhaps without knowing it, always admired their classically serene appearance in the countryside.

There is, however, an abundance of evidence from this era and from this house type that our agrarian ancestors set the stage for our modern world by acting on beliefs and a set of values that furthered change and promoted challenging and difficult situations. It is true that the consumption of patent medicines and amputations have changed to doses of antibiotics and organ transplants; that the "three Rs" have been greatly modified to become language skills, electronic calculations, and computer programs; and that one's life vocation can now be a tailor-made lifestyle packaged in appropriate domestic and work environments. Contemporary decisions seem different from those of the past, but the beliefs and values that motivate our choices were handed down from our great-grandparents' day.

Whether we are planning a balloon frame farmhouse for a Minnesota farm in the 1880s or selecting a computer for home or work in the twenty-first century, the qualities we seek in the product are the same. We want the product to fit our budget and be cost effective to own and operate. We look for a house or machine that is easy and convenient to use. We expect some assurance against malfunction and damage and guarantees for repairs. Further, we prefer that there be a personal quality in the ownership and operation of the product—the house as our home, the computer as "user-friendly."

The acquisition of such products is made more secure if there is a rational basis to their structure and function. Some confidence is gained in learning how the parts of the product relate to the whole and how they operate together. We can then rely upon some of our own skills or upon trained technicians to assemble, operate, and maintain the product. We naturally expect easy delivery and a local outlet from which to obtain replacement parts. We look for the quod erat demonstrandum, the proof, the logical clarity of form, that convinces us we have made a good purchase and have acquired the right and good product.

The reactions that many experience toward the plain, regular geometry of balloon frame farmhouses resonates with an admiration for what is perceived and valued as a simple, certain way of life. This simplicity, however, was not a quality that made life easy. Simplicity was the outcome of a harsh and unrelenting effort to realize desired results by employing the least means. Certainty arose from convictions based on truths tested in the difficulties of one's own experience and the successes and failures of others. Here was an ingrained standard for beauty and a practical test for truth. These were the operational guides three and four generations ago when joists, rafters, studs, and nails became the assembly parts of a new way of building. After a period of cautious testing, balloon frame construction was judged to be the best and most expedient way to achieve a better life by planning and realizing structures that would become homes for farm families in the heartland of the nation.

NOTES

INTRODUCTION

1. Studies in vernacular architecture differ from those in architectural history because the former discover, define, and analyze groups of structures that can be understood as building types while the latter focus upon the achievements of an individual architect or the particular qualities of a single architectural monument. See Dell Upton, "The Power of Things: Recent Studies in American Vernacular Architecture," *American Quarterly* 35 (1983): 262–79, and "Ordinary Buildings: A Bibliographic Essay on American Vernacular Architecture," *American Studies International* 19 (Winter 1981): 57–75. Studies in architectural history tend to treat monuments as if they were isolated from their environment, framed as a painting is on a museum wall, so that attention can be given primarily to the monument as a work of art. It is possible to analyze and interpret such isolated monuments without even referring to the structural system by which or the function for which they were built. Research in vernacular architecture deals with building-types as groups of structures, such as multistory apartment buildings in cities, I-houses on the eastern seaboard, fast-food stands practically everywhere, or farmhouses. The definition of a building-type almost always directly relates to the function and location of the building. In order to thoroughly understand a building's function, it is necessary to note where examples of the building-type are located and how they relate to and operate in their environment. Multistory buildings and fast-food stands are not found on secondary rural roads; that is the habitat of the farmhouse.

2. Seymour Martin Lipset and Richard Hofstadter, *Sociology and History: Methods* (New York: Basic Books, 1968), and David S. Landes and Charles Tilly, eds., *History as Social Science* (Englewood Cliffs, N.J.: Prentice Hall, 1971).

3. Meyer Shapiro, "Style," in A. L. Kroeber, ed., *Anthropology Today* (Chicago: University of Chicago Press, 1953), 287–312.

CHAPTER ONE. THE BALLOON FRAME STRUCTURAL SYSTEM

1. "Nails," *Carpentry and Building* 1 (January 1879): 20.

2. This error in the assembly of a balloon frame house was especially dangerous when wood- and coal-burning cooking ranges and heating stoves were a constant fire hazard. Even when central heating furnaces were installed in basements, the danger of fire continued. See "How Fire Sweeps a Wooden House," *Lumberman's Gazette* 21 (13 December 1882): 4–5.

3. The balloons to which the new structural system were compared were at the time also relatively new instruments of the art, science, and sport of aerostation, i.e., lighter-than-air travel in large inflated balloons. In the 1780s the French were the first to venture into the skies with these craft. Ballooning was still considered new and dangerous in the 1830s in America; people apparently thought that the thin membrane of a balloon encased in a network of ropes or cables was like the frame and sheathing of the new wooden framing system. During this period, numerous posters illustrated real and fictional balloons, some announcing and celebrating various ascents. These images provided inspiration for the phrase for a house built according to "the balloon plan." See Charles Dollfus, The Orion Book of Balloons (New York: Orion Press, 1961), and Svante Stubelius, Balloon, Flying Machine, Helicopter: Further Study in the History of Terms for Aircraft in English (Goteborg, Sweden: Carl Bloms Boktryckeri A.-B., 1960), 104-25.

4. Irving Adler and Ruth Adler, Learning about Steel through the Story of a Nail (New York: John Day, 1961), 12.

5. Alex W. Bealer, The Tools That Built America (New York: Bonanza Books, 1975), 59-63.

6. See "An Interesting Nail Test," Carpentry and Building 10 (March 1888): 49.

7. For a discussion of the origin of the balloon frame structural system, see Walker Field, "A Reexamination into the Invention of the Balloon Frame," Journal of the Society of Architectural Historians (October 1942): 3-29. See also John C. Hudson, "The Middle West as Cultural Hybrid," Transactions 6 (1984): 35-45.

8. John T. Schlebecker, Whereby We Thrive: A History of American Farming, 1607-1972 (Ames: Iowa State University Press, 1975), 30.

9. For a discussion of the experience of American farmers in relation to changes caused by the industrialization and commercialization of society, see Earl W. Hayter, The Troubled Farmer, 1850-1900: Rural Adjustment to Industrialism (De Kalb: Northern Illinois University Press, 1968).

10. Solon Robinson, "A Cheap Farm-House," American Agriculturist 5 (February 1846): 57.

11. See Paul E. Sprague, "Chicago Balloon Frame," in H. Ward Jandl, ed., Technology of Historic American Buildings (Washington, D.C.: Foundation for Preservation Technology and the Association for Preservation Technology, 1983), 35-53.

12. "Plans of Farm Houses," Cultivator 6 (November 1839): 164.

13. Josiah T. Marshall, The Farmer's and Emigrant's Handbook (Hartford, Conn.: O. D. Case, 1851), 61-66.

14. George E. Woodward, "Balloon Frames—III," Cultivator 8 (June 1860): 147.

15. George E. Woodward, "Balloon Frames—IVth Article," Cultivator 8 (August 1860): 249.

16. George E. Woodward, "Balloon Frames—5th Article," Cultivator 8 (September 1860): 276.

17. George E. Woodward, "Balloon Frames—7th Article," Cultivator 8 (December 1860): 366.

18. Compare Woodward, "Balloon Frames—III," 147, with Woodward's Architecture and Rural Art, No., 2—1868 (New York: George E. Woodward, 1868), 54-56. In the 1860 version, the sizes of the members of the balloon frame are: sills—3 × 8; corner studs—4 × 4; other studs—2 × 4; plates—1 × 4; side strips or side girts—1 × 4; rafters—3 × 6 or 2½ × 5; collars—1 × 4; floor joists—3 × 8, or may be 2 × 7; rafters, studding, and joists—16 inches on center. In the 1868 version, the sizes of the members of the balloon frame are: sills—3 × 8; corner posts—4 × 6; studs—2 × 4; door and window studs—3 × 4; side girts—1 × 6 gained in; plates—3 × 4; floor beams—3 × 8, well bridged; rafters—3 × 6; studs, floor beams, and rafters—all 16 inches on center.

Another instance of Woodward's ambiguous position on balloon frame construction is found in his *Country Homes* (1865). Here he states that although timber is abundant, it is the least desirable building material. He encourages the use of stone or brick for lasting homesteads and criticizes "thin lath and plaster constructions which rattle in every wind and leak in every rain, [and] do not afford very good centers for these [home] associations." Between Design 31 for a headstone and Design 32 for remodeling an old farmhouse, Woodward inserts a fifteen-page description of and argument for balloon frames. The section contains the essentials of the *Cultivator* articles of 1860-61. After his advice against building wooden structures, Woodward's position on balloon frame construction appears to be founded upon popularity, practicality, and economy, and not necessarily durability. See George E. Woodward, *Woodward's Country Homes* (New York: George E. Woodward, 1865), 16-18 and 151-66.

19. James H. Monckton, *The National Carpenter and Joiner* (New York: George E. Woodward, 1872), plate 80.

20. Bell's system of framing seems to be based upon the practices of George Snow. See Sprague, "Chicago Balloon Frame," 41.

21. Suel Foster, "Balloon Frames," *Cultivator* 8 (July 1860): 224.

22. H. Hudson Holly, *Modern Dwellings in Town and Country* (New York: Harper and Brothers, 1878), 56.

23. E. C. Gardner, *Homes and How To Make Them* (Boston: James R. Osgood, 1874), 126-27.

24. E. C. Gardner, *Farm Architecture: Houses and Barns* (Holyoke, Mass.: Clark W. Bryan, 1882), 24.

25. E. C. Hussey, *Home Building* (New York: Leader and Van Hoesen, 1876), plate I.

26. Ibid., 208.

27. See A. J. Bicknell, *Bicknell's Village Builder* (Troy, N.Y.: A. J. Bicknell, 1870), *Cottage and Constructive Architecture* (New York: A. J. Bicknell, 1873), and *Bicknell's Cottage and Villa Architecture* (New York: A. J. Bicknell, 1878).

28. See S. B. Reed, *House Plans for Everybody* (New York: Orange Judd, 1884), 55-61.

29. Yearly temperature ranges in the Upper Midwest normally vary from winter nights at 40 degrees below zero Farenheit to harvest afternoons rising close to 110 to 115 degrees above zero Farenheit. Strong winds can intensify the low temperatures and humidity can increase the oppressive heat of the summer sun. The extremes of climate in the region made it necessary to devise additional ways to make life in a balloon frame house somewhat comfortable. Storm windows were used to provide double-glazed protection against winter cold and prevent thick slabs of ice from forming on the inside of windows. Window screens and screen doors allowed for adequate ventilation in the heat of the summer and some freedom from the hordes of invading insects that could make life miserable during spring, summer, and fall. As difficult as it may be for present-day sensibilities to accept, the comfort offered by a shelter or a house was not always considered important. It would be inaccurate to claim that people adapted. One simply did not question domestic environments that did not provide constant and consistent comfort. The thin envelope of a balloon frame farmhouse was sometimes inadequate protection against the climate, but its occupants did not necessarily expect much more than shelter.

30. The majority of balloon frame farmhouses were not insulated by any of these techniques. The use of wood ashes for insulation was found in a German-Russian balloon frame farmhouse in North Dakota. The structure was only one story with a loft. It is possible that the spaces between the studs were gradually filled over many winters of burning wood for heat and disposing of the cooled ashes in the walls of the house. The stovewood technique is documented in William H. Tishler, "Stovewood Architecture," *Landscape* 23 (1979): 28-31. See also "Building Farm Houses," *Carpentry and Building* 8 (May 1886): 94.

CHAPTER TWO. A TYPOLOGY FOR BALLOON FRAME
FARMHOUSES IN THE UPPER MIDWEST

1. For a brief history of the origin of architectural typologies in nineteenth-century France and England, see Anthony Vidler, "The Idea of Type: The Transformation of the Ideal, 1750–1830," *Oppositions* 8 (1977): 95–115.

2. The nature and function of interior spaces as abstracted in a floor plan cannot be considered as the primary criteria for classification. Evidence from the history of changes in many farmhouses indicates that farm families did not think and plan in terms of specialized functions for specific domestic spaces. Families often changed functions for spaces in a farmhouse when a new wing or second story was added to the initial structure. Even when there were no fundamental changes in the floor plan of a farmhouse, the functions of rooms changed. In these instances, floor plans of farmhouses become relevant in the context of a discussion of the history of the house or the various ways the chambers of a house functioned at different times.

3. In his history of building types, Nikolaus Pevsner identifies seventeen kinds of structures, noting that his primary intention is to follow changes in function and planning in each building type. Pevsner also traces the order in which styles follow one another in the history of each type but recognizes that style is not a determinant of function and planning, especially in the nineteenth century when style was used to evoke associations proper to each building type, e.g., the Gothic style for churches or the classical style for schools and universities. See Nikolaus Pevsner, *A History of Building Types* (London: Thames and Hudson, 1976).

4. Edward Hogan and Joseph F. Roybal, *South Dakota House Types: Our Architectural Heritage* (Sioux Falls: South Dakota State University News Bureau, 1978).

5. Jean Sizemore, *The Iowa Farmhouse (1857–1950): A Literature Survey* (Iowa City: Historical Preservation Division, State Historical Society, 1979).

6. *Vernacular Form in Wisconsin: A Guide to Identification* (Madison, Wis.: Historic Preservation Division, State Historical Society, 1984). At a two-day meeting in Minneapolis in July 1984, a group working in state historical societies and historic preservation offices from Nebraska, Kansas, Wisconsin, Iowa, Ohio, Minnesota, Illinois, South Dakota, and Missouri discussed ways in which house types might be given standardized labels so that an identification system could be computerized for common use in all states involved in locating, identifying, and preserving structures. Because of the wide variety of house types represented in the states listed above, the differences in approach to classification, and the limited time available for discussion, no consensus was reached on how to accurately assign appropriate labels to the house types. The meeting was productive in identifying questions that seemed necessary to answer before further work in typing houses could occur. The importance in distinguishing between traditional ethnic forms in building and construction realized in the recently invented system of the balloon frame seemed to be one significant issue that would help simplify the problem of classification by reducing the number of house types that remained after ethnic house types were clearly identified. The final results of these discussions have been presented in draft form to the National Register of Historic Places from the Midwest Vernacular Architecture Committee. The "morphological approach" taken to classification of house types in the document is not greatly different from the one presented in this study.

7. Herbert Gottfried and Jan Jennings, *American Vernacular Design, 1870–1940: An Illustrated Glossary* (New York: Van Nostrand Reinhold, 1985), xvi.

8. Virginia McAlester and Lee McAlester, *A Field Guide to American Houses* (New York: Alfred A. Knopf, 1984), 4–61.

9. John A. Jakle, Robert W. Bastien, and Douglas K. Meyer, *Common Houses in America's Small Towns: The Atlantic Seaboard to the Mississippi Valley* (Athens: University of Georgia Press, 1989), 207-24.

10. Katherine Cole Stevenson and H. Ward Jandl, *Houses by Mail: A Guide to Houses by Sears, Roebuck, and Company* (Washington, D.C.: Preservation Press, 1986), 38-43.

11. See Henry Glassie, *Folk Housing in Middle Virginia: A Structural Analysis of Historic Artifacts* (Knoxville: University of Tennessee Press, 1975).

12. For two other early approaches to identifying house types, see Edna Scofield, "The Evolution and Development of Tennessee House Types," *Journal of the Tennessee Academy of Science* 11 (October 1936): 229-40, and Fred B. Kniffen, "Louisiana House Types," *Annals of the Association of American Geographers* 36 (December 1936): 179-93.

13. Reference to the nature of ideal types as formulated by the sociologist Max Weber might be helpful here. Weber recognized that the study of any historical phenomenon is preceded by a value judgment on the part of the inquirer that attributes significance to aspects of the empirical reality under study. The results of this historical investigation are ideal types. These are statements of empirical reality that describe the common features of all empirical phenomena to which they refer. These are only approximately correct because characteristic and significant elements that exist in gradations in empirical reality are common and constant in ideal types. An ideal type is an exaggerated abstraction that more or less incorporates the features of all concrete phenomena under consideration. The construction of an ideal type depends upon the point of view from which the historian studies historical evidence. Different points of view require different ideal types. The type 3 farmhouse might be understood as an ideal type in this study insofar as it is an abstraction from the diversity of actual farmhouses that more or less embody elements of the ideal type, i.e., gabled rectangular units joined at right angles with one another, each one or one-and-a-half stories in height, and enclosing interior spaces of kitchen, pantry, living room (parlor and dining room), halls, and bedrooms. From another point of view, a different set of elements could be abstracted from the same number of actual farmhouses that would identify the ideal type as a Victorian Cottage or as a Prairie-Style House. The former approach emphasizes historical cultural aspects of the design and decoration of the house; the latter focuses upon regional, geographic elements that characterize the structure. Whether a type 3 farmhouse, Victorian Cottage, or Prairie-Style House, each ideal type becomes significant in the context of the point of view of the historian who postulated it. Discussion and debate about house types, therefore, is likely to continue and contribute to the creative ferment in studies of material culture and vernacular architecture.

14. Thomas C. Hubka, "In the Vernacular: Classifying American Folk and Vernacular Architecture," *Forum: Bulletin of the Committee on Preservation of the Society of Architectural Historians* 8 (December 1985).

15. See Fred A. Shannon, *The Farmer's Last Frontier: Agriculture, 1860-1897*, vol. 5 of *The Economic History of the United States* (New York: Holt, Rinehart, and Winston, 1963).

16. For examples of the windshield survey technique, see Fred B. Kniffen, "Folk Housing: Key to Diffusion," *Annals of the Association of American Geographers* 55 (Fall 1965): 549-77, and Robert Finley and E. M. Scott, "Great Lakes to Gulf: Profile of Dispersed Building Types," *Geographical Review* 30 (July 1940): 412-19.

17. Thomas C. Hubka identifies windshield survey results as "the Myth of Adequate Data" when used without numerous, detailed studies of individual structures. See Hubka, "In the Vernacular." Hubka's cautionary note seems to be substantiated by a report on a windshield survey of houses along highways from Madison, Wisconsin, to Beaumont, Texas, that concludes with the statement: "As the detailed and extensive research required makes adequate interpretation impossible at the present time, all at-

tempts at explanation are purposely omitted" (Finley and Scott, "Great Lakes to Gulf," 412–19).

18. Visual documentation for this study from all sources totals approximately two thousand four hundred photographs. These images record not only farmhouses but also numerous aspects of life and labor on farms in the Upper Midwest.

19. This discussion of artistic style is based upon Meyer Shapiro, "Style," in A. L. Kroeber, ed., Anthropology Today (Chicago: University of Chicago Press, 1953), 287–312.

20. The concept of artistic style will also be used as a tool of aesthetic evaluation later in this study when I compare the aesthetics of professional Victorian American architects with the practical aesthetics of vernacular builders. See Chapter Five, pages 96–135, of this volume.

CHAPTER THREE. SETTLEMENT AND SHELTER

1. John T. Schlebecker, Whereby We Thrive: A History of American Farming, 1607–1972 (Ames: Iowa State University Press, 1975), 82.

2. J. F. Hamburg, The Influence of the Railroad on the Processes and Patterns of Settlement in South Dakota (Chapel Hill: University of North Carolina Press, 1969).

3. Paul W. Gates, Landlords and Tenants on the Prairie Frontier (Ithaca, N.Y.: Cornell University Press, 1973), 310.

4. Herbert Anthony Kellar, ed., Solon Robinson, Pioneer and Agriculturist, 2 vols. (New York: Da Capo Press, 1968), 1:346.

5. Horace Greeley, An Overland Journey (New York: C. M. Saxton, Barker, 1860), 67–68.

6. R. Carlyle Buley, The Old Northwest Pioneer Period, 1815–1840, vol. 1 (Bloomington: Indiana University Press, 1978), 167.

7. Gustav O. Sandro, The Immigrant's Trek: A Detailed History of the Lake Hendricks Colony in Brookings County, Dakota Territory, from 1873–1881 (Hendricks, S.D.: Gustav O. Sandro, 1929), 19.

8. John C. Hudson, "Frontier Housing in North Dakota," North Dakota History 42 (Fall 1975): 4–15.

9. For a full discussion of the origin and dispersion of the log cabin, see Harold R. Shurtleff, The Log Cabin Myth, ed. Samuel Eliot Taylor (Gloucester, Mass.: Peter Smith, 1967), and Fred B. Kniffen and Henry Glassie, "Building in Wood in the Eastern United States," Geographical Review 56 (1966): 40–66.

10. Olaf Erickson, "Olaf Erickson—Scandinavian Frontiersman," Wisconsin Magazine of History 31 (1947): 11–12.

11. For more complete accounts of sod house construction, see R. G. Newton, "The Far-West Pioneer's Home," American Agriculturist 83 (1884): 158; Donald Gates, "The Sod House," Journal of Geography 32 (1933): 353–59; and Roger L. Welsch, "Sod Construction on the Plains," Pioneer America 1-2 (1969): 13–17.

12. The author has not lived in a sod house or log cabin but has shared a small balloon frame farmhouse with numerous uninvited creatures such as mice, squirrels, bees, hornets, wasps, mink, and sparrows. The insects built hives in the roof and walls, squirrels inhabited the porch roof, mice favored the kitchen, mink set up housekeeping under the porch, and sparrows dropped in by way of the chimney into the heating stove. Meanwhile the elements aged the house so that continual repairs were needed to keep it habitable. All this is noted here to remind the reader of the incessant, inhospitable forces and elements of nature that make life in any isolated rural area a day-to-day, season-to-season struggle to persist.

13. Lorna B. Herseth, ed., "A Pioneer's Letter," *South Dakota History* 6 (Summer 1976): 309.

14. Mr. and Mrs. John Schade, Bowman County, interviewed by Larry J. Spunk, North Dakota Oral History Project, July 1974–June 1975, State Historical Society, Bismarck. The Schade family lived in their sod house in North Dakota from 1908 to 1916, long after one customarily thinks of the frontier as existing.

15. E. C. Hussey, *Home Building* (New York: Leader and Van Hoesen, 1876), 378.

16. "The Sod House," *American Agriculturist* 33 (1874): 179–80.

17. Elsie E. Otto, Barnes County, interviewed by Larry J. Spunk, North Dakota Oral History Project, July 1974–June 1975, State Historical Society, Bismarck.

18. Hudson, "Frontier Housing in North Dakota," 7.

19. Ibid.

20. Richard K. Hofstrand, *With Affection, Marten: A Swedish Immigrant's Letters about His Struggles and Triumphs Homesteading on the Frontier* (Charleston, Ill.: Bench Mark, 1983), 49.

CHAPTER FOUR. FARMHOUSE TYPES 1 AND 2:
WHAT MAKES A HOUSE A HOME?

1. A clearer distinction between one- and two-story houses can be made when the structure is a traditional house type because builders learned the plan of the structure through experience and constructed it according to traditional scale and proportions. If an I-house were to be built of a wooden frame, the housewright determined the size of the frame according to what he had learned were proper dimensions. Scale, proportion, and dimensions were conceived of in whole numbers because traditional house types were either one or two stories tall.

2. Many of the examples of small one- to one-and-a-half-story gabled rectangular farmhouses cited in this study are in western Minnesota and South Dakota and North Dakota. These areas were the last to be settled and still contain some rudimentary balloon frame dwellings that are in good condition. Most of them have been abandoned because they were too small to add on to and because they could not readily incorporate the amenities expected in later, more comfortable dwellings.

3. Attributing a date of construction to farmhouses for which no specific information is available has been done by following four guidelines: (1) noting the year of settlement and establishment of the county and township in which the structure is located, (2) identifying the farmhouse type as one built earlier or later in the history of the region, (3) ascertaining the style of any architectural embellishments or ornament on the structure, and (4) identifying general and specific processes of construction—i.e., how the members were joined, the dimensions of frame members, the type of nails used, and the design of doors and windows.

4. Floor plans and elevations in nineteenth-century pattern books frequently relay inadequate or inaccurate information. Interior walls are sometimes omitted or the dimensions of the interior space of a room does not coincide with the external dimensions of the house. The illustrations for these publications were delegated to engravers who apparently did not always understand what they were doing and could either allow original errors to slip by them or introduce mistakes of their own.

5. E. F. Brewer, "A Progressing Dakota Farm House," *American Agriculturist* 43 (1884): 54.

6. Thomas Taylor, *Tom's Experience in Dakota* (Minneapolis: C. D. Whitall, 1883), 28–49.

7. Mary Mix Foley, *The American Home* (New York: Harper and Row, 1980), 28–29.

8. Many two-story gabled rectangular houses were built in towns and cities as either single-family dwellings or buildings containing two large apartments. Because of the restrictions of narrow building lots, these "urban" versions of the two-story gabled rectangular house usually oriented the principal façade on a gable end facing the street. Rural versions of this house are frequently oriented with the long side of the structure toward the lane or county road and the major entrance accented by a full-length porch.

9. The restoration of the interiors of farmhouses and the replication of work and leisure in these homes is informed by numerous sources. Some photographs have been preserved that show farmhouse interiors. Detailed descriptions of farmhouse rooms by writers of memoirs and diaries are also primary sources of information. Letters from and articles by farm wives that appeared in agricultural journals reveal current interests in interior decoration and practical considerations for rooms. Advertisements and catalogues from that period supply a large amount of information about the kinds of chairs, dishes, curtains, wallpaper, etc., available, the price range of the articles, and changes in design and decoration. Architectural stylebooks also listed and sometimes illustrated furniture essential to a proper household. Downing's The Architecture of Country Houses includes a section relating general principles for and illustrations of furnishings. Furniture in Grecian, modern, or Gothic styles was much in demand. More practical than Downing, Lewis Allen advised his readers to use strong, plain, durable furniture rather than that which reflected the current fashion rage. See Andrew Jackson Downing, The Architecture of Country Houses (New York: D. Appleton, 1850), 406–60; and Lewis Allen, Rural Architecture (New York: C. M. Saxton, 1852), 235–45. Other sources for farmhouse furnishings are state and county historical museums in which chambers have been reconstructed and furnished with period pieces; studies of nineteenth-century furniture, such as Ralph Kovel and Terry Kovel, American Country Furniture, 1780–1875 (New York: Crown, 1975), and George Talbot, At Home: Domestic Life in the Post-Centennial Era, 1876–1920 (Madison, Wis.: State Historical Society, 1976); and books on period antiques, such as Robert Swedberg and Harriet Swedberg, Victorian Furniture: Styles and Prices (Des Moines: Wallace-Homestead, 1981) and Country Pine Furniture: Styles and Prices (Des Moines: Wallace-Homestead, 1983). Visits to secondhand shops and antique stores in the region are also informative.

10. Sally McMurry, "Progressive Farm Families and Their Houses, 1830–1855: A Study in Independent Design," Agricultural History 58 (July 1984): 330–46.

11. Kathryn Kish Sklar, Catherine Beecher: A Study in American Domesticity (New York: W. W. Norton, 1973), 151–55.

12. For Catherine Beecher's specifications for a "wise" house plan, see Beecher and Harriet Beecher Stowe, The American Woman's Home (New York: J. B. Ford, 1869), 23–42. Another treatise on home economy that may have influenced farmhouse plans is E. H. Leland, Farm Homes Indoors and Outdoors (New York: Orange Judd, 1882). Leland does not sketch plans for a farmhouse as Beecher does, but he does provide numerous suggestions for do-it-yourself projects to make the house a pleasant, healthy, and efficient place to live and work.

13. Beecher and Stowe, American Woman's Home, 23.

14. Christine Frederick, The New Housekeeping: Efficiency Studies in Home Management (New York: Curtis, 1912), 5–6.

15. David P. Handlin, "Efficiency and the American Home," Architectural Association Quarterly 5 (October/November 1973): 50–55.

16. E. D. L. Seymour, Farm Knowledge, vol. 3 (Garden City, N.Y.: Doubleday, Page, 1918): 326–60. Another relevant farm-oriented publication is William Alonzo Etherton, The Farm House Improved, Kansas State Agricultural College Bulletin, vol. 1 (May 1, 1917), no. 8, Manhattan. Etherton urged the farm family to plan their own house, and

he advised them that home improvements were necessary to realize the most worthwhile things in life.

17. Barbara Levorsen, *The Quiet Conquest. A History of the Lives and Times of the First Settlers of Central North Dakota* (Hawley, Minn.: Hawley Herald, 1974), 21-22.

18. E. C. Hussey, *Home Building* (New York: Leader and Van Hoesen, 1876), 221-22, for "List of House Furnishing Goods for the Various Departments of the Modern Home." Hussey itemizes over two hundred utensils for the kitchen alone without including major pieces of furniture such as the kitchen range or dining table and chairs. Farm wives had a reputation for buying labor-saving devices whether they seemed reliable or not. The kinds and models of household items steadily increased to supply a profitable rural market. See Earl W. Hayter, *The Troubled Farmer, 1859-1900: Rural Adjustment to Industrialism* (De Kalb: Northern Illinois University Press, 1968), 145-63. See also Earl Lifshey, *The Housewares Story: A History of the American Housewares Industry* (Chicago: National Housewares Manufacturers Association, 1973).

19. Marjorie Kriedberg, *Food on the Frontier: Minnesota Cooking from 1850 to 1900* (St. Paul: Minnesota State Historical Society Press, 1975), passim.

20. Merrill E. Jones, "Life on a Jones County Farm, 1873-1912," *Iowa Journal of History* 49 (October 1951): 318. For another account of work in and around the farmhouse, see Norton Juster, *So Sweet to Labor. Rural Women in America, 1865-1895* (New York: Viking Press, 1979).

21. Kerosene lamps were used on most farms until the 1930s and 1940s when rural electrification programs were completed. Some farmers built wind generator electricity plants backed up with storage batteries.

22. The history of some farmhouses in the region documents the enormous change that took place in the manufacturing of material, the making of clothing, and the availability of other material goods for the house. In some farmhouses a special room was designated for a loom. After wool had been sheared and processed and spun, it was woven on a loom into material for clothing. The loom was also used to weave scraps of old material into carpets. In one abandoned farmhouse in Ottertail County, Minnesota, a dismantled loom was found in a shed, an old sewing machine was still in the dining room, and a carpet woven on the loom was rotting on the dining room floor while a machine-made Victorian carpet was decaying on the parlor floor.

23. Beecher and Stowe, *American Woman's Home*, 59-65, and William W. Hill, "Farmers' Houses," *United States Department of Agriculture Report* (Washington, D.C.: Department of Agriculture, 1863): 313-19.

24. Richard K. Hofstrand, *With Affection, Marten: A Swedish Immigrant's Letters about His Struggles and Triumphs Homesteading on the Frontier* (Charleston, Ill.: Bench Mark, 1983), 116-17.

25. Ben Logan, *The Land Remembers: The Story of a Farm and Its People* (New York: Viking Press, 1975), 95.

26. For other detailed accounts of life on farms in the Upper Midwest, see Ruben L. Parson, *Ever the Land: A Homestead Chronicle* (Staples, Minn.: Adventure, 1978), and Erna Oleson Xan, *Wisconsin My Home* (Madison: University of Wisconsin Press, 1950).

CHAPTER FIVE. FARMHOUSE TYPES 3 AND 4:
A VERNACULAR AESTHETICS

1. Dell Upton, "Pattern Books and Professionalism: Aspects of the Transformation of Domestic Architecture in America, 1800-1860," *Winterthur Portfolio* 19 (Summer/Autumn 1984): 107-50. Upton identifies the house types noted here as the "bent house." Another identification for these house types is "cross-wing" (see Thomas Carter and Pe-

ter Gass, *Utah's Historic Architecture, 1847–1940: A Guide* [Salt Lake City: University of Utah Press, 1988]).

2. Balloon frame farmhouses were made of dimension materials. The clapboard siding when overlapped and nailed in place usually left a face of 4¼ inches of the 6-inch board. Windows were almost always 32 inches wide and exterior doors were 3 feet wide. The firebricks were 4 × 8 × 2¼ inches. Counting and multiplying and dividing these standard-size members from a structure in a photograph enables one to determine the dimensions of the dwelling. With knowledge of other farmhouses of a particular type, it is possible to determine divisions and functions of interior spaces with considerable accuracy. In this hypothetical plan, the staircase was positioned so that it ascends to the half story, the one place that allowed head room at the top of the stairs, i.e., at the intersection of the two roof lines where the ceiling space was the highest. I made hypothetical plans of other ell- or T-plan farmhouses from one or two photographs. Two of these farmhouses were in existence and could be measured on site for a floor plan. One hypothetical floor plan was in error by less than 1 foot. The other measurements corresponded to those deduced from the photographs.

3. As will be discussed later, the origins of farmhouse types 3 and 4 are varied and complex. These types were usually the first to appear on the frontier in the Upper Midwest as completed dwellings that acted as models for houses built by newcomers.

4. For a discussion of an "add-on" T-plan farmhouse in north-central Iowa, see Susan Thompson Good, "Interior Life: An Iowa Farmhouse in the Later 1800's," *Palimpsest* 60 (March/April 1979): 34–47.

5. Kniffen identifies this process as the concept of "initial occupance." See Fred B. Kniffen, "Folk Housing: Key to Diffusion," *Annals of the Association of American Geographers* 55 (Fall 1965): 551. The practice of extending a structure with wings or added units has been characterized as a particularly British and Anglo-American way of building. Colonial ell-plan houses and New England connected farmhouses and barns have been cited as two kinds of domestic structures in America that manifest such a pattern of construction. See Mary Mix Foley, *The American House* (New York: Harper and Row, 1980), 20, and Thomas C. Hubka, *Big House, Little House, Back House, Barn: The Connected Farm Buildings of New England* (Hanover, N.H.: University Press of New England, 1984).

6. Andrew Jackson Downing, *The Architecture of Country Houses* (New York: D. Appleton, 1850), 140.

7. Ibid., 78–83.

8. Ibid., 140.

9. Ibid. A contemporary reaction to Downing's work is significant because it reveals a rural perception of the planner's ideas and ideals. The editor of the *Cultivator* reviewed *The Architecture of Country Houses* in 1850. The editor claimed that "a cottage may be adopted for a small farmhouse, and a villa for that of a decidedly wealthy farmer," despite Downing's efforts to establish the cottage as a suburban dwelling. Although not specifically identified, some of the designs in *Country Houses* were characterized as "awkward or grotesque." Whatever the debate about the quality of some designs, the reviewer singled out the ell- or T-plan cottage as a suitable house for the farm. This house type appeared with some variations in virtually every architectural stylebook for the rest of the century. See "Rural Architecture: Downing's Country Houses," *Cultivator* (New Series) 7 (1850): 305–7.

10. "Small, Convenient, Cheap Houses," *American Agriculturist* 25 (1886): 53, and 26 (1886): 14, and "A Convenient Farm-House," *American Agriculturist* 33 (1874): 217–18.

11. "Country House, Costing $600–$800," *American Agriculturist* 41 (1882): 238–39; "Prairie Cottage, Costing $800–$1,000," *American Agriculturist* 41 (1882): 360–61.

12. "Country House," 238.

13. *Rural Architecture* was also published in Chicago in 1885 by George W. Ogilvie under the title *Architecture Simplified, or How to Build a House.*

14. The designs in the Adams-Horr pattern book are similar to a stripped-down version of Downing's Design I from *Country Houses.* See Upton, "Pattern Books and Professionalism," 142.

15. Henry Glassie, "Artifact and Culture, Architecture and Society," in Simon J. Bronner, ed., *American Material Culture and Folklife* (Ann Arbor, Mich.: UMI Research Press, 1985), 47–61.

16. Upton, "Pattern Books and Professionalism," 107–50.

17. Ibid., 130–31.

18. Another significant issue that can pervade a discussion of aesthetic preference and practice is the author's experience and judgments in questions of quality. However carefully and thoroughly one might base arguments upon evidence at hand, one's own perceptions and values are involved in the initial selection and subsequent interpretation of the data. It should be recognized that in the best of circumstances the discussion of aesthetic issues is a subjective process in which judgments are made in part on the basis of intuition or feeling rather than reason and logic. Knowledge based on practical long-term experience provides the foundation for that kind of intuitive knowing and adds to the discussion another intangible element that hopefully refines perceptions and judgments of quality. This mark of the critic should not be viewed as an elitist trait. It is simply a result of time, effort, and discipline in the study of a particular form of artistic expression.

19. For an excellent description of farming as a process, see Ben Logan, *The Land Remembers: The Story of a Farm and Its People* (New York: Viking Press, 1975).

20. Kniffen identifies this prevailing preference for a particular house type as "the principle of Dominance of Contemporary Fashion." See Kniffen, "Folk Housing," 558.

21. It was not unusual to build a frame house that adjoined a sod house or incorporated a log cabin. See Ruben L. Parson, *Ever the Land: A Homestead Chronicle* (Staples, Minn.: Adventure, 1978), 244–46 and Chap. 4, Fig. 3.

22. Ann Davidson, "Diary," manuscript, 15–16, Stevens County Historical Museum, Morris, Minnesota.

23. T-plan farmhouses were sometimes developed to become double-wing dwellings with the addition of a wing equal to the unit on the opposite side of the central gabled rectangle. See Chapter Six of this volume for a discussion of farmhouse types 5 and 6.

24. Barbara Levorsen, *The Quiet Conquest: A History of the Lives and Times of the First Settlers of Central North Dakota* (Hawley, Minn.: Hawley Herald, 1974), 3–4.

25. Arthur A. Hart, "M. A. Disbrow & Company: Catalogue Architecture," *Palimpsest* 56 (July/August 1975): 98–119. The F. Mastvetten farmhouse (Figure 5.5) exhibits most of these commonly used ornamental elements.

26. In some cases it cost less to have carpenters finish the lumber than to purchase machine-milled materials. Lumber was available in various states at varying costs. Boards could be surfaced on one side or two sides, on one side and one edge, on just one edge, on two sides and one edge, or on one side and two edges. "Finished" lumber that was surfaced on all sides usually cost twice as much as "common" boards. Other states of finish raised the price of lumber at a proportional rate. Lumber descriptions and prices are based upon contemporary listings, such as J. J. Howe and Company (Brainerd, Minnesota), "Lumber Quotations," 1881, 1883, and 1884, in Thomas N. Putnam File, North Dakota State University Manuscript Archives, Grand Forks.

27. See Ronald Rees and Carl J. Tracie, "The Prairie House," *Landscape* 22 (1978): 3–8.

28. See John William Ward, "The Politics of Design," in Lawrence B. Holland, ed.,

Who Designs America? (New York: Doubleday, 1965), 51-85, for the social and political aspects of Downing's views on architectural design.

29. Downing, *Country Houses*, xx.

30. Ibid., 8-9.

31. Ibid., 23.

32. Ibid., 24.

33. Downing's *Cottage Residences* (New York: John Wiley and Sons, 1848) and *Country Houses* argued against these aspects of the useful and pragmatic in vernacular building. Other authors of stylebooks from 1850 through the 1870s repeated Downing's belief that aesthetic sensitivity and educated taste should inform social, moral, and religious issues in domestic architecture.

34. However accidental it may seem, the placement and poses of the family members in front of their houses communicate something of how each person related to his or her home. The Pladsons are casually spread out near the side entrance of their house and some seem to be pretending that their picture is not being taken as they look away from the camera. A studied self-consciousness similar to the deliberately unique decorations of the house is generated from such attitudes. In the photograph of the Douglas County farmhouse, the family stand on the porch stolidly staring at the camera with a directness that parallels the design of their house. Each member seems to be in his or her place in a measured hierarchy.

CHAPTER SIX. FARMHOUSE TYPES 5 AND 6:
STYLE, SUBSTANCE, AND COMMUNITY

1. Earlier plans for Monticello indicate that Jefferson was thinking of a cruciform plan for the country villa that was quite similar in basic architectural composition to farmhouse types 5 and 6. See Gene Waddell, "The First Monticello," *Journal of the Society of Architectural Historians* 46 (March 1987): 5-29.

2. Mary Mix Foley, *The American House* (New York: Harper and Row, 1980), 114-15.

3. See Allen G. Noble, *Wood, Brick, and Stone: The North American Settlement Landscape*, vol. 1 (Amherst: University of Massachusetts Press, 1984), 48-56.

4. An Italianate version of an elaborated cruciform-plan house was billed as the "new American style of architecture" in an 1859 issue of the *American Agriculturist*. It was conceded by "Messrs. Saeltzer and Valk" that the design "may not be entirely new"; the editor agreed and added that the work suffered from "too much ornament and angles." See "New American Style of Architecture," *American Agriculturist* 18 (1859): 297.

5. George E. Woodward, *Woodward's Architecture and Rural Art, No. 1—1867* (New York: George E. Woodward, 1867), 62-65.

6. S. B. Reed, *House Plans for Everybody* (New York: Orange Judd, 1886), 152.

7. Ibid., 157.

8. See Rudolf Heberle, "The Application of Fundamental Concepts in Rural Community Studies," *Rural Sociology* 6 (1941): 203-15.

9. "Lac Qui Parle County," *Immigration Tract* (Dawson, Minn., 1896), n.p.

10. Ibid.

11. George T. Wallace, "Madison and Lac Qui Parle Co.," *Madison* (Minn.) *Independent Press*, 15 December 1899, 9.

12. Ibid., 11.

13. Olivia H. Rudd, "Trapper's Cabin Was First Home for Ole Holtans," *Dawson* (Minn.) *Sentinel*, 19 June 1959, 7.

14. "Early Settlers in Providence Township of Lac Qui Parle County, Mr. and Mrs. A.

O. Ness," manuscript, 9–10, Lac Qui Parle County Historical Museum, Madison, Minnesota, n.d.

15. See John Unseem and Ruth Hill Unseem, "Minority Group Patterns in Prairie Society," *American Journal of Sociology* 50 (1945): 377–85.

16. "Andrew O. Ness," *Compendium of History and Biography of Central and Northern Minnesota* (Chicago: George A. Ogle, 1904), 469–70.

17. Rudd, "Trapper's Cabin," 7.

18. For those involved in this Lac Qui Parle building boom, the average number of years between living in the first, small farmhouse and living in the new large one was twenty years. In most instances, both families and farms had grown to the extent that a larger home was as much a necessity as a show of achievement.

19. The prices for these farmhouses are based upon figures that appeared in Lac Qui Parle County newspapers describing the cost for comparable farmhouses built by neighbors of the Nesses and Holtans. Further information about how the costs were covered has come from interviews with various local farmers.

20. See "Wheat Statistics, 1866–1898," in Fred A. Shannon's *The Farmer's Last Frontier: Agriculture, 1860–1897* (New York: Holt, Rinehart, and Winston, 1963), 417; and Henrietta Larson, *The Wheat Market and the Farmer in Minnesota, 1858–1900* (New York: Columbia University Studies in History, Economics, and Public Law, 1926), 160–64.

21. Norwegians in Providence township were easily able to integrate with the Swedish settlement there because the two languages are sufficiently similar to permit communication. These two groups also joined together in Lutheran congregations in the township. Norway was a nation that was divided into distinct provinces from which Lac Qui Parle farmers had emigrated. They maintained these provincial identities and labeled themselves Trondheimers or Stavangers. This recognition of self and others did contribute to competition among Norwegians, but it did not seem to weaken any sense of national identity.

22. Jon Gjerde, *From Peasants to Farmers: The Migration from Balestrand, Norway, to the Upper Middle West* (Cambridge: Cambridge University Press, 1985), 51.

23. Rudd, "Trapper's Cabin," 5.

24. For perceptions of this aspect of life in rural America, see E. V. Smalley, "The Isolation of Life on Prairie Farms," *Atlantic Monthly* 72 (September 1893): 379–82, and Jas. R. Hanna, "The Isolation of Farm Life," *Wallace's Farmer* 34 (February 1909): 193. Both authors suggested that farmhouses be built at the center of intersections of land so that they would be close to one another.

25. See Jane Marie Pederson, "The Country Visitor: Patterns of Hospitality in Rural Wisconsin, 1880–1925," *Agricultural History* 58 (July 1984): 347–64.

26. June D. Holmquist, ed., *They Chose Minnesota: A Survey of the State's Ethnic Groups* (St. Paul: Minnesota Historical Society Press, 1981), 226–29.

27. George E. Lund, "History of Providence Valley Lutheran Church, 1878–1978," *Providence Valley Lutheran Church* (Skokie, Ill.: Lemann and Associates, 1976), 7–8. For a study of the importance of the church as a focal point for the rural community and of the nature and size of the rural parish in western Minnesota, see John G. Rice, "Patterns of Ethnicity in a Minnesota County, 1880–1905," *Geographical Reports* (Umea, Sweden) 4 (1973): 33–48, and Jon Gjerde, "The Development of Church Centered Communities among European Immigrants: A Case Study of Three Minnesota Townships" (Master's thesis, University of Minnesota, Minneapolis, 1978).

28. Dawson History Book Committee, eds., *Dawson, Minnesota, History: The First Hundred Years, 1884–1894* (Dawson, Minn.: Dawson Sentinel, 1984), 93.

29. For a first-person account of socioreligious life in the rural Midwest, see Mrs. R.

O. Brandt, "Social Aspects of Prairie Pioneering: Extracts from Reminiscences of a Pioneer Pastor's Wife," *Norwegian-American Studies and Records* 7 (1933): 1-46.

30. Martin Luther, *Sermons on the Gospels for Sundays and the Principal Festivals of the Church Year*, vol. 2, trans. M. Loy (Columbus, Ohio: Schulze and Gassmann, 1871), 452-55.

31. Anna Amrud, "Early Recollections of My Childhood," manuscript, 4, Lac Qui Parle County Historical Museum, Madison, Minnesota, n.d.

32. Rudd, "Trapper's Cabin," 7.

33. Luther, *Sermons on the Gospels*, 1:239.

34. See Odd Brochmann, *Bygget i Norge*, 2 Bind [Building in Norway, 2 vols.] (Oslo: Gyldendal Norsk Forlag, 1981), 2:7-76, and Arne E. Oldem, *Sveitserstil—1800-Årenes Byggestil* [The Swiss style—Nineteenth-century building style] (Oslo: Institut for Ethnologi, Universitet, 1984).

35. H. K. Daniels, *Home Life in Norway* (New York: Macmillan, 1911), 111.

36. Tore Drange et al., *Gamle Trehus: Reparasjon og Vedlikehold* [Old wooden houses: Repairs and maintenance] (Oslo: Universitets Forlaget, 1980), 160-66.

37. For a similar transfer of ethnic traits in Norwegian-American farmhouses, see Fred W. Peterson, "Norwegian-American Farm Homes in Steele and Traill Counties, North Dakota: The American Dream and the Retention of Roots, 1890-1914," *North Dakota History* 51 (Winter 1984): 4-13.

38. The interpretation of Norwegian-American farmhouses offered in this study does not intend to establish cause and effect relationships between the faith and the piety of the Holtans and Nesses and the form and function of their farmhouses. The meaning of the farmhouses can be interpreted by relating relevant aspects of the lifestyle of the families to their domestic environments and understanding how the members of these families and the members of the church parishes perceived these homes. The reader should not imagine that Lac Qui Parle folks enjoyed an idyllic all-American lifestyle in a pastoral environment. The social and religious aspects of their communities exercised significant control over individuals within each rural parish. These controls enforced a rather stern preservation of Old World village traditions and order. See Utz Jeggle, "The Rules of the Village: On the Cultural History of the Peasant World in the Last 150 Years," in Richard J. Evans and W. R. Lee, eds., *The German Peasantry: Conflict and Community in Rural Society from the Eighteenth to the Twentieth Century* (London: Croom Helm, 1986), 265-89.

39. "Early Settlers in Lac Qui Parle County," 8.

CHAPTER SEVEN. FARMHOUSE TYPES 8 AND 9:
CONSOLIDATION AND STANDARDIZATION

1. Another name given farmhouse type 8 is the workingman's foursquare. Farmhouse type 9 has also been called the Cornbelt Cube, the Two-Story Cube, the Box House, and the square two-story pyramidal-roof house.

2. Farmhouse type 8 may have been built as a home for elderly couples who were retiring from farming but still lived on or near the "home place." The type may also have been a structure that economically housed tenant farmers. Early in the twentieth century this house type was also frequently used as a model for portable or prefabricated structures designed to be used primarily as vacation homes. Their small scale and compact design were well suited to the sectional construction used in these kinds of shelters.

3. In addition to these popular labels given to the house type, it has been suggested that it originated from two distinctly different folk traditions in the United States. As a "southern pyramid-roof house" its origins have been in part traced to French influences

from New Orleans. Examples of this dwelling have been embellished with stylistic features ranging from Georgian to Queen Anne. The product of another folk tradition is called "the western bungalow." Its range is broad, extending from the Middle West to the Far West, and its origin has been attributed to a specific German-Russian house type imported to the Great Plains in the second half of the nineteenth century. See Allen G. Noble, *Wood, Brick, and Stone: The North American Settlement Landscape*, vol. I (Amherst: University of Massachusetts Press, 1984), 99-100 and 124.

4. Mary Mix Foley, *The American House* (New York: Harper and Row, 1980), 108-11.

5. "Building Plans: The Lumberman's Low Priced Houses, Design No. 7," *American Lumberman* I (May 1899): 17.

6. George K. Holmes, "Progress of Agriculture in the United States," *U.S. Department of Agriculture Yearbook, 1899*, as reprinted in Wayne D. Rasmussen, ed., *Agriculture in the United States: A Documentary History*, vol. 2 (New York: Random House, 1975), 1659-60.

7. See Adam Ward Rome, "American Farmers as Entrepreneurs, 1870-1900," *Agricultural History* 56 (January 1982): 37-49.

8. W. J. Spillman, "Systems of Farm Management in the United States," *U.S. Department of Agriculture Yearbook, 1902*, as quoted in Rasmussen, ed., *Agriculture in the United States*, 2:1759 and 1761.

9. See D. Jerome Tweeten, "The Golden Age of Agriculture, 1897-1917," *North Dakota History* 37 (Winter 1970): 41-55.

10. George F. Barber of Knoxville, Tennessee, and Robert W. Shoppell of New York City entered the mail-order house business in the 1880s, expanding the market for this kind of merchandising to a national level.

11. T. W. Harvey Lumber Company, *Architectural Designs Issued by T. W. Harvey Lumber Co.* (Chicago: By the company, 1889), 13.

12. "Ready Made Houses," *Lumberman's Gazette* 23 (November 1883): 4.

13. Ibid.

14. Sears, Roebuck, and Company entered the market with mail-order houses in 1909. In addition to supplying complete precut, ready-to-assemble structures, the company also furnished mortgage loans to its clients. See Gordon L. Weil, *Sears, Roebuck, U.S.A.: The Great American Catalogue Store and How It Grew* (New York: Stein and Day, 1977), 68-69.

15. The vertical studs in the exterior wall of a balloon frame house are continuous from the sill to the top plate and could be 18 to 20 feet long for a two-story house. A platform frame system is built so that the studs for the first story are only as long as that space is high. The second story is built on the platform that the first story provides.

16. The development of home economics and the standardization of household tasks for the sake of greater efficiency has already been discussed in relation to farmhouse types 1 and 2. What is presented in that context is also applicable to the design and functions intended for the two-story foursquare house. The layout of the Oscar Borass farmhouse in Chapter Four is quite similar to the floor plans of the mail-order houses offered in this chapter. See Chapter Four of this volume, pp. 61-95.

17. Information about the fire that destroyed the first house and the many portals of the new house was collected in an interview with a member of the Van Amstel family in 1975.

18. The Van Amstel farmhouse is at the end of a long glacial wash, built on light gravel soil under which an enormous amount of naturally filtered water flows. Instead of incurring the costs of digging a deep well, a "dry point" pipe can be driven into the earth to a depth of approximately 12 feet to tap the abundant natural resource. In many areas of the region natural springs make water supply equally accessible, but in most ar-

eas wells must be dug, sometimes to depths of 200 to 300 feet. In some locales in North Dakota, artesian wells are used. Some of these wells are so heavily fluoridated that the water tends to stain anything it comes into contact with for any duration. These are geographic and geological factors that influenced decisions to add indoor plumbing to farmhouses in the region.

19. "Plumbing in a Farmhouse," *Carpentry and Building* 29 (January 1907): 25–26.

20. For a discussion of the development of the indoor bathroom in the nineteenth century, see Sigfried Giedion, *Mechanization Takes Command* (New York: W. W. Norton, 1969), 659–712.

CHAPTER EIGHT. FARMHOUSE TYPE 10: RURAL IMAGES OF SUCCESS

1. "The Pioneer Farm" and "The Prosperous Farm," *Independent Farmer and Fireside Companion* 1 (1879): 164 and 170.

2. See "American Farmhouses," *The Plow* 1 (1852): 88–89 and Beverly Seaton, "Idylls of Agriculture, Or Nineteenth Century Success Stories of Farming and Gardening," *Agricultural History* 55 (January 1981): 21–31.

3. Robert Wiebe, *The Search for Order, 1877–1920* (New York: Hill and Wang, 1967), 136.

4. See Margaret L. Woodward, "The Northwestern Farmer, 1868–1876: A Tale of Paradox," *Agricultural History* 37 (July 1963): 134–42, and Robert F. Berkhofer, Jr., "Space, Time, Culture, and the New Frontier," *Agricultural History* 38 (January 1964): 21–30.

5. Mrs. H. H. Charlton, "Life on the Farm," *Western Farmer* 8 (August 1889): 518.

6. "Does Farming Pay?" *Western Farmer* 8 (June 1889): 352. For a recent and well-informed discussion of what constitutes success or failure in upper midwestern farming, see Gilbert C. Fite, "Failure on the Last Frontier: A Family Chronicle," *Western Historical Quarterly* (January 1987): 4–14.

7. See Jan Cohn, *The Palace or the Poorhouse: The American Home as Cultural Symbol* (East Lansing: Michigan State University Press, 1979), 115–71.

8. See Thomas E. Hill, *Never Give a Lady a Restive Horse* (Berkeley, Calif.: Diablo Press, 1967), 128–29. Reprint of *Hill's Manual of Social and Business Forms*, 1873.

9. "President Thrifty's Home," "Old Slovenly's 'Den,'" *Wisconsin Farmer* 10 (August 1858): 294–95, and "Two Kinds of Houses," *Cultivator* 10 (1862): 120. See also "Tumbledown Mansion: The House of Farmer Slack and the House of Farmer Snug," *The Plough, the Loom, and the Anvil* 5 (1852): 120–21.

10. Structural information about the Flinn farmhouse as well as its floor plan is derived from James S. Cook, "A Mid-Nineteenth Century Iowa Farmhouse," the Wolf Collection, State Historical Society of Iowa Archives.

11. The photograph is from T. A. Hoverstad, *The Norwegian Farmers in the United States* (Fargo, N.D.: Hans Jervell, 1915), n.p. Hoverstad actually concentrated his study on successful farmers in the Red River valley in North Dakota and contrasted photographs of the log cabins of these Norwegian pioneer farmers with photographs of their later manorial farmhouses. Although based upon the good fortune of many Scandinavian farmers in the area, the format of the book is structured on the before-and-after rhetorical contrast of the rags-to-riches American success story.

12. Biographical information on Fingal Enger is from Clarence H. Tolley, "Fingal Enger, King of the Goose River," *North Dakota History* 26 (July 1959): 107–22; "Fingal Enger: Necrological Remarks," *Mayville* (N.D.) *Tribune*, 4 September 1913, 1–2; and Enger files of the Historical Data Project, Archives of the State Historical Society of North Dakota, Bismarck.

13. A local story explains that it was Enger's wife who caused the new house to be built. Enger was planning a trip to Norway about 1888. His wife, it is claimed, made him promise to build a new house when he returned. If he refused to do this, he need not go anywhere. The house was finished and furnished after Enger enjoyed a visit to his homeland. This story is told by a great-granddaughter of Enger, Mrs. Nina Lee.

14. Enger's large farmhouse of 1889 was not the first or the only one of its size and style to be built in that rural community. See Fred W. Peterson, "Norwegian-American Farm Homes in Steele and Traill Counties, North Dakota: The American Dream and the Retention of Roots, 1890–1914," *North Dakota History* 51 (Winter 1984): 4–13.

15. Tolley, "Fingal Enger," 113.

16. See Chapter Six of this volume, 136–73.

17. See Marilyn Brinkman, ed., *Bringing Home the Cows: Family Dairy Farming in Stearns County* (St. Cloud, Minn.: Stearns County Historical Society, 1988).

18. An analysis of the frame of this farmhouse indicates that the carpenter placed each window and door opening at intervals that consistently correspond with the regular placement of studs and joists on a 16-inches-on-center interval. For instance, the placement of windows 5½ feet from each corner of the house allows for the space of the doubled stud at the corner of the balloon frame and space for four more studs to total 66 inches, or 5½ feet. The windows and doors are either 48 inches or 32 inches in width so they can be introduced into the network of the structure at those regular intervals predetermined by the builder. I have worked with farmers in this area and can attest that this careful, methodical approach to any practical task is a trait common to many German-American farmers. This does not mean that other ethnic groups do not have this trait; it just seems to be especially strong among German-Americans.

19. See Chapter Seven of this volume, pp. 174–213.

CHAPTER NINE. CONCLUSION: BRICKS, BALLOON FRAMES, AND HI-TECH

1. See John F. Kasson, *Civilizing the Machine: Technology and Republican Values in America, 1776–1900* (New York: Grossman, 1976), passim.

2. Dorothy Gahring Clark, *Daniel Nelson, His Family, and Homestead, Mahaska County, Iowa* (Oskaloosa, Iowa: Clarkcraft, 1973), 7–10, 26–29.

3. Interviews with Walter and Pearl Hanse, August-September 1981.

4. Upton has argued that the history of timber framing in America reveals a consistent and continuous direction toward a flexible and labor-efficient structural system. The development of balloon frame construction can be perceived as one result of the tendencies toward simplification and industrialization of building materials and methods in the United States from the seventeenth century through the nineteenth century. See Dell Upton, "Traditional Timber Framing," in Brooke Hindle, ed., *Material Culture of the Wooden Age* (Tarrytown, N.Y.: Sleepy Hollow Press, 1981), 35–93.

SELECTED BIBLIOGRAPHY

PRIMARY SOURCES

Books

Adams-Horr Company (Minneapolis). *Rural Architecture*. Chicago: Northwestern Lumberman Print, 1884.

Aladdin Homes Company. *Aladdin Homes: Catalogue #29*. Bay City, Mich.: By the company, 1917.

Allen, Lewis. *Rural Architecture*. New York: C. M. Saxton, 1852.

Andreas, Alfred T. *Illustrated Historical Atlas of Dakota*. Chicago: Andreas Atlas, 1884.

———. *Illustrated Historical Atlas of the State of Iowa*. Chicago: Andreas Atlas, 1875.

———. *Illustrated Historical Atlas of the State of Minnesota*. Chicago: Andreas Atlas, 1876.

Atwood, D. T. *Atwood's Country and Suburban Homes*. New York: Orange Judd, 1871.

Bascom, John. *Aesthetics, or The Science of Beauty*. New York: Ainsworth, 1872.

Beecher, Catherine, and Harriet Beecher Stowe. *The American Woman's Home*. New York: J. B. Ford, 1869.

Bell, William. *Carpentry Made Easy*. Philadelphia: James Challen and Sons, 1858.

Bicknell, A. J. *Bicknell's Cottage and Villa Architecture*. New York: A. J. Bicknell, 1878.

———. *Cottage and Constructive Architecture*. New York: A. J. Bicknell, 1873.

Blodgett and Osgood Company. *Ready-Made Houses*. St. Paul: By the company, 189[?].

Bond, J. W. *Minnesota and Its Resources*. New York: Redfield, 1853.

Breeder's Gazette. *Farm Buildings*. Chicago: Breeder's Gazette, 1911.

Cleaveland, Henry W., William Backus, and Samuel D. Backus. *Village and Farm Cottages*. New York: D. Appleton, 1856.

Cummings, M. F., and C. C. Miller. *Modern American Architecture*. Toledo: S. Bailey, 1868.

Davis, Alexander Jackson. *Rural Residences*. New York: N.p., 1837.

Downing, Andrew Jackson. *The Architecture of Country Houses*. New York: D. Appleton, 1850.

———. *Cottage Residences*. New York: John Wiley and Putnam, 1842.

———. *Rural Essays*. New York: G. P. Putnam, 1853.

———. *A Treatise on the Theory and Practice of Landscape Gardening Adapted to North America*. New York: Wiley and Putnam, 1841.

Dwyer, Charles P. *The Economic Cottage Builder*. Buffalo: Wenzer, McKim, 1856.
————. *The Immigrant Builder*. Philadelphia: Claxton, Remsen, and Haffelfinger, 1872.
Eggleston, Nathaniel H. *The Home and Its Surroundings*. New York: Harper and Brothers, 1883.
Etherton, William Alonzo. *The Farm House Improved*. Kansas State Agricultural College Bulletin, vol. 1 (May 1, 1917), no. 8. Manhattan.
Frederick, Christine. *The New Housekeeping: Efficiency Studies in Home Management*. New York: Curtis, 1912.
Fuller, Albert W. *Artistic Homes in City and Country*. Boston: James R. Osgood, 1882.
Gardner, E. C. *Farm Architecture: Houses and Barns*. Holyoke, Mass.: Clark W. Bryan, 1882.
————. *Homes and All about Them*. Boston: James R. Osgood, 1885.
————. *Homes and How to Make Them*. Boston: James R. Osgood, 1874.
————. *The House That Jill Built, After Jack's Had Proved a Failure*. New York: Fords, Howard, and Hulbert, 1882.
Geib-Carl Lumber Company. *Modern American Homes*. Chicago: C. L. Bowes, 1918.
Gibson, Louis H. *Convenient Houses*. New York: Thomas Y. Crowell, 1889.
Gorden-Van Tine Company. *Architectural Details*. Davenport, Iowa: By the company, 1915.
Greeley, Horace. *An Overland Journey*. New York: C. M. Saxton, Barker, 1860.
Gregg, Josiah. *Commerce of the Prairie*. New York: Henry G. Langley, 1844.
Hall, William W. "Farmers' Houses." In *United States Department of Agriculture Report*, 313–37. Washington, D.C.: Department of Agriculture, 1863.
Harvey, T. W., Lumber Company. *Architectural Designs Issued by T. W. Harvey Lumber Co.* Chicago: By the company, 1889.
Hill, Thomas E. ("Prof"). *Never Give a Lady a Restive Horse*. Reprint of *Hill's Manual of Social and Business Forms*, 1873. Berkeley, Calif.: Diablo Press, 1967.
Hodgson, Fred T. *Modern Carpentry: A Practical Manual*. Chicago: Frederick J. Drake, 1902.
Hodgson, Fred T., ed. *Practical Bungalows and Cottages for Town and Country*. Chicago: Frederick J. Drake, 1912.
Holly, H. Hudson. *Holly's Country Seats*. New York: D. Appleton, 1863.
————. *Modern Dwellings in Town and Country*. New York: Harper and Brothers, 1878.
Hussey, E. C. *Home Building*. New York: Leader and Van Hoesen, 1876.
Illustrated Historical Atlas of Traill and Steele Counties, North Dakota. Mayville, N.D.: J. J. Kelley, 1892.
Jacques, Daniel H. *The House: A Pocket Manual of Rural Architecture*. New York: Fowler and Wells, 1859.
Keith, M. L. *Keith's Book of Plans*. Minneapolis: M. L. Keith, 1912.
Kellar, Herbert Anthony, ed. *Solon Robinson: Pioneer and Agriculturist*. 2 vols. New York: Capo Press, 1968.
Leland, E. H. *Farm Homes Indoors and Outdoors*. New York: Orange Judd, 1882.
Loudon, John Claudius. *An Encyclopedia of Cottage, Farm, and Villa Architecture and Furniture*. London: Longman, Brown, Green and Longmans, 1846.
Luther, Martin. *Sermons on the Gospels for Sundays and the Principal Festivals of the Church Year*. 3 vols. Trans. M. Loy. Columbus, Ohio: Schulze and Gassmann, 1871.
Mason, George C. *The Old House Altered*. New York: Putnam's and Sons, 1878.
Nowlin, William. *The Bark Covered House*. Detroit: N.p., 1876.

Ogilvie, George W. *Architecture Simplified, or How to Build a House.* Chicago: George W. Ogilvie, 1885.

Olson, Nils W., ed. *A Pioneer in Northwest America, 1841–58: The Memoirs of Gustav Unonius.* Minneapolis: University of Minnesota Press, 1950.

Osborne, Charles Francis. *The Family House.* Philadelphia: Penn Publishing, 1910.

Palliser, Palliser, and Company. *Palliser's American Cottage Homes.* Bridgeport, Conn.: Palliser, Palliser, and Company, 1877.

————. *Palliser's Model Homes for the People.* Bridgeport, Conn.: Palliser, Palliser, and Company, 1878.

————. *Palliser's New Cottage Homes and Details.* New York: Palliser, Palliser, and Company, 1887.

The Radford American Homes. Chicago: Montgomery Ward, 1903.

The Radford Home Builder. Chicago: Radford Architecture, 1909.

The Radford Ideal Homes. Chicago: Radford Architecture, 1903.

Radford's Artistic Homes. Chicago: Radford Architecture, 1908.

Reed, S. B. *Dwellings for Village and Country.* New York: N.p., 1885.

————. *House Plans for Everybody.* New York: Orange Judd, 1884.

Saxton, Glen L. *The Plan Book of American Dwellings.* Minneapolis: Glen L. Saxton, 1914.

Scott, Frank J. *The Art of Beautifying Suburban Home Grounds.* New York: D. Appleton, 1872.

Shoppel, Robert W. *Artistic Modern Houses at Low Cost.* New York: Co-operative Building Plan Associates, 1881.

————. *Shoppel's Model Houses.* New York: Co-operative Building Plan Associates, 1890.

Sloan, Samuel. *Sloan's Homestead Architecture.* Philadelphia: J. B. Lippincott, 1861.

Taylor, Thomas. *Tom's Experience in Dakota.* Minneapolis: C. D. Whitehall, 1883.

Thompson Yards, Inc. *The Model Farm and Home Exhibit.* Minneapolis: By the company, 1920.

Vaux, Calvert. *Villas and Cottages.* New York: Harper and Brothers, 1857.

Walter, Thomas U. *Two Hundred Designs for Cottages and Villas.* Philadelphia: Carey and Hart, 1846.

Wheeler, Gervaise. *Homes for the People in Suburb and Country.* New York: Charles Scribner, 1855.

Woodward, George E. *Cottages and Farm Houses.* New York: George E. Woodward and F. W. Woodward, 1867.

————. *Woodward's Architecture and Rural Art, No. 1.—1867.* New York: George E. Woodward, 1867.

————. *Woodward's Architecture and Rural Art, No. 2—1868.* New York: George E. Woodward, 1868.

————. *Woodward's Country Homes.* New York: George E. Woodward, 1865.

————. *Woodward's Suburban and Country Houses.* New York: Excelsior, 1871.

Diaries, Manuscripts, and Periodicals

"American Farmhouses." *The Plow* 1 (1852): 88–89.

Amrud, Anna. "Early Recollections of My Childhood." Manuscript. Lac Qui Parle County Historical Museum, Madison, Minn., n.d.

Austin, Joseph C. "An Iowa Farm in the Making." *Annals of Iowa* 40 (Spring 1970): 306–18.

Brandt, Mrs. R. O. "Social Aspects of Prairie Pioneering: Extracts from Reminiscences of a Pioneer Pastor's Wife." *Norwegian-American Studies and Records* 7 (1933): 1–46.

Brewer, E. F. "A Progressing Dakota Farm House." *American Agriculturist* 43 (1884): 54–55.

Buck, Solon J., ed. "Making a Farm on the Frontier: Extracts from the Diaries of Mitchell Young Jackson." *Agricultural History* 4 (July 1930): 92–120.

Charlton, Mrs. H. H. "Life on the Farm." *Western Farmer* 8 (August 1889): 518.

Davidson, Ann. "Diary." Manuscript. Western Minnesota Historical Research Center, Morris, n.d.

Detzler, Jack J. "I Live Happily Here: A German Immigrant in Territorial Wisconsin." *Wisconsin Magazine of History* 50 (1967): 254–59.

"Documents Immigrant Letter: Letter from Gerhard Kremers, July 26, 1848." *Wisconsin Magazine of History* 21 (1937): 68–84.

"Does Farming Pay?" *The Western Farmer* 8 (June 1889): 352.

"Early Settlers in Providence Township of Lac Qui Parle County, Mr. and Mrs. A. O. Ness." Madison, Minn.: Lac Qui Parle County Museum, n.d.

Erickson, Olaf. "Olaf Erickson—Scandinavian Frontiersman." *Wisconsin Magazine of History* 31 (1947): 7–26, 186–207, 236–38.

Felton, O. J. "Pioneer Life in Jones County." *Iowa Journal of History and Politics* 29 (April 1931): 233–81.

"Fingal Enger." Historical Data Project. Archives of the State Historical Society of North Dakota, Bismarck.

"Fingal Enger: Necrological Remarks." *Mayville* (N.D.) *Tribune*, 4 September 1913, 1–2.

Foster, Suel. "Balloon Frames." *Cultivator* 8 (July 1860): 224.

Hanna, Jas. R. "The Isolation of Farm Life." *Wallace's Farmer* 34. (February 1909): 193.

Herseth, Lorna B., ed. "A Pioneer's Letter." *South Dakota History* 6 (January 1976): 306–15.

"How Fire Sweeps a Wooden House." *Lumberman's Gazette*, 13 December 1882, 306–15.

"An Interesting Nail Test." *Carpentry and Building* 10 (March 1888): 49.

J. J. Howe and Company (Brainerd, Minn.). "Lumber Quotations," 1881, 1883, and 1884. In Thomas N. Putnam File, North Dakota State University Manuscript Archives, Grand Forks.

Jones, Merrill E. "Life on a Jones County Farm, 1873–1912." *Iowa Journal of History* 49 (October 1951): 311–38.

Low, Ann Marie. *Dust Bowl Diary*. Lincoln: University of Nebraska Press, 1984.

"Nails." *Carpentry and Building* 1 (January 1879): 20.

"New American Style of Architecture." *American Agriculturist* 18 (1859): 297.

Newton, R. G. "The Far-West Pioneer's Home." *American Agriculturist* 43 (1884): 158.

Pederson, Thomas. "Some Recollections of Thomas Pederson." *Wisconsin Magazine of History* 21 (1936): 16–34, 129–38, 175–90.

"The Pioneer Farm" and "The Successful Farm." *Independent Farmer and Fireside Companion* 1 (1879): 164, 170.

"Plans of Farm Houses." *Cultivator* 6 (November 1839): 164.

"Small, Convenient, Cheap Houses." *American Agriculturist* 25 (1886): 53; 26 (1886): 14.

Smalley, E. V. "The Isolation of Life on Prairie Farms." *Atlantic Monthly* 72 (September 1893): 370–82.

"The Sod House." *American Agriculturist* 33 (1874): 179–80.

Throne, Mildred, ed. "Document Iowa Farm Letters, 1856–1865." *Iowa Journal of History* 58 (January 1960): 37–88.

Torgils, Utne. *Grass and People: A History of Lac Qui Parle County*. Madison, Minn.: Lac Qui Parle County Museum, n.d.

"Tumbledown Mansion: The House of Farmer Slack and the House of Farmer Snug." *The Plough, the Loom, and the Anvil* 5 (1852): 120–21.

"Two Kinds of Houses." *Cultivator* 10 (1862): 120.

Wallace, George T. "Madison and Lac Qui Parle County." *Madison* (Minn.) *Independent Press*, 15 December 1899, 9.
Woodward, George E. "Balloon Frames." *Cultivator* 8 (January 1860): 20–21.
―――― . "Balloon Frames—III." *Cultivator* 8 (June 1860): 147.
―――― . "Balloon Frames." *Cultivator* 8 (July 1860): 224.
―――― . "Balloon Frames—IVth Article." *Cultivator* 8 (August 1860): 249.
―――― . "Balloon Frames—5th Article." *Cultivator* 8 (September 1860): 276–77.
―――― . "Balloon Frames—7th Article." *Cultivator* 8 (December 1860): 366.
―――― . "Balloon Frames—9th Article." *Cultivator* 9 (January 1861): 39.
―――― . "Balloon Frames—11th Article." *Cultivator* 9 (February 1861): 50.
―――― . "Balloon Frames—12th Article." *Cultivator* 9 (March 1861): 86–7.
―――― . "Balloon Frames—13th Article." *Cultivator* 9. (May 1861): 146.
―――― . "Balloon Frames—14th Article." *Cultivator* 9 (July 1861): 226–27.

Interviews

North Dakota Oral History Project, July 1974–June 1975. Interviews by Larry J. Spunk. State Historical Society, Bismarck.
    Berkom, J. H. van (Burke County).
    Bloomquist, Ross (Foster County).
    Bohlin, Walter (Emmons County).
    Carpenter, Warren and Alma (Steele County).
    Hooefs, Rudolph H. (Richland County).
    Kraft, Pius (Emmons County).
    Lasher, Mr. and Mrs. William (Sheridan County).
    Linn, Thomas (Steele County).
    McCloud, N. F. (Richland County).
    Medahl, Mrs. Adelene (Steele County).
    Otto, Elsie E. (Burnes County).
    Rasmussen, Mike (Steele County).
    Schade, Mr. and Mrs. John (Bowman County).
    Schmid, John (Foster County).
    Setterland, M. A. (Burke County).
    Stevens, Everett (Sargant County).
    Stokkeland, Sophia (Griggs County).

SECONDARY SOURCES

Books

Adler, Irving, and Ruth Adler. *Learning about Steel through the Story of a Nail*. New York: John Day, 1961.
Ames, Kenneth L., ed. *Victorian Furniture*. Philadelphia: Victorian Society in America, 1982.
A:son-Palmquist, Lena. *Building Traditions among Swedish Settlers in Rural America*. Uddevalla, Sweden: Risbergs Trykeri, 1983.
Bealer, Alex W. *The Tools That Built America*. New York: Bonanza Books, 1975.
Bealer, Alex W., and John O. Ellis. *The Log Cabin: Homes of the North American Wilderness*. Barre, Mass.: Barre Publishing, 1978.
Bender, Thomas. *Community and Social Change in America*. Baltimore: Johns Hopkins University Press, 1978.

Benson, Mabel. *The Home of the Brave: A Story of the Pioneers.* Bismarck, N.D.: N.p., 1984.

Beyer, Glenn H., and J. Hugh Rose. *Frame Housing.* New York: John Wiley and Sons, 1957.

Billington, Ray Allen. *Land of Savagery, Land of Promise: The European Image of the American Frontier.* New York: W. W. Norton, 1981.

Blegen, Theodore C. *Minnesota: A History of the State.* Minneapolis: University of Minnesota Press, 1978.

Blum, Jerome. *The End of the Old Order in Rural Europe.* Princeton, N.J.: Princeton University Press, 1978.

Blumenson, John J. G. *Identifying American Architecture: A Pictorial Guide to Styles and Terms, 1600–1945.* Nashville: American Association for State and Local History, 1977.

Borchert, John R. *America's Northern Heartland: An Economic and Historical Geography of the Upper Midwest.* Minneapolis: University of Minnesota Press, 1987.

Borgedal, Paul, ed. *Norske Gards Bruk.* Bind III. [Norwegian farms. vol. 3.] Oslo: Forlaget Norske Gards Bruk, 1943.

Bowers, Douglas E., and James B. Hoehn. *A List of References for the History of Agriculture in the Midwest, 1840–1900.* Davis: Agricultural History Center, University of California, 1973.

Bowers, William L. *The Country Life Movement in America, 1900–1920.* Port Washington, N.Y.: Kennikat Press, 1974.

Brinkman, Marilyn, ed. *Bringing Home the Cows: Family Dairy Farming in Stearns County.* St. Cloud, Minn.: Stearns County Historical Society, 1988.

Brinkman, Marilyn Salzi, and Wm. Towner Morgan. *Light from the Hearth: Central Minnesota Pioneers and Early Architecture.* St. Cloud, Minn.: North Star Press, 1982.

Brochmann, Odd. *Bygget i Norge.* 2 Bind. [Building in Norway. 2 vols.] Oslo: Gyldenal Norsk Forlag, 1981.

Bruce, Alfred, and Harold Sandbank. *The History of Prefabrication.* New York: Arno Press, 1974.

Buck, Solon Justus. *The Granger Movement.* Lincoln: University of Nebraska Press, 1913.

Buley, R. Carlyle. *The Old Northwest Pioneer Period, 1815–1840.* 2 vols. Bloomington: Indiana University Press, 1978.

Burger, Thomas. *Max Weber's Theory of Concept Formation: History, Laws, and Ideal Types.* Durham, N.C.: Duke University Press, 1976.

Carlsson, Gustaf. *Gamla Svenska Allmogehem.* [Old Swedish country houses.] Stockholm: C. E. Fritzes Bokforlags, 1912.

Carroll, Peter N., and David W. Noble. *The Free and the Unfree: A New History of the United States.* New York: Penguin Books, 1977.

Century Farms of Wisconsin. Shawnee Mission, Kans.: Intercollegiate Press, 1984.

Clark, Clifford Edward, Jr. *The American Family Home, 1800–1960.* Chapel Hill: University of North Carolina Press, 1986.

Clawson, Marion. *Man and Land in the United States.* Lincoln: University of Nebraska Press, 1964.

Cochrane, Willard W. *The Development of American Agriculture: A Historical Analysis.* Minneapolis: University of Minnesota Press, 1979.

Cohn, Jan. *The Palace or the Poorhouse: The American Home as Cultural Symbol.* East Lansing: Michigan State University Press, 1979.

Collin, T. Byard. *The New Agriculture.* New York: Munn, 1906.

Conrat, Masie, and Richard Conrat. *The American Farm.* San Francisco: California Historical Society, 1977.

Curti, Merle. *The Making of an American Community: A Case Study of Democracy in a Frontier County.* Stanford, Calif.: Stanford University Press, 1959.
Cuthbert, John A., and Maggie Keeler. *Vernacular Architecture in America: A Selective Bibliography.* Boston: G. K. Hall, 1985.
Daniels, H. K. *Home Life in Norway.* New York: Macmillan, 1911.
Dawson History Book Committee, eds. *Dawson, Minnesota, History: The First Hundred Years, 1884-1984.* Dawson, Minn.: Dawson Sentinel, 1984.
Diede, Pauline Hener. *Homesteading on the Knife River.* Bismarck, N.D.: Germans from Russia Heritage Center, 1983.
Dollfus, Charles. *The Orion Book of Balloons.* New York: Orion Press, 1961.
Drache, Hiram. *The Day of the Bonanza.* Fargo: North Dakota Institute for Regional Studies, 1964.
Drange, Tore, et al. *Gamle Trehus: Reparasjon og Vedlikehold.* [Old wooden houses: Repairs and maintenance.] Oslo: Universitets Forlaget, 1980.
Dutton, Ralph. *The Victorian Home.* London: B. T. Batsford, 1959.
Eliassen, Georg, et al. *Norwegian Architecture throughout the Ages.* Oslo: H. Aschehoug, 1950.
Emmons, David M. *Garden in the Grasslands: Boomer Literature of the Central Great Plains.* Lincoln: University of Nebraska Press, 1971.
Erickson, Charlotte. *Invisible Immigrants: The Adaptation of English and Scottish Immigrants in Nineteenth-Century America.* London: Leicester University Press, 1972.
Fitch, James Marsten. *American Building: The Historical Forces That Shaped It.* New York: Schocken Books, 1973.
———. *Architecture and the Esthetics of Plenty.* New York: Columbia University Press, 1961.
Foley, Mary Mix. *The American House.* New York: Harper and Row, 1980.
Friedman, Lawrence J. *Inventors of the Promised Land.* New York: Alfred A. Knopf, 1975.
Gard, Robert, and Maryo Gard. *My Land, My Home, My Wisconsin: The Epic Story of the Wisconsin Farm and Farm Family from Settlement Days to the Present.* Milwaukee: Milwaukee Journal, 1978.
Gates, Paul W. *Landlords and Tenants on the Prairie Frontier.* Ithaca, N.Y.: Cornell University Press, 1973.
Giedion, Sigfried. *Mechanization Takes Command.* New York: W. W. Norton, 1969.
Ginger, Ray. *Age of Excess: The United States from 1877 to 1914.* New York: Macmillan, 1975.
Gjerde, Jon. *From Peasants to Farmers: The Migration from Balestrand, Norway, to the Upper Middle West.* Cambridge: Cambridge University Press, 1985.
Glassie, Henry. *Folk Housing in Middle Virginia: A Structural Analysis of Historic Artifacts.* Knoxville: University of Tennessee Press, 1975.
———. *Patterns of Folk Culture of the Eastern United States.* Philadelphia: University of Pennsylvania Press, 1968.
Gottfried, Herbert, and Jan Jennings. *American Vernacular Design, 1870-1940: An Illustrated Glossary.* New York: Van Nostrand Reinhold, 1985.
Gowans, Alan. *The Comfortable House: North American Suburban Architecture, 1890-1930.* Cambridge, Mass.: MIT Press, 1986.
———. *Images of American Living: Four Centuries of Architecture and Furniture as Cultural Expression.* New York: Harper and Row, 1976.
Greenberg, Joseph. *Language Typology: A Historical and Analytical Overview.* The Hague: Mouton, 1974.
Griswold, A. Whitney. *Farming and Democracy.* New Haven, Conn.: Yale University Press, 1952.

Grow, Lawrence. *The Old House Book of Cottages and Bungalows*. Pittstown, N.J.: Main Street Press, 1987.

Haber, Samuel. *Efficiency and Uplift: Scientific Management in the Progressive Era, 1890–1920*. Chicago: University of Chicago Press, 1964.

Hall, Bolton. *A Little Land and a Living*. New York: Arcadia Press, 1908.

Hamburg, J. F. *The Influence of the Railroad on the Processes and Patterns of Settlement in South Dakota*. Chapel Hill: University of North Carolina Press, 1969.

Handlin, David. *The American Home*. Boston: Little, Brown, 1979.

Hayden, Delores. *The Grand Domestic Revolution: A History of Feminist Designs for American Homes, Neighborhoods, and Cities*. Cambridge, Mass.: MIT Press, 1981.

Hayter, Earl W. *The Troubled Farmer, 1850–1900: Rural Adjustment to Industrialism*. De Kalb: Northern Illinois University Press, 1968.

Higham, John. *From Boundlessness to Consolidation: The Transformation of American Culture, 1848–1860*. Ann Arbor: University of Michigan Press, 1969.

Hitchcock, Henry Russell. *American Architectural Books*. Minneapolis: University of Minnesota Press, 1962.

Hofstrand, Richard K. *With Affection, Marten: A Swedish Immigrant's Letters about His Struggles and Triumphs Homesteading on the Frontier*. Charleston, Ill.: Bench Mark, 1983.

Hogan, Edward, and Joseph F. Roybal. *South Dakota House Types: Our Architectural Heritage*. Sioux Falls: South Dakota State University News Bureau, 1978.

Holmes, Fred L. *Old World Wisconsin: Around Europe in the Badger State*. Eau Claire, Wis.: E. M. Hale, 1944.

Holmquist, June D., ed. *They Chose Minnesota: A Survey of the State's Ethnic Groups*. St. Paul: Minnesota Historical Society Press, 1981.

Hoverstad, T. A. *The Norwegian Farmers in the United States*. Fargo, N.D.: Hans Jewell, 1915.

Howe, Daniel Walker, ed. *Victorian America*. Pittsburgh: University of Pennsylvania Press, 1976.

Hubka, Thomas C. *Big House, Little House, Back House, Barn: The Connected Farm Buildings of New England*. Hanover, N.H.: University Press of New England, 1984.

Humphrey, Seth K. *Following the Prairie Frontier*. Minneapolis: University of Minnesota Press, 1931.

Hurt, R. Douglas. *American Farm Tools*. Manhattan, Kans.: Sunflower University Press, 1982.

Hussey, Christopher. *The Picturesque: Studies in a Point of View*. London: Frank Cass, 1967.

Jackson, John Brinkerhoff. *American Space*. New York: W. W. Norton, 1972.

Jacobs, Wilbur R., et al. *Turner, Bolton, Webb: Three Historians of the American Frontier*. Seattle: University of Washington Press, 1965.

Jarchow, Merrill E. *The Earth Brought Forth: A History of Minnesota Agriculture to 1885*. St. Paul: Minnesota Historical Society Press, 1949.

Johnson, Hildegard Binder. *Order upon the Land: The United States Rectangular Land Survey and the Upper Mississippi Country*. New York: Oxford University Press, 1976.

Jones, Howard Mumford. *The Age of Energy: Varieties of American Experience, 1865–1915*. New York: Viking Press, 1970.

Jones, Raymond P., and John E. Ball. *Framing, Sheathing, and Insulation*. New York: Van Nostrand Reinhold, 1973.

Juster, Norton. *So Sweet to Labor: Rural Women in America, 1865–1895*. New York: Viking Press, 1979.

Karp, Ben. *Ornamental Carpentry on Nineteenth-Century American Houses*. New York: Dover Publications, 1981.

Kasson, John F. *Civilizing the Machine: Technology and Republican Values in America, 1776–1900*. New York: Grossman, 1976.

Kidney, Walter C. *The Architecture of Choice: Eclecticism in America, 1880–1930*. New York: Braziler, 1974.

King, Anthony D. *The Bungalow: The Production of a Global Culture*. London: Routledge and Kegan Paul, 1984.

Koop, Michael, and Stephen Ludwig. *German-Russian Folk Architecture in South Eastern South Dakota*. Vermillion, S.D.: State Historical Preservation Center, 1984.

Kouwenhoven, John A. *The Arts in Modern American Civilization*. New York: W. W. Norton, 1975.

Kovel, Ralph, and Terry Kovel. *American Country Furniture, 1780–1875*. New York: Crown, 1975.

Kraenzel, Carl F. *Great Plains in Transition*. Norman: University of Oklahoma Press, 1955.

Kriedberg, Marjorie. *Food on the Frontier: Minnesota Cooking from 1850 to 1900*. St. Paul: Minnesota State Historical Society Press, 1975.

Lancaster, Clay. *The American Bungalow, 1889–1930*. New York: Abbeville Press, 1985.

Landes, David S., and Charles Tilly, eds. *History as Social Science*. Englewood Cliffs, N.J.: Prentice Hall, 1971.

Larson, Agnes M. *History of the White Pine Industry in Minnesota*. Minneapolis: University of Minnesota Press, 1949.

Levorsen, Barbara. *The Quiet Conquest: A History of the Lives and Times of the First Settlers of Central North Dakota*. Hawley, Minn.: Hawley Herald, 1974.

Lifeshey, Earl. *The Housewares Story: A History of the American Housewares Industry*. Chicago: National Housewares Manufacturers Association, 1973.

Lipset, Seymour Martin, and Richard Hofstadter. *Sociology and History: Methods*. New York: Basic Books, 1968.

Logan, Ben. *The Land Remembers: The Story of a Farm and Its People*. New York: Viking Press, 1975.

Lovell, Odd S. *The Promise of America: A History of the Norwegian-American People*. Minneapolis: University of Minnesota Press, 1984.

Lovell, Odd S., ed. *Cultural Pluralism versus Assimilation*. Northfield, Minn.: Norwegian-American Historical Society, 1977.

Lund, George E. *Providence Valley Lutheran Church*. Skokie, Ill.: LeMann and Associates, 1976.

Lynes, Russell. *The Domesticated Americans*. New York: Harper and Row, 1957.

McAlester, Virginia, and Lee McAlester. *A Field Guide to American Houses*. New York: Alfred A. Knopf, 1984.

McConner, Grant. *The Decline of Agrarian Democracy*. Berkeley and Los Angeles: University of California Press, 1959.

MacFarlane, Alan. *Reconstructing Historical Communities*. Cambridge: Cambridge University Press, 1977.

Marc, Oliver. *Psychology of the House*. Trans. Jesse Wood. London: Thames and Hudson, 1977.

Marx, Leo. *The Machine in the Garden: Technology and the Pastoral Ideal in America*. London: Oxford University Press, 1964.

Mass, John. *The Victorian Home in America*. New York: Hawthorn Books, 1972.

Merk, Frederick. *History of the Westward Movement*. New York: Alfred A. Knopf, 1980.

Meyers, Marvin. *The Jacksonian Persuasion: Politics and Belief*. Stanford, Calif.: Stanford University Press, 1957.

Moholy-Nagy, Sibyl. *Native Genius in Anonymous Architecture.* New York: Horizon Press, 1957.

Mondy, Robert William. *Pioneers and Preachers: Stories of the Old Frontier.* Chicago: Nelson-Hall, 1980.

Morris, Lucy Leavenworth Wilder, ed. *Old Fence Rail Corners: Frontier Tales Told by Minnesota Pioneers.* St. Paul: Minnesota Historical Society Press, 1976.

Moyer, L. R., and O. G. Dale. *History of Chippewa and Lac Qui Parle Counties, Minnesota.* 2 vols. Indianapolis: B. F. Bowen, 1916.

Murray, Stanley Norman. *The Valley Comes of Age: A History of Agriculture in the Valley of the Red River of the North, 1812-1920.* Fargo: North Dakota Institute for Regional Studies, 1967.

Nash, Roderick. *Wilderness and the American Mind.* New Haven, Conn.: Yale University Press, 1973.

Nelson, E. C., and Eugene L. Fevold. *The Lutheran Church among Norwegian-Americans.* 2 vols. Minneapolis: Augsburg, 1960.

Nesbit, Robert C. *Wisconsin, a History.* Madison: University of Wisconsin Press, 1973.

Newcomb, Rexford. *Architecture of the Old West Territory: A Study of Early Architecture in Ohio, Indiana, Illinois, Michigan, Wisconsin, and Part of Minnesota.* Chicago: University of Chicago Press, 1950.

Noble, Allen G. *Wood, Brick, and Stone: The North American Settlement Landscape.* 2 vols. Amherst: University of Massachusetts Press, 1984.

Norske Gardsbruk: Oppland, Valdres. Fylke I. [Norwegian farms: Oppland, Valdres. Area I.] Oslo: Forlaget Norske Gardsbruk, 1950.

Øien, Einar. *Bondegarden Hus Tun Hage.* [Rustic farms—House, courtyard.] Oslo: Grøndahl and Søns Forlag, 1947.

Oldem, Arne E. *Sveitserstil—1800-Årenes Byggestil.* [The Swiss style—Nineteenth-century building style.] Oslo: Institut for Ethnologi, Universitet, 1984.

Oliver, Paul, ed. *Shelter, Sign, and Symbol.* Woodstock, N.Y.: Overlook Press, 1977.

Olssen, Nils William. *A Pioneer in Northwest America, 1841-1858: The Memoirs of Gustaf Unonius.* 2 vols. Minneapolis: University of Minnesota Press, 1950.

Osborne, Charles Francis. *The Family House.* Philadelphia: Penn, 1910.

Parson, Ruben L. *Ever the Land: A Homestead Chronicle.* Staples, Minn.: Adventure, 1978.

Perin, Constance. *Everything in Its Place: Social Order and Land Use in America.* Princeton, N.J.: Princeton University Press, 1977.

Perrin, Richard W. E. *Historic Wisconsin Buildings: A Survey of Pioneer Architecture, 1835-1870.* Milwaukee: Milwaukee Public Museum Press, 1962.

Peterson, Charles E., ed. *Building Early America.* Randor, Pa.: Chilton, 1962.

Pevsner, Nikolaus. *A History of Building Types.* London: Thames and Hudson, 1976.

Pickering, Ernest. *The Homes of America.* New York: Bramhall House, 1961.

Pressly, Thomas. *Farm Real Estate Values in the United States by County, 1850-1959.* Seattle: University of Washington Press, 1965.

Rapoport, Amos. *House Form and Culture.* Englewood Cliffs, N.J.: Prentice Hall, 1969.

Rasmussen, Wayne D., ed. *Agriculture in the United States: A Documentary History.* 4 vols. New York: Random House, 1975.

Reese, John B. *Some Pioneers and Pilgrims on the Prairies of Dakota.* Mitchell, S.D.: N.p., 1920.

Robertson, James Oliver. *American Myth, American Reality.* New York: Hill and Wang, 1980.

Robinson, Elwyn B. *History of North Dakota.* Lincoln: University of Nebraska Press, 1966.

Rockswold, E. Palmer. *Per, Immigrant and Pioneer.* Staples, Minn.: Adventure, 1981.

Rybcjynski, Witold, *Home: A Short History of an Idea*. New York: Viking Press, 1986.

Sage, Leland L. *A History of Iowa*. Ames: Iowa State University Press, 1974.

Sallet, Richard. *Russian-German Settlements in the United States*. Trans. Laverne Rippley and Armand Bauer. Fargo: North Dakota Institute for Regional Studies, 1974.

Sandro, Gustav O. *The Immigrants' Trek: A Detailed History of the Lake Hendricks Colony in Brookings County, South Dakota Territory, from 1873-1881*. Hendricks, Minn.: Gustav O. Sandro, 1929.

Schaefer, Erwin. *Nineteenth Century Modern: The Functional Tradition in Victorian Design*. New York: Praeger, 1970.

Schafer, Joseph. *A History of Agriculture in Wisconsin*. Madison: State Historical Society of Wisconsin Press, 1922.

Schlebecker, John T. *Whereby We Thrive: A History of American Farming, 1607-1972*. Ames: Iowa State University Press, 1975.

Schell, Herbert S. *History of South Dakota*. Lincoln: University of Nebraska Press, 1961.

Schweitzer, Robert, and Michael W. R. Davis. *America's Favorite Homes: Mail-Order Catalogues as a Guide to Popular Early 20th-Century Houses*. Detroit: Wayne State University Press, 1990.

Scott, Roy V. *The Reluctant Farmer: The Rise of Agricultural Extension to 1914*. Urbana: University of Illinois Press, 1978.

Semmingson, Ingrid. *Norway to America: A History of the Migration*. Minneapolis: University of Minnesota Press, 1978.

Shank, Wesley. *The Iowa Catalogue: Historic American Buildings Survey*. Iowa City: University of Iowa Press, 1979.

Shannon, Fred A. *The Farmer's Last Frontier: Agriculture, 1860-1897*. Vol. 5 of *The Economic History of the United States*. New York: Holt, Rinehart, and Winston, 1963.

Shaw, Joseph M. *Pulpit under the Sky: A Life of Hans Nielson Hauge*. Minneapolis: Augsburg, 1955.

Shi, David E. *The Simple Life: Plain Living and High Thinking in American Culture*. New York: Oxford University Press, 1985.

Shurtleff, Harold R. *The Log Cabin Myth*. Ed. Samuel Eliot Taylor. Gloucester, Mass.: Peter Smith, 1967.

Sizemore, Jean. *The Iowa Farmhouse (1857-1950): A Literature Survey*. Iowa City: Historical Preservation Division, State Historical Society, 1979.

Sklar, Kathryn Kish. *Catherine Beecher: A Study in American Domesticity*. New York: W. W. Norton and Company, 1973.

Smith, Henry Nash. *Virgin Land: The American West as Symbol and Myth*. New York: Vintage Books, 1959.

Stephanson, George M. *The Religious Aspects of Swedish Immigration: A Study of Immigrant Churches*. Minneapolis: University of Minnesota Press, 1932.

Stevenson, Katherine Cole, and H. Ward Jandl. *Houses by Mail: A Guide to Houses by Sears, Roebuck, and Company*. Washington, D.C.: Preservation Press, 1986.

Strasser, Susan. *Never Done: A History of American Housework*. New York: Pantheon Books, 1982.

Stubelius, Svante. *Balloon, Flying Machine, Heliocopter: Further Study in the History of Terms for Aircraft in English*. Goteborg, Sweden: Carl Bloms Boktryckeri A.-B., 1960.

Stumpp, Karl. *The German Russians*. Bonn, Brussels, and New York: Edition Atlantic-Forum, 1971.

Swedberg, Robert, and Harriet Swedberg. *Country Pine Furniture: Styles and Prices*. Des Moines: Wallace-Homestead, 1983.

———. *Victorian Furniture: Styles and Prices*. Des Moines: Wallace-Homestead, 1981.

Swierenga, Robert P. *Pioneers and Profits: Land Speculation on the Iowa Frontier.* Ames: Iowa State University Press, 1968.

Talbot, George. *At Home: Domestic Life in the Post-Centennial Era, 1876–1920.* Madison, Wis.: State Historical Society, 1976.

Tavuchis, Nicholas. *Pastors and Immigrants: The Role of a Religious Elite in the Absorption of Norwegian Immigrants.* The Hague: Martin Nyhoff, 1963.

Taylor, Henry C. *Tarpleywick: A Century of Iowa Farming.* Ames: Iowa State University Press, 1970.

Tilly, Charles. *As Sociology Meets History.* New York: Academie Press, 1981.

Tomisch, John. *A Genteel Endeavor: American Culture and Politics in the Gilded Age.* Stanford, Calif.: Stanford University Press, 1971.

Truesdell, Leon E. *Farm Population of the United States.* Vol. 6 of *Census Monographs.* Westport, Conn.: Greenwood Press, 1978; reprint of 1926 edition.

Tryon, Rolla Milton. *Household Manufacturers in the United States, 1640–1860.* Chicago: University of Chicago Press, 1917.

Tuan, Yi-Fu. *Space and Place: The Perspective of Experience.* Minneapolis: University of Minnesota Press, 1977.

————. *Topophilia.* Englewood Cliffs, N.J.: Prentice Hall, 1974.

Tweeton, D. Jerome and Theodore B. Jelliff. *North Dakota: The Heritage of the People.* Fargo: North Dakota Institute for Regional Studies, 1976.

Vernacular Form in Wisconsin: A Guide to Identification. Madison, Wis.: Historic Preservation Division, State Historical Society, 1984.

Webb, Walter. *The Great Plains.* Boston: Ginn, 1931.

Weil, Gordon L. *Sears, Roebuck, U.S.A.: The Great American Catalogue Store and How It Grew.* New York: Stein and Day, 1977.

Wheeley, Thomas C., ed. *The Immigrant Experience: The Anguish of Becoming an American.* New York: Dial Press, 1917.

Williams, Mary A. Barnes. *Fifty Pioneer Mothers of McClean County, North Dakota.* Washburn, N.D.: Washburn Leader, 1932.

Witsell, Rebecca Rogers, and Suzanne Kettrell, eds. and comps., *Authentic Stencil Patterns, 1890–1930.* Little Rock, Ark.: Designed Communications, 1985.

Wolf, Peter. *Land in America: Its Value, Use, and Control.* New York: Pantheon Books, 1981.

Woodforde, John. *The Truth about Cottages.* London: Routledge and Kegan Paul, 1969.

Wright, Gwendolyn. *Moralism and the Modern Homes: Domestic Architecture and Cultural Conflict in Chicago, 1873–1913.* Chicago: Chicago University Press, 1980.

Xan, Erna Oleson. *Wisconsin My Home.* Madison: University of Wisconsin Press, 1950.

Articles

Ames, Kenneth L. "Meaning in Artifacts: Hall Furnishings in Victorian America." *Journal of Interdisciplinary History* 9 (Summer 1987): 19–46.

Ankli, Robert E. "Farm-Making Costs in the 1850's." *Agricultural History* 48 (January 1974): 51.

Argersinger, Peter H. and Jo Ann E. Argersinger. "The Machine Breakers: Farmworkers and Social Change in the Rural Midwest of the 1870's." *Agricultural History* 58 (July 1984): 393–410.

Atack, Jeremy. "Farm and Farm-Making Costs Revisited." *Agricultural History* 56 (October 1982): 663–76.

Barns, Evadine A. "Building the Frontier Home." *Minnesota History* 15 (1934): 34–55.

————. "Furnishing the Frontier Home." *Minnesota History* 15 (1934): 181–93.

————. "Keeping House on the Minnesota Frontier." *Minnesota History* 14 (1933): 263-82.

Berkhofer, Robert F., Jr. "Space, Time, Culture, and the New Frontier." *Agricultural History* 38 (January 1964): 21-30.

Borchert, James. "Historic Photo-Analysis: A Research Method." *Historical Methods* 15 (Spring 1982): 35-44.

Breugman, Robert. "Central Heating and Forced Ventilation: Origins and Effects of Architectural Design." *Journal of the Society of Architectural Historians* 37 (October 1978): 143-61.

Brown, Richard D. "Modernization and the Modern Personality in Early America, 1600-1685: A Sketch of a Synthesis." *Journal of Interdisciplinary History* 2 (1972): 201-28.

Carson, Cary. "Doing History with Material Culture." In Ian M. G. Quimby, ed., *Material Culture and the Study of American Life*, 41-46. New York: W. W. Norton, 1978.

Clark, Clifford, Jr. "Domestic Architecture as an Index to Social History: The Romantic Revival and the Cult of Domesticity in America, 1840-1870." *Journal of Interdisciplinary History* 7 (Summer 1976): 33-56.

Field, Walker. "A Reexamination into the Invention of the Balloon Frame." *Journal of the Society of Architectural Historians* (October 1942): 3-29.

Fancaviglia, Richard V. "Some Comments on the Historic and Geographic Importance of Railroads in Minnesota." *Minnesota History* 43 (Summer 1972): 58-62.

Finley, Robert, and E. M. Scott. "Great Lakes to Gulf: Profile of Dispersed Building Types." *Geographical Review* 30 (July 1940): 412-19.

Fite, Gilbert C. "Failure on the Last Frontier: A Family Chronicle." *Western Historical Quarterly* (January 1987): 4-14.

————. "Some Farmers' Accounts of Hardships on the Frontier." *Minnesota History* 37 (March 1961): 204-11.

Gallaher, Ruth A. "Around the Fireplace." *Palimpsest* 8 (January 1927): 18-23.

Garvin, James C. "Mail-Order House Plans and Victorian Architecture." *Winterthur Portfolio* 16 (Winter 1981): 309-34.

Gates, Donald. "The Sod House." *Journal of Geography* 32 (1933): 353-59.

Gates, Paul W. "The Homestead Law in Iowa." *Agricultural History* 38 (April 1964): 67-78.

Gebhard, David. "Fifty Years of the American Home." *Landscape* 8 (1958): 5-9.

Gjerde, John A. "The Effects of Community on Migration." *Journal of Historical Geography* 5 (October 1979): 103-22.

Glassie, Henry. "Artifact and Culture, Architecture and Society." In Simon J. Bronner, ed., *American Material Culture and Folklife*, 47-62. Ann Arbor, Mich.: UMI Research Press, 1985.

Good, Susan Thompson. "Interior Life: An Iowa Farmhouse in the Later 1880's." *Palimpsest* 60 (March/April 1979): 34-47.

Hanchert, Thomas W. "Abstract: The Four Square House Type in the United States." In Camille Wells, ed., *Perspectives in Vernacular Architecture*, 51-53. Annapolis, Md.: Vernacular Architecture Forum, 1982.

Hanson, Susan Atherton. "Home Sweet Home: Industrialization's Impact on Rural Households, 1865-1925." Ph.D. dissertation, University of Maryland, College Park, 1986.

Hart, Arthur A. "M. A. Disbrow and Company: Catalogue Architecture." *Palimpsest* 56 (July/August 1975): 98-119.

Heberle, Rudolf. "The Application of Fundamental Concepts in Rural Community Studies." *Rural Sociology* 6 (1941): 203-15.

Henke, Warren A. "Imagery, Immigration, and the Myth of North Dakota." *North Dakota History* 38 (Fall 1971): 412–19.

Henretta, James A. "Families and Farms: *Mentalité* in Pre-Industrial America." *William and Mary Quarterly* 35 (January 1978): 3–32.

Hersey, George L. "Godey's Choice." *Journal of the Society of Architectural Historians* 18 (1959): 104–11.

Hubka, Thomas C. "In the Vernacular: Classifying American Folk and Vernacular Architecture." *Forum: Bulletin of the Committee on Preservation of the Society of Architectural Historians* 8 (December 1985).

Hudson, John C. "Frontier Housing in North Dakota." *North Dakota History* 42 (Fall 1975): 4–15.

————. "The Middle West as Cultural Hybrid." *Transactions* 6 (1984): 34–45.

Jackson, James Brinkerhof. "The Westward Moving House: Three American Houses and the People Who Made Them." *Landscape* 2-3 (1953): 8–21.

Jakle, John A. "The Testing of a House Typing System in Two Midwestern Counties: A Comparative Analysis of Rural Houses." In Susan Gross, ed., *Occasional Publications of the Department of Geography*, Paper No. 2 (August 1976): 1–36.

Jarchow, Merrill E. "Social Life of an Iowa Family, 1872–1912." *Iowa Journal of History* 5 (April 1952): 123–54.

Jeggle, Utz. "The Rules of the Village: On the Cultural History of the Peasant World in the Last 150 Years." In Richard J. Evans and W. R. Lee, eds., *The German Peasantry: Conflict and Community in Rural Society from the Eighteenth to the Twentieth Century*, 265–89. London: Croom Helm, 1986.

Johnson, Hildegard B. "Factors Influencing the Distribution of the German Pioneer Population in Minnesota." *Agricultural History* 19 (January 1945): 39–57.

Jordan, T. G. "Between the Forest and the Prairie." *Agricultural History* 38 (1964): 205–16.

Karstad, Ruby G. "The New York Times and the Minnesota Frontier." *Minnesota History* 17 (1936): 411–20.

Kirk, Jeffrey. "The Family as Utopian Retreat from the City: The Nineteenth-Century Contribution." *Soundings* 15 (1972): 21–41.

Kniffen, Fred B. "Folk Housing: Key to Diffusion." *Annals of the Association of American Geographers* 55 (Fall 1965): 549–77.

————. "Louisiana House Types." *Annals of the Association of American Geographers* 36 (December 1936): 179–93.

Kniffen, Fred B., and Henry Glassie. "Building in Wood in the Eastern United States." *Geographical Review* 56 (1966): 40–66.

Kornwolf, James D. "High Victorian Gothic: The Dilemma of Style in Modern Architecture." *Journal of the Society of Architectural Historians* 34 (March 1975): 37–47.

Larsen, Arthur J. "Roads and Settlements in Minnesota History." *Minnesota History* 21 (September 1940): 225–44.

Lawrence, Roderick J. "The Comparative Analysis of Homes: Research Method and Application." *Social Science Information* 22 (1983): 461–85.

Limmer, George E. "The Agricultural Press: Early Agricultural Editors and Their Farm Philosophies." *Agricultural History* 31 (October 1957): 3–22.

Loehr, Rodney C. "Farmers' Diaries: Their Interest and Value as Historical Sources." *Agricultural History* 12 (October 1938): 312–25.

Lowenthal, David. "The American Scene." *Geographical Review* (1968): 61–87.

McMurry, Sally. "Progressive Farm Families and Their Houses, 1830–1855: A Study in Independent Design." *Agricultural History* 58 (July 1984): 330–46.

Marin, William A. "Sod Houses and Prairie Schooners." *Minnesota History* 12 (1931): 135–56.

Mattson, Richard. "The Bungalow Spirit." *Journal of Cultural Geography* 1 (1981): 135–56.

Moneo, Raphael. "On Typology." *Oppositions* 13 (1978): 22–45.

Nelson, Marion J. "The Material Culture and Folk Arts of the Norwegians in America." In Ian M. G. Quimby, ed., *Perspectives on American Folk Art*, 79–133. New York: W. W. Norton, 1980.

Nordbo, Artha, ed. "Torgo Midboe Family History." Manuscript. Griggs County, North Dakota, n.d.

Olson, V. J. "A Statistical Study of Factors Affecting Farmers' Earnings in Stevens County." Master's Thesis, University of Minnesota, Minneapolis, 1927.

Ostergren, Robert C. "European Settlement and Ethnicity Patterns on the Agricultural Frontiers of South Dakota." *South Dakota History* 13 (1983): 49–82.

Pederson, Jane Marie. "The Country Visitor: Patterns of Hospitality in Rural Wisconsin, 1860–1925." *Agricultural History* 58 (July 1984): 347–64.

Peterson, Charles E. "Early American Prefabrication." *Gazette des Beaux Arts* 33 (January 1948): 37–46.

Peterson, Fred W. "Norwegian-American Farm Homes in Steele and Traill Counties, North Dakota: The American Dream and the Retention of Roots, 1890–1914," *North Dakota History* 51 (Winter 1984): 4–13.

————. "Substance, Style, and Community: Selected Farmhouses of Lac Qui Parle County, Minnesota." In Thomas Carter and Bernard Herman, eds., *Perspectives in Vernacular Architecture III*, 176–84. Columbia: University of Missouri Press, 1989.

————. "Vernacular Building and Victorian Architecture: Midwestern American Farm Homes." *Journal of Interdisciplinary History* 12 (Winter 1981): 409–27.

Qualey, Carlton C. "A New Eldorado: Guides to Minnesota, 1850's–1880's." *Minnesota History* 42 (Summer 1971): 215–24.

Raitz, K. B. "Wisconsin Tobacco Sheds: A Key to Ethnic Settlement and Diffusion." *Landscape* 20 (1975): 32–37.

Rees, Ronald, and Carl J. Tracie. "The Prairie House." *Landscape* 22 (1978): 3–8.

Rice, John G. "Patterns of Ethnicity in a Minnesota County, 1880–1905." *Geographical Reports* (Umea, Sweden) 4 (1973): 33–48.

Riley, Glenda. "Women Pioneers in Iowa." *Palimpsest* 57 (March/April 1976): 34–53.

Riviere, G. H. "Folk Architecture: Past, Present, and Future." *Landscape* 4 (1954): 5–12.

Rome, Adam Ward. "American Farmers as Entrepreneurs, 1870–1900." *Agricultural History* 56 (January 1982): 37–49.

Rudd, Olivia H. "Trapper's Cabin Was First Home for Ole Holtans." *Dawson* (Minn.) *Sentinel*, 19 June 1959, 7.

Sanderson, Dwight. "The Rural Community in the United States as an Elementary Group." *Rural Sociology* 1 (1936): 142–50.

Scofield, Edna. "The Evolution and Development of Tennessee House Types." *Journal of the Tennessee Academy of Science* 11 (October 1936): 229–40.

Scully, Vincent J., Jr. "Romantic Rationalism and the Expression of Structure in Wood." *Art Bulletin* 35 (1953): 121–43.

Seaton, Beverly. "Idylls of Agriculture, Or Nineteenth Century Success Stories of Farming and Gardening." *Agricultural History* 55 (January 1981): 21–31.

Shapiro, Meyer. "Style." In A. L. Kroeber, ed., *Anthropology Today*, 287–312. Chicago: University of Chicago Press, 1953.

Spencer, J. E. "House Types in Southern Utah." *Geographical Review* 35 (1945): 444–57.

Sprague, Paul E. "Chicago Balloon Frame." In *Technology of Historic American Buildings*, ed. H. Ward Jandl, 35–53. Washington, D.C.: Foundation for Preservation Technology and the Association for Preservation Technology, 1983.

Stone, Lawrence. "The Revival of Narrative: Reflections on a New Old History." *Past and Present: A Journal of Scientific History* 85 (1979): 3–24.

Tishler, William H. "Built from Tradition: Wisconsin's Rural Ethnic Folk Architecture." *Wisconsin Academy Review* (March 1984): 14–18.

————. "The Landscape: An Emerging Historic Preservation Resource." *APT* 11 (1979): 9–25.

————. "The Site Arrangement of Rural Farmsteads." *APT* 10 (1978): 63–77.

————. "Stovewood Architecture." *Landscape* 23 (1979): 28–31.

Tolley, Clarence H. "Fingal Enger, King of the Goose River." *North Dakota History* 26 (July 1959): 107–22.

Trewartha, G. T. "Some Regional Characteristics of American Farmsteads." *Annals of the Association of American Geographers* 38 (September 1948): 169–225.

Tweeten, D. Jerome. "The Golden Age of Agriculture, 1897–1917." *North Dakota History* 37 (Winter 1970): 41–55.

Unseem, John, and Ruth Hill Unseem. "Minority Group Patterns in Prairie Society." *American Journal of Sociology* 50 (1945): 377–85.

Upton, Dell. "Pattern Books and Professionalism: Aspects of the Transformation of Domestic Architecture in America, 1800–1860." *Winterthur Portfolio* 19 (Summer/Autumn 1984): 107–50.

————. "The Power of Things: Recent Studies in American Vernacular Architecture." *American Quarterly* 35 (1983): 262–79.

————. "Toward a Performance Theory of Vernacular Architecture: Early Tidewater Virginia as a Case Study." *Folklore Forum* 12 (1979): 173–96.

Vidler, Anthony. "The Idea of Type: The Transformation of the Ideal, 1750–1830." *Oppositions* 8 (1977): 95–115.

Vogeler, Inholf. "The Roman Catholic Culture Region of Western Minnesota." *Pioneer America* 2 (1976): 71–83.

Vogt, E. Z. Jr. "Social Stratification in the Rural Midwest: A Structural Analysis." *Rural Sociology* 12 (1947): 364–75.

Waddell, Gene. "The First Monticello." *Journal of the Society of Architectural Historians* 46 (March 1987): 5–29.

Welsch, Roger L. "Sod Construction on the Plains." *Pioneer America* 1-2 (1969): 13–17.

West, Pamela. "The Rise and Fall of the American Porch." *Landscape* 20 (1976): 42–47.

Wik, Reynold M. "Henry Ford's Tractors and American Agriculture." *Agricultural History* 38 (April 1964): 79–86.

Woodward, Margaret L. "The Northwestern Farmer, 1868–1876: A Tale of Paradox." *Agricultural History* 37 (July 1963): 134–42.

Wyatt, Barbara, ed. and comp. "Surveying and Evaluating Vernacular Architecture." *National Building Register Bulletin* 31 (1987), draft version.

INDEX